Holocaust Memoir Digest

Holocaust Memoir Digest

A Digest of Published Survivor Memoirs
With Study Guide and Maps

Volume 3

Compiled and Edited by

Esther Goldberg

With an Introduction and
30 colour maps by

Sir Martin Gilbert

VALLENTINE MITCHELL
LONDON • PORTLAND, OR

First published in 2006 in Great Britain by
VALLENTINE MITCHELL
Suite 314, Premier House, 112–114 Station Road
Edgware, Middlesex HA8 7BJ

and in the United States of America by
VALLENTINE MITCHELL
c/o ISBS, 920 N. E. 58th Avenue, Suite 300
Portland, Oregon 97213-3786

Website: www.vmbooks.com

British Library Cataloguing in Publication Data

Holocaust memoir digest: a digest of published survivor
  memoirs with study guide and maps
  vol. 3
  1. Holocaust, Jewish (1939–1945) – Personal narratives
  I. Goldberg, Esther
  940.5'319

ISBN 0 85303 724 8
ISBN 978 0 85303 724 8

Library of Congress Cataloging-in-Publication Data
A catalog record for this book is available.

Cover illustrations Front cover: At a railway station in the Balkans, a passenger train (left) is opposite a train (right) carrying Jewish deportees from Macedonia to the Treblinka death camp. Back cover: The spur railway line leading into the Theresienstadt Ghetto, photograph taken in 1996.

Typeset in 11/13pt Ehrhardt by FiSH Books, London
Printed in Great Britain by MPG Books Ltd, Bodmin, Cornwall

"What does it mean to remember?

It is to live in more than one world,

to prevent the past from fading,

and to call upon the future to illuminate it."

Elie Wiesel

"...a country is considered the more civilized

the more the wisdom and efficiencies of its laws

hinder a weak man from becoming too weak

or a powerful one too powerful.

But in the Lager things are different...."

Primo Levi

CONTENTS

Study Guide Maps

INTRODUCTION BY SIR MARTIN GILBERT

The third volume of Esther Goldberg's *Holocaust Memoir Digest* provides an opportunity to reflect on the importance of memoirs across the whole spectrum of recent history, from the Armenian genocide during the First World War to the Rwandan genocide at the end of the twentieth century. Inevitably, the main focus of historians has been the written record set down at the time of the tragedies: both the official documents of the time preserved by the perpetrators of the killings, and the diaries and the letters of the victims written at the very moment when the terrible events were taking place. This contemporary record is the basic source for facts and narrative.

Once the events of each mass murder began to recede into history, a different source began to emerge: the recollections, written in tranquillity – or comparative tranquillity – of the time of torment. As years, and eventually decades, separated the events from those who were writing about them, there emerged a different scale of understanding and recording.

The nature of pre-war Jewish life – so different in different countries – was seen as relevant to the Holocaust experience. The part played by resistance in all its forms, including the resistance of trying to maintain a life of humanity amid the destruction of human values, was seen as an important element of the story. As interest grew in the role of the bystanders, the help given by non-Jews, often at the risk of their own lives, it assumed a major part in understanding the events.

Each of the memoirs in this volume sheds light on these aspects of the Holocaust. As in the two previous volumes, the twenty-six topics through the memoirs give a rich texture to the otherwise difficult narrative that is inevitably dominated by persecution and destruction.

The first memoir in this volume is Primo Levi's *Survival in Auschwitz*, originally published as *If This is a Man*. As with Elie Wiesel's *Night*, one of the memoirs in Volume One, Primo Levi's memoir has become one of the iconic memoirs of the Holocaust. An Italian Jew, deported to Auschwitz in early 1944, Levi's recollections cast considerable light on many facets of the Holocaust. As late as February 1944, the destination of the deportation to Auschwitz was unknown. As Levi writes: "Nobody knew."

Even at the time of his deportation from Italy, Levi experienced the brutality of the guards. His comment reflects the bewilderment of all those caught up in the reign of terror that engulfed German-dominated Europe. "Here we received the first blows," he writes, "and it was so new and senseless that we felt no pain, neither in body nor in spirit. Only a profound amazement: how can one hit a man without anger?"

The second iconic memoir in this volume is that of Leon Weliczker Wells, *The Janowska Road*. Wells was born in Eastern Galicia, survived the destruction of the Lvov Ghetto, and was a prisoner in the notorious Janowska Concentration Camp on the outskirts of Lvov. "Every male individual in the camp never knew when he woke up in the morning whether he would be going to work or death that day. Only infants and children, the old, the sick and for the most part, women, could be certain the Germans would kill them as soon as they arrived at Janowska."

Wells was made a member of the "Death Brigade" – Jewish prisoners whose task was to dig up the corpses of those who had earlier been murdered at Janowska. His memoir begins with a vivid account of pre-war Jewish life in a small Eastern Galician town. There, once a week, his mother took part in a rota for feeding the poor: "Mother served as many as forty beggars; and including her own family, she would cook for and serve fifty people."

Wells's mother was killed in the final round-up in the Lvov ghetto. He dedicates his memoir to the eight members of his immediate family who were murdered during the Holocaust: his mother and father, his two brothers, and his four sisters, the youngest, Bina, seven years old.

The Janowska Road contains a powerful account of a camp that is seldom written about. The next memoir in this volume, *By Bread Alone, The Story of A-4685*, contains an equally powerful account of the best known of all camps, Auschwitz. Mel Mermelstein was born in Ruthenia when it was part of Czechoslovakia. It was under Hungarian rule when the deportations to Auschwitz took place in 1944, by train. "The darkness that accompanied the closing of the doors came as a shock, and what arose among us was a collective sigh and whimpering sound. It was as if the mass within the boxcar had given up hope, as if the sliding door that sealed us in had also sealed our lives for ever."

Mermelstein's account of the arrival at Auschwitz makes it clear how desperately the human mind searches for a normal explanation, even after the men were separated from the women and children, and, as we now know, were destined for the gas chambers. "Surprisingly there was no expression of dismay at the separation.... We told ourselves that this was temporary and that we would be re-united as soon as our accommodations were arranged." In addition, Mermelstein recalled, "We were too demoralized by the long journey in the sealed boxcar to do anything but obey."

After slave labour camps and death marches, Mermelstein was among those liberated at Buchenwald by American forces. He writes, of a photograph taken by one of the liberators: "That photograph turned out to be one of the most widely circulated and published photographs of the camps.... Our deep eyes, full of pain and suffering and sickness and fatigue, were already telling the tales which we could not put into words."

Each memoir in this volume tells of some act of generosity by the non-Jews, and of the impact made by such acts. Mermelstein recalled how, during a Death March through Germany in the closing months of the war, the villagers called out in greeting and then threw bread from their tables to the marchers. "More important than the pieces of bread we snatched," Mermelstein wrote, "was the unexpected surge of hope within us.... In a face-to-face, people-to-people experience there had been a shower of bread that carried the rain of compassion."

There is an instance of that "rain of compassion" in the next memoir in this volume of the *Digest, Fragments of Memory* by Hana Greenfield. This is the story of a Czech Jewish girl who was initially taken from her home town of Kolin to the Theresienstadt Ghetto, and then to Auschwitz, before deportation to slave labour camps in the Hamburg area, and liberation in Bergen-Belsen. She recalls, while working in open countryside near Hamburg, managing, on the pretext of running to the trees to relieve herself, to find a house. It was winter. Her feet were frozen. The woman invited her in, served her warm soup, and invited her to return if possible. She managed to return. "After serving me a bowl of thick, sweet porridge," Hana recalled, "she murmured something to her husband and handed me an old pair of men's shoes with new soles that her husband had prepared for me."

Hana Greenfield reflects: "I never learned the names of those good people nor their address, but for the rest of the winter I blessed them, while my frozen feet recovered thanks to their kindness and humanity."

Fragments of Memory is the first memoir in the Digest that includes Theresienstadt, the so-called Model Ghetto established by the Nazis for tens of thousands of Jews from Germany,

Austria and Czechoslovakia, many of them elderly. Starvation was widespread there. Most of those who did not die of starvation were deported to Auschwitz and killed.

While at Theresienstadt, Hana Greenfield was a witness to a unique event there, and in the history of the Holocaust. It took place in August 1943, the arrival of 1,196 children from the distant Bialystok Ghetto in Poland. "A column of marching ghosts," she recalled, "with wet rags clinging to their emaciated bodies, accompanied by a large number of SS men." The children were housed in a barrack outside the ghetto walls. Fifty-three doctors and nurses from the ghetto volunteered to join them and look after them. It was thought that the children had been brought to Theresienstadt en route to freedom in neutral Switzerland, as part of an exchange scheme for German prisoners of war being held by the Allies. Together with the doctors and nurses, the children left Theresienstadt by train. Their destination was not Switzerland but Auschwitz, where they and their helpers – Hana Greenfield's mother among them – were murdered.

Each memoir in this volume, as in the two previous volumes, contains eyewitness testimony of places, episodes and reflections that are seldom found elsewhere. The final memoir in this volume of the *Digest* is of a young woman, Eva Gossman, from Slovakia. When she was born, Slovakia was part of the Czechoslovak republic. With the coming of war in 1939 it was an independent state that supported Nazi Germany. Slovak Jews were among the first to be deported across the international border into Greater Germany.

Eva Gossman and her brother were fortunate to be sent in December 1942 across the border in another direction, to Hungary. When the Germans occupied Hungary in March 1944 the children managed to return to Slovakia, where they were deported to the town of Nitra. There, she and her brother, then her parents, sister and a cousin, were given shelter by a Slovak woman and her 11-year-old daughter. When the war intensified, the whole family, eight people in all, were hidden by their rescuers in a specially built underground bunker. Here they survived until liberation by Soviet troops in the spring of 1945.

Eva Gossman describes the rapid imposition of anti-Jewish laws in Slovakia from the first days of its independence. "Decrees excluding Jews from business, the professions and government service came in rapid succession. We felt besieged; outcasts in our own country and among our own people." Two years after Slovakia had come into existence as an independent state, it was "fully equipped" for the persecution of the Jews. "It had an ideology that demanded it, a government agency that oversaw it, a legal framework that justified it, and an internal military force that, with the blessing of the German government, would enforce it."

It was to the saviour of her family, Maria Krescankova, that Eva Gossman devotes some of the most powerful pages of her memoir. Not only did this brave woman hide the family in Presov, at the risk of her own life and that of her daughter, but, when danger threatened, she travelled with them to Nitra to find a hiding place for them there. "She was brave to offer a temporary shelter to my family during an unexpected roundup of Jews. But it was a giant leap to go from there to uprooting herself and her child, leaving everything that was familiar and secure behind, riding a train into darkness."

Eva Gossman notes another feature of the life of those who tried to save Jews. "During the war they were enemies of the 'law' and the 'state', subject to harassment by neighbours, betrayal by informers, and death at the hands of the Nazi collaborators and local police. At best they were unpatriotic, at worst they were traitors. After the war they were commonly viewed with suspicion, either because they were thought to have obtained material rewards (greed being more comprehensible than altruism) or, even more perniciously, because they had robbed the Final Solution of its ultimate success."

Each of those whose memoirs is examined in these pages not only tells their personal story and that of their family and friends, but also reflects on the deeper meaning and implication of the events. Primo Levi's memoir was first published, in Italian, in 1958, a mere thirteen years after the Holocaust. Yet already the implications of that time are the subject of the writer's personal retrospective. "Man's capacity to dig himself, to secrete a shell, to build around himself a tenuous barrier of defence, even in apparently desperate circumstances, is astonishing," Primo Levi writes, and he goes on to note each human being's "invaluable activity of adaptation, partly passive and partly active...."

There was no limit to what had to be adapted to. If "the most immediate cause of stress comes to an end," Levi points out, "you are grievously amazed to see that another one lies behind; and in reality a whole series of others. So that as soon as the cold, which throughout the winter had seemed our only enemy, had ceased, we became aware of our hunger...."

Another feature of this adaptability was the sense that somehow, things could always be worse. In his memoir, Primo Levi recalls a November day in the Buna Monowitz slave labour camp attached to Auschwitz, after it had been raining for ten days and the ground was like "the bottom of a swamp". On that tenth day there was one piece of luck for the prisoners, it was not windy. Levi reflects: "Strange, how in some way one always has the impression of being fortunate, how some chance happening, perhaps infinitesimal, stops us crossing the threshold of despair and allows us to live."

Leon Weliczker Wells first published his memoir in 1963, twenty years after he was sent to Janowska camp. He stressed the extent to which the scale of the Holocaust gave those caught up in it a certain strength. If the tragedy had been on a much smaller scale, he believed, "it would have been harder to take, for it would have been pain within limits of endurance. Beyond that limit one ceases to feel anything more.... Living with and meeting people who shared a similar fate, it seemed that this was the 'normal' life." At the same time, Wells "began to observe to my disgust that I, too, was coming very near to developing the indifference and apathy of so many others". He was saved from that apathy by thinking of "those at home, and the determination that my mother should see me alive. These ideas kept me from yielding, and gave me a positive ideal to strive for."

Wells survived, but his mother did not. His hopes that she would see him again saved him from descending into the apathy of those who gave up hope. In Mel Mermelstein's *By Bread Alone*, published thirty-four years after the end of the Second World War, is memory of a wartime conversation he has with his uncle, to whom he asks: "Do you want me to bless God for this unbearable pain?" His uncle answers: "the Jewish way is to bless and to hope... until hope and blessing surmount the pain and even the bitterness, and the living learn how to go on."

Each memoir in this volume, as in its two predecessors, is the story of someone who learned how to "go on", how to maintain hope. In her memoir written fifty-three years after the end of the war, Hana Greenfield reflects on the part played by two non-Jews – "good people" – in restoring and maintaining hope. Sharing such few good moments as could be found was also a means of survival. On one occasion, while working in the kitchen at Theresienstadt, Hana Greenfield was able to smuggle two potatoes to her grandfather, which he then shared with her. "We looked at each other with a smile and felt like co-conspirators. That was a moment of happiness we shared amidst the sad realities of our daily life in the ghetto."

Among Hana Greenfield's reflections is one that was shared by many survivors in the months and years after liberation, and which she is able powerfully to articulate. "Nobody realised in those days," she wrote, "that we, the survivors, were ravaged in our souls, our emotions; that we were one great pain filling every crevice of our guts. The outside was a camouflage, a protective cover that enabled us to live among normal people. Had the outside resembled the inside, we would have looked like lepers among the others."

How can the experiences of the Holocaust be transmitted? Hana Greenfield, having attended the trial of an alleged former concentration camp guard, writes: "The prosecutor could not understand what he was asking, and the words of the witnesses could not describe what they had lived through."

Eva Gossman has a similar warning about the attempt to transmit the facts and emotions of the past. Writing of why so many survivors were silent when asked by their children about their experiences, she writes: "We fear that by sharing our experiences we may kill their optimism, their joy in life, their confidence that the world is a hospitable place and above all, that we can and will protect them from evil. If there were times within our own memories when parents could not protect their children, can we protect them?" As to the retrospect of more than half a century, she writes that, in assessing the gradual unfolding of the events of the Holocaust "from the secure position of the present, we may have to accept the fact that we suffered from a lack of imagination about the depth of depravity and inhumanity that a legitimately constituted government could act against its own citizens." The Jews of her native land, Slovakia, "and those in most other countries occupied or allied with the Reich, paid a high price for living with hope."

And yet, as is clear from each of the memoir writers in this volume, and in the two previous volumes, without hope, survival was almost impossible.

The reader of each of the volumes of the *Holocaust Memoir Digest* will find that the grim aspects of the story, which make it as hard to read and absorb for the editor as for her readers, are offset by the very fact of the survival of the memoir writer, and by several elements that feature in the topics covered. Pre-war Jewish life is the story of the warmth of family life and community cohesion. Resistance tells of the bravery of men and women facing death, yet able to find means to challenge their persecutors, often by small yet always meaningful and uplifting acts of defiance. The category of Righteous sheds light on the selflessness of the human spirit. In every category, there are examples of human resilience and dignity. The Holocaust was a black era in European and world history, nothing can minimise its horrors; but within the darkness are shafts of light that can teach each generation that there is a way forward for humanity that brings out and elevates the noblest instincts of the human heart.

Martin Gilbert
Merton College
Oxford
2 April 2006

EDITOR'S ACKNOWLEDGEMENTS

Between the publication of Volume 1 of my *Holocaust Memoir Digest*, and Volume 2, I had the fortunate experience of meeting a relative whom I had not previously known, the last member of my family to leave Europe. Due to the diligent genealogical work of two cousins, I have a family tree that reaches back to the early 1800s. It is fairly easy to surmise from it which relatives were buried in the town's cemetery before the Second World War, and which ones in the mass grave in the forest nearby in 1942. The family tree shows another cousin, with children born after the war. In the last year I found this cousin, living in Detroit, and heard some of his story: how he and his parents, who had lost two children in the Nazi era, had fled into the Soviet Union in 1941, how they had returned to their hometown after it was liberated, and how they had eventually emigrated to the United States.

To anyone who has lost family to genocide, to find a cousin who has appeared out of the ashes – even sixty-two years later – is a miracle. It is a moment that immediately connects us to a past: to a way of life that was his childhood, and in which the lives of many of those on the family tree had shared; to the months that led up to the final moments in the forest, and the chaos that became the way of life for those who wanted only to live; to the rebuilding of life and sanity in a new world while carrying the memory and the hopes of those who were murdered.

Arthur Byck was born in Klesow, then Poland, now Ukraine, in 1933. He was eight years old when his parents fled with him eastward, away from the advancing German Army. He was eighteen when he came to the United States, to get an education and begin to build a stable, fulfilling life. He was seventy-two when he died in his sleep in late October 2005.

In addition to being connected with our family's past, in meeting him I also became connected with our family's future: his children and grandchildren carry his attributes and the names of his murdered family members and, together with his wife, carry his story. The news of his sudden and untimely death was a reminder of the precariousness of life, the value of time and relationships, and the need to remember the past and to learn from it.

We are fortunate to live at a time when survivors are among us and we can benefit from hearing their voices and their concerns. They have made an enormous contribution to Holocaust education in their willingness to recall, record and remind us of their experiences. They have created a body of knowledge to which survivors of bullying and racial hatred, and survivors of genocide, can relate.

Karen Murphy, who is developing the International Program for Facing History and Ourselves, told me she used my *Holocaust Memoir Digest* in Rwanda, where history is very close and very painful. In hearing the words of survivors of the Holocaust, Rwandans are able to gain strength in the rebuilding of their own lives, and of their own families. In this way, Holocaust survivors have given us all their example in their choice to rebuild their lives, memorialize their dead, record the evil perpetrated against them, honour those who helped them, and teach that we all have moral choices.

Sixty years after their liberation, the survivors are aging, and their ranks thinning. It is now our obligation to take their recollections and their wisdom to the next generations. This is what the *Holocaust Memoir Digest* seeks to do. I am particularly grateful to the survivors whose memoirs have been included in Volumes 1 and 2, and now Volume 3, for their encouragement and for their belief in the *Digest* and the way it represents their memoirs, and as an "appetizer" to further interest in their memoirs.

I am grateful to Frank Cass for publishing so many survivor memoirs in his Library of Holocaust Testimonies, and for including *Holocaust Memoir Digest* among his Vallentine Mitchell publications. I am grateful to my editor Mark Anstee and to Toby Harris at Vallentine Mitchell, and to my North American distributor ISBS, particularly Lenny Gerson, for meeting all delivery challenges.

The encouragement of survivors who talk in schools and who understand the use of the *Digest* has been very important to me. Many survivors speak to children in schools, children who are the same ages as the survivors were during the events they describe. It is hoped that the survivors who have not yet done so will write their memoirs, and publishers who have not yet done so will publish them, so future generations will continue to gain from their insights.

The encouragement from professors, educators, teachers, librarians and students of the Holocaust and genocide has shown that the written recollections of survivors have an important place in our understanding of what happens during the breakdown of civilization. I am particularly grateful to the following professors who have understood the need for and the uses of the *Digest* since it was in its infancy, and have cheered me on from their distant corners for now more than four years: Stephen Norwood, University of Oklahoma, in Norman; David Patterson, University of Memphis, Tennessee; Eunice Pollack, University of North Texas, in Denton; and Haim Shaked, University of Miami, Florida.

Educators who run teacher-training programmes have offered their encouragement and their endorsement, among them: David J. Bobb, Director, Hoogland Center for Teacher Excellence, Hillsdale College, Michigan; Jeffrey Morry, Director, The Asper Foundation Holocaust and Human Rights Studies Program, Winnipeg, Canada; Karen Pollock, Chief Executive, and Anita Parmar, Education Officer, Holocaust Education Trust, UK; Leonid Saharovici, Memphis, and Executive Director Ruth K. Tanner of the Tennessee Holocaust Commission, Nashville; Mark Skvirsky, National Program Director, Facing History and Ourselves; Eva Unterman, Chair, Council for Holocaust Education, Jewish Federation of Tulsa, Oklahoma.

In many of the states in the United States, the Second Generation – known affectionately as "2Gs" – have taken on the task of ensuring that Holocaust education, and the voices of survivors, finds its place in the curriculum. I am especially grateful to Esther Finder in Rockville, Maryland, Barbara Wind in Whippany, New Jersey, and Lillian Gerstner in Skokie, Illinois.

Sir Martin Gilbert, whose Holocaust histories helped me to understand the history, the geography and the context, has been a pioneer in the use of eyewitness accounts. His maps for the individual memoirs, based on the places mentioned in each memoir, and his general maps in the Study Guide section, will help the reader visualize the enormous expanses covered within the history of the Holocaust period.

Shi Sherebrin has consistently stayed ahead of my technological quagmires and is always ready to keep my technical skills and the project moving forward. Geoff Cain and Earl Pinsky of Digital Internet Group created and maintain the website (www.holocaustmemoirdigest.org) on which all three volumes can be explored, and purchased through a direct link with Amazon. Tim Aspden has prepared all of the maps for publication with patience and expertise.

This project is funded in part by the Conference on Jewish Material Claims Against Germany (Claims Conference), which represents world Jewry in negotiating for compensation and restitution for victims of Nazi persecution and their heirs. The Claims Conference administers compensation funds, recovers unclaimed Jewish property, and allocates funds to institutions that provide social welfare services to Holocaust survivors, and preserves the memory and lessons of the Shoah. I am grateful to Ilana Sperling who has been my liaison at the Claims Conference, and to Bernie Zaifman, President, and Esther Marcus, Executive Director of the London Jewish Federation, London, Ontario, Canada who provided a home for the *Digest* through which I could apply for funding.

It is due to my mother, Helen Goldberg, and her speaking of her early life that I have sought to understand what happened, how it could have happened, and what its moral implications mean to me. From my late father, Ben Goldberg, I inherited a love of reading, especially biography, the story of people's lives; and from my brother Rick, I got my early collection of Holocaust memoirs. I am grateful to my daughters Shoshana and Mirit for their approaches to "tikun olam" the healing of the world. They, and their cousins, carry the hopes and dreams of the Byk family of Klesow, the Flejsz family of Kiev, the Goldberg family of Czartorysk, the Szapiro family of Sarny, and the Poznanski family of Lodz.

Esther Goldberg
London, Ontario, Canada
2 April 2006

THE DIGEST

The aim of the *Holocaust Memoir Digest* is to make the contents of each survivor's memoir available to schools, libraries and institutions that deal with the Holocaust. Using the *Digest*, teachers, students and researchers will know what is in the memoirs, and will be able to use them easily and effectively.

The memoirs appear in the order of their first publication. The memoirs chosen for this third volume of the *Digest* cover a range of regions and experiences, and include the earliest to the most recently published memoirs. Subsequent volumes of the *Digest* will continue to present a range of regions and experiences.

Outline

Each entry of the *Digest* covers the following:
Personal Chronology
Author
Title
Publishing details
Focus of the memoir: age of the writer, time frame, geographic locations
Features of the memoir: foreword, photographs, documents, works cited, maps, afterword, appendices, footnotes, glossary, bibliography, index
Topics particular to each memoir, with the page numbers from the memoir (given for every reference), according to the following themes:

 1. Pre-war Jewish home and community life
 2. Pre-war anti-Semitism
 3. The coming of war
 4. Life under German occupation
 5. Creation of the ghetto
 6. Daily life in the ghetto
 7. Deportation
 8. Mass murder sites
 9. Transit camps
10. Death camps
11. Slave labour camps and factories
12. Theresienstadt/Terezin
13. Auschwitz-Birkenau
14. Death marches
15. Concentration camps
16. Witness to mass murder
17. Resistance, ghetto revolts, individual acts of courage and defiance
18. Partisan activity
19. Specific escapes

20. In hiding, including Hidden Children
21. Righteous Gentiles (also known as Righteous Among the Nations)
22. Liberation
23. Displaced Persons camps (DP camps)
24. Stories of individuals, including family members
25. Post-war life and career
26. Personal reflections

Places mentioned, within Europe, including variant names or spellings, are listed with the page number of first reference. These places are also shown on individual maps, specially drawn for the *Digest* by Sir Martin Gilbert, to illustrate each memoir.

Places mentioned, outside Europe, are listed with the page number of first reference.

Memoir Digest

Primo Levi, *Survival in Auschwitz*

1919: born in Turin, Italy

13 December 1943: captured as a partisan in Northern Italy, aged 24

End of January, 1944: taken to Fossoli transit camp, Italy

February, 1944: German troops enter Fossoli transit camp, Italy

22 February 1944: leaves Fossoli on deportation train

26 February 1944: deportation train arrives in Auschwitz, ninety-six men taken to Buna-Monowitz slave labour camp

Spring 1944: goes to Infirmary, result of accident

Fall 1944: takes an exam to become a Chemistry Specialist at Buna

March through July 1944: works in Buna

August 1944: Allied bombardments of Upper Silesia begin

November 1944: twenty-one still alive of the ninety-six in his convoy who had arrived in February

December 1944: chosen to work in the Chemical Command, Buna

11 January 1945: goes to Infirmary with scarlet fever

18 January 1945: Auschwitz is evacuated, he remains in Infirmary

27 January 1945: Auschwitz is liberated by Soviet troops

Post-war: returns to Turin, Italy; he dies in 1987

Author: Primo Levi

Title: *Survival in Auschwitz, The Nazi Assault on Humanity*

Publishing details

Macmillan Publishing, New York. 1961. 157 pages.
ISBN #0-02-034310-8.
Originally published in Italian in 1958, and in English as *If This is a Man* by Orion Press, 1959.
Translated from the Italian by Stuart Woolf.

Focus:

Primo, a young Italian, who was 20 in 1939, is deported from Italy to Auschwitz where he survives for almost a year; the events recorded take place between his arrest on 13 December 1943 and his liberation by Soviet forces in Auschwitz on 27 January 1945.

Features:

Foreword: Author's Preface, pages 5–6.
　　　　　"You who live safe ...," poem written by the Author, page 8.

Contents: (by topic, with page numbers)

Life under German occupation

(10) At the Italian-run transit camp of Fossoli, February 1944: "The arrival of a squad of German SS men ... inspected the camp with care and had publicly and loudly upbraided the Italian commissar for the defective organization of the kitchen service and for the scarce amount of wood distributed for heating; they even said an infirmary would soon be opened. But on the morning of the 21st we learned that on the following day the Jews would be leaving."

Deportation

(10) Notification of deportation from Fossoli for all the Jews: "Our destination? Nobody knew. We should be prepared for a fortnight of travel. For every person missing at the roll call, ten would be shot."

(12) 22 February 1944, they are deported, first by bus to Carpi: "Here we received the first blows: and it was so new and senseless that we felt no pain, neither in body nor in spirit. Only a profound amazement: how can one hit a man without anger?"

(12–13) Loaded onto the train: "There were twelve goods wagons for six hundred and fifty men; in mine we were only forty-five, but it was a small wagon. ... Among the forty-five people in my wagon only four saw their homes again; and it was by far the most fortunate wagon."

(14) The train reaches its destination: "Now in the hour of decision, we said to each other things that are never said among the living. We said farewell and it was short; everybody said farewell to life through his neighbour. We had no more fear."

(106) 1944: "Throughout the spring, convoys arrived from Hungary; one prisoner in two was Hungarian, and Hungarian had become the second language in the camp after Yiddish."

(123) The survival rate of his convoy by November 1944: "We were ninety-six when we arrived, we, the Italians of convoy 174,000; only twenty-nine of us survived until October, and of these, eight went in the selection. We are twenty-one now and the winter has hardly begun. How many of us will be alive at the new year? How many when spring begins?"

(124) "Three hundred prisoners have arrived in the Lager from the Lodz ghetto, transferred by the Germans before the Russian advance ... ." August 1944.

Transit camps

(10) He is sent upon capture to Fossoli: "At the moment of my arrival, that is, at the end of January, 1944, there were about one hundred and fifty Italian Jews in the camp, but within a few weeks their number rose to more than six hundred."

(11–12) The last night in Fossoli before deportation to the unknown: "... we experienced within ourselves a grief that was new for us, the ancient grief of the people that has no land, the grief without hope of the exodus which is renewed every century." 21 February 1944.

Slave labour camps and factories

(15, 21) After their arrival at Auschwitz on 26 February 1944 and after selection, ninety-six men of his convoy remain; they are taken to Buna-Monowitz (Auschwitz III): "We are at Monowitz, near Auschwitz, in Upper Silesia, a region inhabited by both Poles and Germans. This camp is a work-camp, in German one says 'Arbeitslager'; all the prisoners (there are about ten thousand) work in a factory which produces a type of rubber called Buna, so that the camp itself is called Buna."

(30–2) Two weeks after his convoy had entered Buna-Monowitz: "I push wagons, I work with a shovel, I turn rotten in the rain, I shiver in the wind; already my own body is no longer mine: my belly is swollen, my limbs emaciated, my face is thick in the morning, hollow in the evening; some of us have yellow skin, others grey. When we do not meet for a few days we hardly recognize each other."

(39–41) An accident at Buna allows him to seek medical treatment: "Ka-Be is the abbreviation of Krankenbau, the infirmary. There are eight huts ... . They permanently hold a tenth of the population of the camp, but there are few who stay there longer than two weeks and none more than two months: within these limits they are held to die or be cured. Those who show signs of improvement are cured in Ka-Be, those who seem to get worse are sent from Ka-Be to the gas chamber."

(41–4) Being admitted to Ka-Be, the infirmary at Buna: "The life of Ka-Be is a life of limbo. The material discomforts are relatively few, apart from hunger and the inherent pains of illness. It is not cold, there is no work to do, and unless you commit some grave fault, you are not beaten."

(45) The band at Buna which plays as the workers leave and return to the camp: "The tunes are few, a dozen, the same ones every day, morning and evening: marches and popular songs dear to every German. They lie engraven on our minds and will be the last thing in Lager that we shall forget: they are the voice of the Lager, the perceptible expression of its geometrical

madness, of the resolution of others to annihilate us first as men in order to kill us more slowly afterwards."

(52–3) The nights in the bunk in Buna: "I do not know who my neighbour is; I am not even sure that it is always the same person because I have never seen his face except for a few seconds amidst the uproar of the reveille, so that I know his back and his feet much better than his face."

(53–5) The dreams in the night: "I remember that I have recounted it to Alberto and that he confided to me, to my amazement, that it is also his dream and the dream of many others, perhaps of everyone. ... Why is the pain of every day translated so constantly into our dreams, in the ever-repeated scene of the unlistened-to story?"

(55–7) The nights in Buna: "... the suffering of the day, composed of hunger, blows, cold, exhaustion, fear and promiscuity, turns at night-time into shapeless nightmares of unheard-of violence, which in free life would only occur during a fever. One wakes up at every moment, frozen with terror, shaking in every limb, under the impression of an order shouted out by a voice full of anger in a language not understood."

(59–63) Their work at Buna, two men carrying 175 pound wooden "sleepers" which will lay the path for moving a cast-iron cylinder: "I bite deeply into my lips; we know well that to gain a small, extraneous pain serves as a stimulant to mobilize our last reserves of energy. The Kapos also know it: some of them beat us from pure bestiality and violence, but others beat us when we are under a load almost lovingly, accompanying the blows with exhortations, as cart-drivers do with willing horses."

(65) Buna the camp, where: "... the only things alive are machines and slaves – and the former are more alive than the latter. ... The Buna is as large as a city; besides the managers and German technicians, forty thousand foreigners work there, and fifteen to twenty languages are spoken. All the foreigners live in different Lagers which surround the Buna ... . Our Lager ('Judenlager') by itself provides ten thousand workers who come from all the nations of Europe. We are the slaves of the slaves, whom all can give orders to, and our name is the number which we carry tattooed on our arm and sewn on our jacket."

(66, 107) Efficiency at Buna: "As will be told, the Buna factory, on which the Germans were busy for four years and for which countless of us suffered and died, never produced a pound of synthetic rubber." In August 1944, Allied bombardments of Upper Silesia begin, later: "The day on which the production of synthetic rubber should have begun, which seemed imminent in August, was gradually postponed until the Germans no longer spoke about it."

(70–8) Commerce in Buna, by trade or theft, driven by hunger, punishable to all: "... but the punishment strikes the thief and the victim with equal gravity."

(75) The "civilian" prisoners who were also known as "forced labourers", caught for "political crimes" such as trading, within Buna, condemned to Primo's Lager for a period of time: "... the Lager is for them a punishment, and if they do not die of exhaustion or illness they can expect to return among men; if they could communicate with us, it would create a breach in the wall which keeps us dead to the world, and a ray of light into the mystery which prevails among free men about our condition. For us, on the contrary, the Lager is not a punishment; for us, no end is foreseen and the Lager is nothing but a manner of living assigned to us, without limits of time, in the bosom of the Germanic social organism."

(82–3) On the Jewish "Prominenz": "When he is given the command of a group of unfortunates, with the right of life or death over them, he will be cruel and tyrannical, because he will understand that if he is not sufficiently so, someone else, judged more suitable, will take over his post. Moreover, his capacity for hatred, unfulfilled in the direction of the oppressors, will double back, beyond all reason, on the oppressed; and he will only be satisfied when he has unloaded onto his underlings the injury received from above."

(83–4) On non-Jewish "Prominenz": "It is difficult to explain how in Auschwitz the political German, Polish and Russian prominents rivalled the ordinary convicts in brutality. But it is known that in Germany the qualifications of political crime also applied to such acts as clandestine trade, illicit relations with Jewish women, theft from Party officials. The 'real' politicals lived and died in other camps, with names now sadly famous, in notoriously hard conditions, which, however, in many aspects differed from those described here."

(84) On survival: "Many were the ways devised and put into effect by us in order not to die: as many as there are different human characters. All implied a weakening struggle of one against all, and a by no means small sum of aberrations and compromises. Survival without renunciation of any part of one's own moral world – apart from powerful and direct interventions by fortune – was conceded only to a very few superior individuals, made of the stuff of martyrs and saints."

(92–4) The possibility of work in the Chemical Kommando: "Although we do not think for more than a few minutes a day, and then in a strangely detached and external manner, we well know that we will end in selections. I know that I am not made of the stuff of those who resist, I am too civilized, I still think too much, I use myself up at work. And now I also know that I can save myself if I become a Specialist, and that I will become a Specialist if I pass a chemistry examination."

(96–8) He takes an examination to become a member of the Chemical Kommando, administered by Doctor Pannwitz who begins the questioning with a look: "… that look was not one between two men; and if I had known how completely to explain the nature of that look, which came as if across the glass window of an aquarium between two beings who live in different worlds, I would also have explained the essence of the great insanity of the third Germany."

(106–7) Five months in Buna: "For living men, the units of time always have a value, which increases in ratio to the strength of the internal resources of the person living through them; but for us, hours, days, months spilled out sluggishly from the future into the past, always too slowly, a valueless and superfluous material, of which we sought to rid ourselves as soon as possible. With the end of the season when the days chased each other, vivacious, precious and irrecoverable, the future stood in front of us, grey and inarticulate, like an invincible barrier. For us, history had stopped." July 1944.

(107–9) The Allies advance: "At Buna the German civilians raged with the fury of the secure man who wakes up from a long dream of domination and sees his own ruin and is unable to understand it."

(112–13) The winter of 1944 arrives: "Just as our hunger is not that feeling of missing a meal, so our way of being cold has need of a new word. We say 'hunger', we say 'tiredness', 'fear', 'pain', we say 'winter' and they are different things. They are free words, created and used by free men who lived in comfort and suffering in their homes. If the Lagers had lasted longer a new, harsh language would have been born; and only this language could express what it means to toil the whole day in the wind, with the temperature below freezing, wearing only a shirt, underpants, cloth jacket and trousers, and in one's body nothing but weakness, hunger and knowledge of the end drawing near."

(113–16) October 1944 selection: "One feels the selections arriving. 'Selekcja': the hybrid Latin and Polish word is heard once, twice, many times, interpolated in foreign conversations; at first we cannot distinguish it, then it forces itself on our attention, and in the end it persecutes us." The selection begins with a bell ringing: "… if it sounds during the day, it means 'Blocksperre', enclosure in huts, and this happens when there is a selection to prevent anyone avoiding it, or when those selected leave for the gas, to prevent anyone seeing them leave."

(116–18) A description of the selection process, then the soup is distributed: "A double ration will be given to those selected. I have never discovered whether this was a ridiculously charitable initiative of the 'Blockältester', or an explicit disposition of the SS, but in fact, in the interval of two or three days (sometimes even much longer) between the selection and the departure, the victims at Monowitz-Auschwitz enjoyed this privilege."

(121) "We have bored our way through all the minutes of the day, this very day which seemed invincible and eternal this morning; now it lies dead and is immediately forgotten; already it is no longer a day, it has left no trace in anybody's memory. … Do you know how one says 'never' in camp slang? 'Morgen früh', tomorrow morning."

(125–6) Primo is chosen for work in the Laboratory: "Häftling 174517 has been promoted as a specialist and has the right to a new shirt and underpants and has to be shaved every Wednesday."

(126–8) Work in the Laboratory: "The smell makes me start back as if from the blow of a whip: the weak aromatic smell of organic chemisty laboratories. For a moment the large semi-dark room at the university, my fourth year, the mild air of May in Italy comes back to me with brutal violence and immediately vanishes. … My comrades in the Kommando envy me, and they are right; should I not be contented? But in the morning, I hardly escape the raging wind and cross the doorstep of the laboratory when I find at my side the comrade of all my peaceful moments, of Ka-Be, of the rest-Sundays – the pain of remembering, the old ferocious longing to feel myself a man, which attacks me like a dog the moment my conscience comes out of the gloom."

(129–30) His discussion in his mind with the girls in the Laboratory for whom the last year "has gone by so quickly": "This time last year I was a free man: an outlaw but free, I had a name and a family, I had an eager and restless mind, an agile and healthy body. … I had an enormous, deep-rooted foolish faith in the benevolence of fate; to kill and to die seemed extraneous literary things to me. My days were both cheerful and sad, but I regretted them equally, they were all full and positive; the future stood before me as a great treasure. Today the only thing left of the life of those days is what one needs to suffer hunger and cold; I am not even alive enough to know how to kill myself."

Auschwitz-Birkenau

(15) Their deportation train stops at the Auschwitz ramp: "Everything was as silent as an aquarium, or as in certain dream sequences. We had expected something more apocalyptic:

they seemed simple police agents. It was disconcerting and disarming. ... They behaved with the calm assurance of people doing their normal duty of every day." 26 February 1944.

(15–17) Separation at the Auschwitz ramp: "In less than ten minutes all the fit men had been collected together in a group. What happened to the others, to the women, to the children, to the old men, we could establish neither then nor later: the night swallowed them up, purely and simply. Today, however, we know that in that rapid and summary choice each one of us had been judged capable or not of working usefully for the Reich; we know that of our convoy no more than ninety-six men and twenty-nine women entered the respective camps of Monowitz-Buna and Birkenau, and that of all the others, more than five hundred in number, not one was living two days later."

(18–23) Description of entering the camp: "Then for the first time we became aware that our language lacks words to express this offence, the demolition of a man. In a moment, with almost prophetic intuition, the reality was revealed to us: we had reached the bottom. It was not possible to sink lower than this; no human condition is more miserable than this, nor could it conceivably be so. Nothing belongs to us anymore; they have taken away our clothes, our shoes, even our hair; if we speak, they will not listen to us, and if they listen, they will not understand. They will even take away our name: and if we want to keep it, we will have to find in ourselves the strength to do so, to manage somehow so that behind the name something of us, of us as we were, still remains."

(23–5) Entrance into the camp; he becomes #174517: "And for many days, while the habits of freedom still led me to look for the time on my wristwatch, my new name ironically appeared instead, its number tattooed in bluish characters under the skin."

(27–30) Description of the camp layout and make-up: "We had soon learned that the guests of the Lager are divided into three categories: the criminals, the politicals and the Jews. All are clothed in stripes, all are 'Häftlinge' (prisoners), but the criminals wear a green triangle next to the number sewn on the jacket; the politicals wear a red triangle; and the Jews, who form the large majority, wear the Jewish star, red and yellow."

(33–5) The routine of the camp: "The confusion of language is a fundamental component of the manner of living here: one is surrounded by a perpetual Babel, in which everyone shouts orders and threats in languages never heard before, and woe betide whoever fails to grasp the meaning." Morning rations: "the distribution of bread, of bread-Brot-Broid-chleb-pain-lechem-kenyér, of the holy grey slab which seems gigantic in your neighbour's hand, and in your own hand so small as to make you cry." Washing: "In this place it is practically pointless to wash every day in the turbid water of the filthy washbasins for purposes of cleanliness and health; but it is most important as a symptom of remaining vitality, and necessary as an instrument of moral survival."

(46–7) Schmulek tries to help him understand about the crematoriums: "'Show me your number: you are 174517. This numbering ... applies to Auschwitz and the dependent camps. There are now ten thousand of us here at Buna-Monowitz; perhaps thirty thousand between Auschwitz and Birkenau. "Wo sind die Andere?" Where are the others?'"

Death marches

(137–41) On 11 January 1945 Primo goes to Ka-Be, the infirmary, with scarlet fever, as the camp prepares for evacuation in the face of the Russian advance: "All the healthy prisoners ... left during the night of January 18, 1945. They must have been about twenty thousand coming from different camps. Almost in their entirety they vanished during the evacuation march: Alberto was among them. ... So we remained in our bunks, alone with our illnesses, and with our inertia stronger than fear. In the whole Ka-Be we numbered perhaps eight hundred."

Witness to mass murder

(45) The work brigades, Buna-Monowitz (Auschwitz III): "At the departure and the return march the SS are never lacking. Who could deny them their right to watch this choreography of their creation, the dance of dead men, squad after squad, leaving the fog to enter the fog? What more concrete proof of their victory?"

(81–2) "All the mussulmans who finished in the gas chambers have the same story, or more exactly, have no story; they followed the slope down to the bottom, like streams that run down to the sea. ... Their life is short but their number is endless; they, the 'Muselmänner', the drowned, form the backbone of the camp, an anonymous mass, continually renewed and always identical, of non-men who march and labour in silence, the divine spark dead within them, already too empty to really suffer. One hesitates to call them living: one hesitates to call their death death, in the face of which they have no fear, as they are too tired to understand."

(124) November 1944, deportees from the Lodz Ghetto bring news: "... they described how the Germans had liquidated the Lublin camp over a year ago: four machine guns in the corners and the huts set on fire ... ." The "Lublin camp" was Majdanek, destroyed in the "Harvest Festival" November 1943.

(126) "The Russians are fifty miles away. ... Prisoners 'reclaimed' from all the camps in east Poland pour into our Lager haphazardly; the minority are set to work, the majority leave immediately for Birkenau and the Chimney."

Resistance, ghetto revolts, individual acts of courage and defiance

(35–6) In Buna, Steinlauf gives him a lesson on survival: "... that precisely because the Lager was a great machine to reduce us to beasts, we must not become beasts; that even in this place one can survive, and therefore one must want to survive, to tell the story, to bear witness; and that to survive we must force ourselves to save at least the skeleton, the scaffolding, the form of civilization. We are slaves, deprived of every right, exposed to every insult, condemned to certain death, but we still possess one power, and we must defend it with all our strength for it is the last – the power to refuse our consent."

(72) In Buna: "These few survivors from the Jewish colony of Salonika ... are the repositories of a concrete, mundane, conscious wisdom, in which the traditions of all the Mediterranean civilizations blend together. That this wisdom was transformed in the camp into the systematic and scientific practice of theft and seizure of positions and the monopoly of the bargaining Market, should not let one forget that their aversion to gratuitous brutality, their amazing consciousness of the survival of at least a potential human dignity made of the Greeks the most coherent national nucleus in the Lager, and in this respect, the most civilized."

(124) Deportees from the Lodz Ghetto bring news: "... they told us rumours about the legendary battle of the Warsaw Ghetto ... ."

(134–6) A prisoner who had connections to the revolt at Birkenau (Auschwitz II), where one of the crematoriums was blown up, is hung at Buna: "Alberto and I went back to the hut, and we could not look each other in the face. That man must have been tough, he must have been made of another metal than us if this condition of ours, which has broken us, could not bend him." (The revolt had taken place on 7 October 1944.)

Partisan activity

(9) He had hoped to establish: "... a partisan band affiliated with the Resistance movement 'Justice and Liberty'. Contacts, arms, money and the experience needed to acquire them were all missing." Northern Italy, 1943.

(9–10) Captured as a partisan, arrested as: "a suspect person" on 13 December 1943, aged twenty-four, in Italy: "During the interrogations that followed, I preferred to admit my status of 'Italian citizen of Jewish race'. I felt that otherwise I would be unable to justify my presence in places too secluded even for an evacuee; while I believed (wrongly as was subsequently seen) that the admission of my political activity would have meant torture and certain death."

(155) 25 January 1945, Auschwitz, recounting their former lives: "Charles almost cried when I told him the story of the armistice in Italy, of the turbid and desperate beginning of the Partisan resistance, of the man who betrayed us and of our capture in the mountains."

In hiding, including Hidden Children

(26) Primo explains in his limited German that his mother is in hiding in Italy: "'... hidden, no one knows, run away, does not speak, no one sees her.'"

Righteous Gentiles

(109–11) "I believe that it was really due to Lorenzo that I am alive today; not so much for his material aid, as for his having constantly reminded me by his presence, by his natural and plain manner of being good, that there still existed a just world outside our own, something and someone still pure and whole, not corrupt, not savage, extraneous to hatred and terror; something difficult to define, a remote possibility of good, but for which it was worth surviving."

(131–2) Lorenzo supplies Alberto and Primo with extra soup: "We speak about Lorenzo and how to reward him; later, if we return, we will of course do everything we can for him; but of what use is it to talk about that? He knows as well as us that we can hardly hope to return. We ought to do something at once; we could try to have his shoes repaired at the cobbler's shop in our Lager ... ." December 1944, Buna.

Liberation

(127–8) Soviet troops close in on Buna (Auschwitz III) December 1944: "But the Germans are deaf and blind, enclosed in an armour of obstinacy and of wilful ignorance. ... They construct shelters and trenches, they repair the damage, they build, they fight, they command, they organize and they kill. What else could they do? They are Germans. This way of behaviour is not meditated and deliberate, but follows from their nature and from the destiny they have chosen. They could not act differently: if you wound the body of a dying man, the wound will begin to heal, even if the whole body dies within a day."

(145) After the Germans flee and Buna is bombed, Primo, Arthur and Charles find a stove and potatoes for the eleven surviving members of their Ka-Be hut: "Towarowski ... proposed to

the others that each of them offer a slice of bread to us three who had been working. And so it was agreed. Only a day before a similar event would have been inconceivable. The law of the Lager said: 'eat your own bread, and if you can, that of your neighbour', and left no room for gratitude. It really meant that the Lager was dead. It was the first human gesture that occurred among us. I believe that that moment can be dated as the beginning of the change by which we who had not died slowly changed from Häftlinge to men again."

(145–50) The situation in the camp and their hut after the Wehrmacht troops retreat: "An indescribable filth had invaded every part of the camp. ... Although suffering from the cold, which remained acute, we thought with horror of what would happen if it thawed: the diseases would spread irreparably, the stench would be suffocating, and even more, with the snow melted we would remain definitively without water."

(151–4) A "trench" of potatoes is found outside the barbed wire: "... for the first time since the day of my arrest I found myself free, without armed guards, without wire fences between myself and home. ... Liberty. The breach in the barbed wire gave us a concrete image of it. To anyone who stopped to think, it signified no more Germans, no more selections, no work, no blows, no roll-calls, and perhaps, later, the return. But we had to make an effort to convince ourselves of it, and no one had time to enjoy the thought. All around lay destruction and death."

(155–6) While waiting for the Soviet troops: "We all said to each other that the Russians would arrive soon, at once; we all proclaimed it, we were all sure of it, but at bottom nobody believed it. Becauses one loses the habit of hoping in the Lager, and even of believing in one's own reason. In the Lager it is useless to think, because events happen for the most part in an unforeseeable manner; and it is harmful, because it keeps alive a sensitivity which is a source of pain, and which some providential natural law dulls when suffering passes a certain limit. Like joy, fear and pain itself, even expectancy can be tiring."

Stories of individuals, including family members

(15) Selection at the ramp upon arrival at Auschwitz Main Camp (Auschwitz I): "But Renzo stayed an instant too long to say goodbye to Francesca, his fiancée, and with a single blow they knocked him to the ground."

(16, 20) Three-year-old Emilia, last seen at the ramp upon arrival at Auschwitz: "Emilia, daughter of Aldo Levi of Milan, was a curious, ambitious, cheerful, intelligent child; her parents had succeeded in washing her during the journey in the packed car in a tub with tepid water which the degenerate German engineer had allowed them to draw from the engine that was dragging us all to death."

(26–7) Schlome, a Polish Jew, in Buna–Monowitz (Auschwitz III), befriends him on the first day: "I have never seen Schlome since, but I have not forgotten his serious and gentle face of a child, which welcomed me on the threshold of the house of the dead."

(35–6) Friend: "... ex-sergeant Steinlauf of the Austro–Hungarian army, Iron Cross of the '14–'18 war... " teaches him about how to survive, and why.

(37–8) A work companion at Buna: "He is Null Achtzehn. He is not called anything except that, Zero Eighteen, the last three figures of his entry number; as if everyone was aware that only man is worthy of a name, and that Null Achtzehn is no longer a man. I think that even he has forgotten his name, certainly he acts as if this was so."

(42) Chajim, his friend in Ka-Be, the infirmary: "He is Polish, a religious Jew, learned in rabbinical law. He is about as old as I, a watchmaker by profession, and here in Buna works as a precision mechanic; so he is among the few who are able to preserve their dignity and self-assurance through the practice of a profession in which they are skilled."

(46–7) His neighbours in the infirmary: "One is Walter Bonn, a Dutchman, civilized and quite well mannered. ... The other one, Walter's neighbour ... is a Polish Jew, albino, with an emaciated and good-natured face, no longer young. His name is Schmulek, he is a smith." Schmulek is taken in the next selection: "When Schmulek left, he gave me his spoon and knife; Walter and I avoided looking at each other and remained silent for a long time."

(48) His friend from Rome, Piero Sonnino has a method to survive in the infirmary among dysentery patients: "Piero knows what he is risking, but it has gone well so far."

(51, 125, 133–4, 141) His friend Alberto, in Block 45, Buna: "Alberto entered the Lager with his head high, and lives in here unscathed and uncorrupted. He understood before any of us that this life is war; he permitted himself no indulgences, he lost no time complaining and commiserating with himself and with others, but entered the battle from the beginning. ... He fights for his life but still remains everybody's friend. He 'knows' whom to corrupt, whom to avoid, whose compassion to arouse, whom to resist. ... I always saw him, and still see in him, the rare figure of the strong yet peace-loving man against whom the weapons of night are blunted." Alberto is evacuated from Buna on the death march, 18 January 1945.

(52) At night, Block 45, Buna: "Engineer Kardos moves around the bunks, tending wounded feet and suppurating corns. This is his trade: there is no one who will not willingly renounce a slice of bread to soothe the torment of those numbed sores which bleed at every step all day. And so, in this manner, honestly, engineer Kardos solves the problem of living."

(58–9) Resnyk, Primo's bed companion in Buna, Polish, deported from Drancy after having lived in Paris for twenty years: "He is thirty, but like all of us, could be taken for seventeen or fifty. He told me his story, and today I have forgotten it, but it was certainly a sorrowful, cruel and moving story; because so are all our stories, hundreds of thousands of stories, all different and all full of a tragic, disturbing necessity. ... simple and incomprehensible like the stories in the Bible. But are they not themselves stories of a new Bible?"

(61, 95) Wachsmann, a rabbi and teacher from Galicia: "... is lit up by an amazing vitality in actions and words and spends long evenings discussing Talmudic questions incomprehensibly in Yiddish and Hebrew with Mendi, who is a modernist rabbi." Mendi: "... comes from sub-Carpathian Russia, from that confusion of peoples where everyone speaks at least three languages, and Mendi speaks seven."

(64–5) The Greeks of Salonika in Buna: "... whom even the Germans respect and the Poles fear. They are in their third year of camp, and nobody knows better than them what the camp means. They now stand closely in a circle, shoulder to shoulder, and sing one of their interminable chants." (The Greeks were deported from Salonika beginning in March 1943. The time to which Primo refers would have been their second year, as is described in Erika Amariglio's memoir "From Thessaloniki and to Auschwitz and Back", included in the *Holocaust Memoir Digest*, Volume 2.)

(67–9) Food and the men: Sigi from Vienna, and Béla from Hungary, speaking of food;

memories of his friends, Vanda, Luciana, and Franco and their last meal together in Fossoli; Fischer, the Hungarian, saves his bread; Templer, "the official organizer of the Komando," finds extra soup: "For a few hours we can be unhappy in the manner of free men."

(84–5) Schepschel, in Buna: "... when the opportunity showed itself, he did not hesitate to have Moischl, his accomplice in a theft from the kitchen, condemned to a flogging, in the mistaken hope of gaining favour in the eyes of the 'Blockältester' and furthering his candidature for the position of 'Kesselwäscher', 'vat-washer'."

(85–7) Alfred L., who works to become head of the Chemical Kommando: "... knew that the step was short from being judged powerful to effectively becoming so, and that everywhere, and especially in the midst of the general levelling of the Lager, a respectable appearance is the best guarantee of being respected."

(87–9) Elias Lindzin, #141565: "... has survived the destruction from outside, because he is physically indestructible; he has resisted the annihilation from within because he is insane. So, in the first place, he is a survivor: he is the most adaptable, the human type most suited to this way of living. If Elias regains his liberty he will be confined to the fringes of human society, in a prison or a lunatic asylum. But here in Lager there are no criminals nor madmen; no criminals because there is no moral law to contravene, no madmen because we are wholly devoid of free will, as our every action is, in time and place, the only conceivable one."

(89–91) "Henri ... is eminently civilized and sane ... . According to Henri's theory, there are three methods open to man to escape extermination which still allow him to retain the name of man: organization, pity and theft. ... Henri has discovered that pity, being a primary and instinctive sentiment, grows quite well if ably cultivated, particularly in the primitive minds of the brutes who command us, those very brutes who have no scruples about beating us up without a reason, or treading our faces into the ground; nor has the practical importance of the discovery escaped him, and upon it he has built up his personal trade."

(91) "doctor Citron and doctor Weiss" at Ka-Be, the infirmary in Buna.

(99–105) Jean the Alsatian picks Primo to carry the soup, receives a lesson on Italian, and Dante's "Divine Comedy": "... perhaps, despite the wan translation and the pedestrian, rushed commentary, he has received the message, he has felt that it has to do with him, that it has to do with all men who toil, and with us in particular; and that it has to do with us two, who dare to reason of these things with the poles for the soup on our shoulders."

(103) Engineer Levi at Kraftwerk, Buna, the "cable-laying Kommando": "He waves to me, he is a brave man, I have never seen his morale low, he never speaks of eating."

(117) "Irregularities" in the selection: "René, for example, so young and robust, ended on the left ... . It must equally have been a mistake about Sattler, a huge Transylvanian peasant who was still at home only twenty days ago; Sattler does not understand German, he has understood nothing of what has taken place, and stands in a corner mending his shirt. Must I go and tell him that his shirt will be of no more use?"

(118) The evening after the selection: "Silence slowly prevails and then, from my bunk on the top row, I see and hear old Kuhn praying aloud ... . Kuhn is thanking God because he has not been chosen. Kuhn is out of his senses. Does he not see Beppo the Greek in the bunk next to

him, Beppo who is twenty years old and is going to the gas chamber the day after tomorrow and knows it and lies there looking fixedly at the light without saying anything and without even thinking anymore? Can Kuhn fail to realize that next time it will be his turn?"

(120–2) The Hungarian Kraus Páli: "He works too much and too vigorously: he has not yet learnt our underground art of economizing on everything, on breath, movements, even thoughts. He doesn't yet know that it is better to be beaten, because one does not normally die of blows, but one does of exhaustion, and badly, and when one grows aware of it, it is already too late."

(138, 143–5) Arthur and Charles, two Frenchmen with him in Ka-Be at the end, only recently captured and brought to Buna: "Charles was courageous and robust, while Arthur was shrewd, with the practical common sense of the peasant."

(137, 140, 157) The twelve other prisoners in his Ka-Be hut, and their fates: the two Hungarians leave on the death march and are killed by the SS: "Sómogyi was the only one to die in the ten days. Sertelet, Cagnolati, Towarowski, Lakmaker and Dorget ... died some weeks later in the temporary Russian hospital of Auschwitz. In April, at Katowice, I met Schenck and Alcalai in good health. Arthur has reached his family happily and Charles has taken up his teacher's profession ... ."

Post-war life and career

(Endpaper) Returned to Turin to manage a chemical factory and write. He died in 1987.

Personal reflections

(5–6) From the author's Preface: "The need to tell our story to 'the rest,' to make 'the rest' participate in it, had taken on for us, before our liberation and after, the character of an immediate and violent impulse, to the point of competing with our elemental needs."

(6) From the author's Preface: "It seems unnecessary to me to add that none of the facts are invented."

(13) "Sooner or later in life everyone discovers that perfect happiness is unrealizable, but there are few who pause to consider the antithesis: that perfect unhappiness is equally unattainable. The obstacles preventing the realization of both these extreme states are of the same nature: they derive from our human condition which is opposed to everything infinite. Our ever-insufficient knowledge of the future opposes it: and this is called, in the one instance, hope, and in the other, uncertainty of the following day. The certainty of death opposes it: for it places a limit on every joy, but also on every grief. The inevitable material cares oppose it: for as they poison every lasting happiness, they equally assiduously distract us from our misfortunes, and make our consciousness of them intermittent and hence supportable."

(23) "Imagine now a man who is deprived of everyone he loves, and at the same time of his house, his habits, his clothes, in short, of everything he possesses: he will be a hollow man, reduced to suffering and needs, forgetful of dignity and restraint, for he who loses all often easily loses himself. He will be a man whose life or death can be lightly decided with no sense of human affinity, in the most fortunate of cases, on the basis of a pure judgement of utility. It is in this way that one can understand the double sense of the term 'extermination camp', and it is now clear what we seek to express with the phrase: 'to lie on the bottom'."

(31) "According to our character, some of us are immediately convinced that all is lost, that one cannot live here, that the end is near and sure; others are convinced that however hard the present life may be, salvation is probable and not far off, and if we have faith and strength, we will see our houses and our dear ones again. The two classes of pessimists and optimists are not so clearly defined, however, not because there are many agnostics, but because the majority, without memory or coherence, drift between the two extremes, according to the moment and the mood of the person they happen to meet."

(49) From the perspective of the infirmary: "In this Ka-Be, an enclosure of relative peace, we have learnt that our personality is fragile, that it is in much more danger than our life; and the old wise ones, instead of warning us 'remember that you must die', would have done much better to remind us of this greater danger that threatens us. If from inside the Lager, a message could have seeped out to free men, it would have been this: take care not to suffer in your own homes what is inflicted on us here."

(50–1) "Man's capacity to dig himself in, to secrete a shell, to build around himself a tenuous barrier of defence, even in apparently desperate circumstances, is astonishing and merits a serious study. It is based on an invaluable activity of adaptation, partly passive and unconscious, partly active ... ."

(66) "For human nature is such that grief and pain – even simultaneously suffered – do not add up as a whole in our consciousness, but hide, the lesser behind the greater, according to a definite law of perspective. It is providential and is our means of surviving in the camp. And this is the reason why so often in free life one hears it said that man is never content. In fact it is not a question of a human incapacity for a state of absolute happiness, but of an ever-insufficient knowledge of the complex nature of the state of unhappiness; so that the single name of the major cause is given to all its causes, which are composite and set out in an order of urgency. And if the most immediate cause of stress comes to an end, you are grievously amazed to see that another one lies behind; and in reality a whole series of others. So that as soon as the cold, which throughout the winter had seemed our only enemy, had ceased, we became aware of our hunger... ."

(79) "... the Lager was pre-eminently a gigantic biological and social experiment. Thousands of individuals, differing in age, condition, origin, language, culture and customs are enclosed within barbed wire: there they live a regular, controlled life which is identical for all and inadequate to all needs, and which is much more rigorous than any experimenter could have set up to establish what is essential and what adventitious to the conduct of the human animal in the struggle for life. We do not believe in the most obvious and facile deduction: that man is fundamentally brutal, egoistic and stupid in his conduct once every civilized institution is taken away, and that the Häftling is consequently nothing but a man without inhibitions. We believe, rather, that the only conclusion to be drawn is that in the face of driving necessity and physical disabilities many social habits and instincts are reduced to silence."

(80–1) "... a country is considered the more civilized the more the wisdom and efficiencies of its laws hinder a weak man from becoming too weak or a powerful one too powerful. But in the Lager things are different... . Whosoever does not know how to become an 'Organisator', 'Kombinator', 'Prominent' (the savage eloquence of these words!) soon becomes a 'mussulman'. In life, a third way exists, and is in fact the rule; it does not exist in the concentration camp."

(119) "It is November, it has been raining for ten days now and the ground is like the bottom of a swamp. ... It is lucky that it is not windy today. Strange, how in some way one always has the impression of being fortunate, how some chance happening, perhaps infinitesimal, stops us crossing the threshold of despair and allows us to live."

Places mentioned in Europe (page first mentioned)

Auschwitz Main Camp/Auschwitz I (13), Birkenau/Brzezinka/Auschwitz II (15), Brenner Pass (13), Buna-Monowitz/Monowice/Auschwitz III (15), Carpi (12), Cracow/Krakow/ Krakau (73), Czestochowa (139), Drancy transit camp (58), Fossoli transit camp (10), Galicia (61), Gleiwitz/Gliwice slave labour camp (75), Heydebreck slave labour camp (Kedzierzyn) (75), Hungary/ Magyarország (106), Italy/Italia (21), Janinagrube slave labour camp (75), Jaworzno slave labour camp (114), Katowice/Kattowitz (157), Liguria (101), Lodz/Litzmanstadt (124), Lorraine/Alsace-Lorraine/Elsass-Lottringen (138), Lublin (124), Metz (140), Milan/ Milano/Mailand (16), Modena (10), Normandy (106), Norway/Norge (59), Paris (59), Poland/Polska (126), Poznan/Posen (115), Provenchères-sur-Fave (155), Rome/Roma (48), Ruthenia/Sub-Carpathia (95), Salonika/Thessaloniki (24), Salzburg (14), Strasbourg (101), Toulouse (148), Transylvania (125), Turin/Torino (97), Ukraine/Ukrajina (59), Upper Silesia/Oberschlesien (21), Vienna/Wien (14), Vosges (143), Warsaw/Warszawa/Warschau (88), Zakopane (139)

Places mentioned outside Europe (page first mentioned)

Algeria/Al Jazair/Algérie (59), Russia/Rossija (95), Tripoli (11)

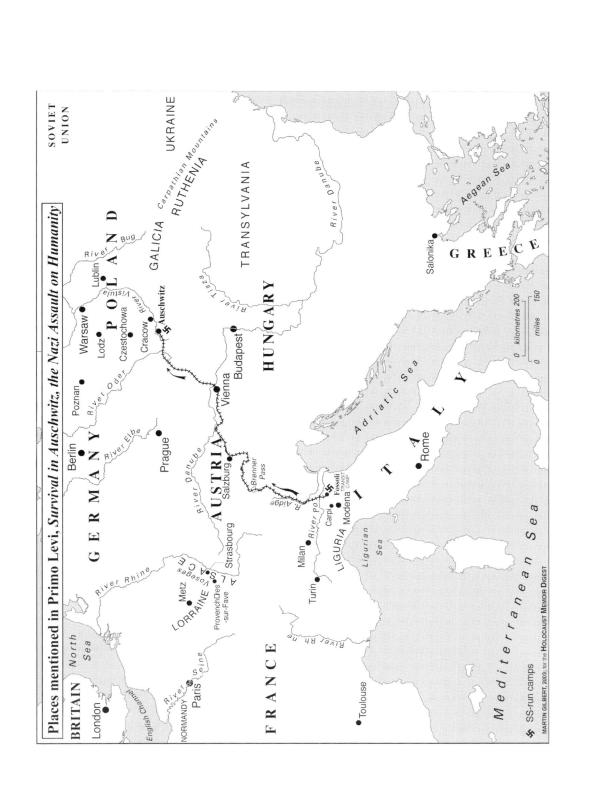

Places mentioned in Primo Levi, *Survival in Auschwitz, the Nazi Assault on Humanity*

BRITAIN

London

SOVIET UNION

North Sea

English Channel

River Seine

Paris

NORMANDY

FRANCE

Toulouse

River Rhine

Metz

LORRAINE

ProvenchDes-sur-Fave

Vosges

ALSACE

Strasbourg

GERMANY

Berlin

River Elbe

Prague

River Oder

Poznan

P O L A N D

Warsaw

Lodz

Czestochowa

River Vistula

Cracow River

Auschwitz

Lublin

River Bug

GALICIA

Carpathian Mountains

RUTHENIA

UKRAINE

River Danube

AUSTRIA

Salzburg

Brenner Pass

River Adige

Vienna

Budapest

HUNGARY

River Tisza

TRANSYLVANIA

River Danube

Milan

River po

Turin

Carpi

Fossoli
TRANSIT CAMP

Modena

LIGURIA

River Rhône

I T A L Y

Rome

Ligurian Sea

Mediterranean Sea

Adriatic Sea

Aegean Sea

GREECE

Salonika

0   kilometres   200

0   miles   150

SS-run camps

MARTIN GILBERT, 2003; for the HOLOCAUST MEMOIR DIGEST

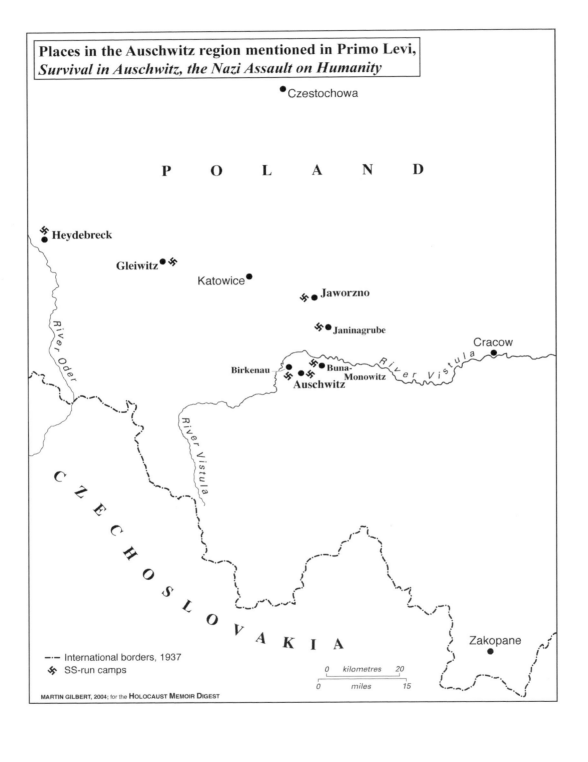

Places in the Auschwitz region mentioned in Primo Levi,
Survival in Auschwitz, the Nazi Assault on Humanity

● Czestochowa

P O L A N D

卐 Heydebreck
●

Gleiwitz ● 卐
Katowice ●

卐 ● Jaworzno

卐 ● Janinagrube

● Cracow
River Vistula

Birkenau ─ 卐 ● Buna-
卐 ● Monowitz
Auschwitz

River Oder

River Vistula

C Z E C H O S L O V A K I A

Zakopane ●

–·– International borders, 1937
卐 SS-run camps

0   kilometres   20

0   miles   15

MARTIN GILBERT, 2004; for the HOLOCAUST MEMOIR DIGEST

"We are slaves,

deprived of every right,

exposed to every insult,

condemned to certain death,

but we still possess one power,

and we must defend it with all our strength

for it is the last

– the power to refuse our consent."

Primo Levi

Leon Weliczker Wells, *The Janowska Road*

---

10 March 1925: born, in Stojanow, Eastern Galicia, to Abraham and Chana (Reiss) Weliczker, the second of six children, after Ellen Lea, and then Aaron, Jacob, Rachaela, Judith and Bina follow

Late March 1933: family moves to Lvov

1–5 September 1939: Lvov is bombed by Germany

Early to late September 1939: family flees to Stojanow to avoid the bombing, then returns to Lvov

October 1939–June 1941: Eastern Galicia under Soviet occupation

22 June 1941: Lvov is bombed by German Air Force as Germany attacks the Soviet Union

30 June 1941: German troops enter Lvov

July 1941: tortured and in hiding in Lvov

August–November 1941: works as a glazier in the Hazet candy factory, Lvov

November 1941: Lvov Ghetto established; obtains work in railway construction

2 March–June 1942: at the Janowska camp

July 1942: escapes from Janowska, recuperates at home and in hospital, flees to Stojanow

Autumn 1942: after Stojanow Aktion, moves to Radziechow

1 December 1942: remaining Jews leave Radziechow, Leon hides in woods until mid-December, returns to Lvov Ghetto

2 January 1943: survives the January Aktion in Lvov, hiding in Ghetto

2 June 1943: transferred to Janowska after complete liquidation of Lvov Ghetto

15 June–19 November 1943: as a member of Janowska "Death Brigade" (Sonderkommando)

19 November 1943: escapes from Janowska with entire Death Brigade, goes into hiding in Lvov

May 1944: is liberated in Lvov by Soviet troops

Fall 1944–June 1945: works for Soviet supply office in Lvov, obtaining and distributing supplies

July 1945: escapes to Gliwice (Gleiwitz) DP Camp, studies at Polytechnic Institute

March 1946: leaves Gliwice for Munich, studies at the Engineering School

Spring 1946: his diary, *The Death Brigade* (Part V *The Janowska Road*) is published in Lodz

Summer 1949: receives PhD in Engineering in Munich, emigrates to the United States

Author: Leon Weliczker Wells

Title: *The Janowska Road*

Publishing details

Holocaust Library, United States Holocaust Memorial Museum, 100 Raoul Wallenberg Place SW, Washington, D.C. 1999. 320 pages.
ISBN #0-89604-159-X.
Originally published as "The Death Brigade", 1963.
One-third of the memoir is taken from a diary the author kept between 15 June and 19 November 1943 during his time as a "Sonderkommando" at the Janowska Camp, and his escape. During these months he was an eyewitness to mass murders as he was forced to dispose of the bodies. He describes acts of resistance and his escape. For the purpose of the *Digest*, this diary is considered a document, and is not therefore included in the events in the *Digest*.

Focus:

Leon, from Lvov in Poland, who was 14 in 1939, survives Soviet occupation and two internments in the Janowska Camp, and in hiding in Lvov. The events described take place between his birth in 1925, and his emigration to the United States in 1949.

Features:

Photographs: Front cover: "... barbed wire fence enclosing Janowska camp" and "Members of Sonderkommando 1005 stand next to a 'bone-crushing machine'."

Documents: A diary, written by the author, covering the period between 15 June 1943, when he becomes a member of the "Death Brigade" at the Janowska Camp, and 19 November 1943, when he escapes and is hidden. It was published by the Central Jewish Historical Commission in Lodz, spring 1946, and is included in this edition as Part V, pages 150–245.

Maps: Regional map of Eastern Galicia, Street plan of Lvov, with detail map, 1941–1942, map of Janowska Camp, Autumn 1942, pages 8–10.

Afterword: Epilogue (1961) written by the author, page 333. Epilogue (1998) written by the author, page 334.

Index: Pages 335–40.

Contents: (by topic, with page numbers)

Pre-war Jewish home and community life

(12–17) Preparation for and description of the Sabbath: "The Sabbath really began on Thursday. That afternoon Mother would go to the stores and markets to shop for the weekend. In the evening the poor would come to those who were better off to borrow money for the Sabbath supply. ... The whole of Friday was taken up with preparations for the next day." The Sabbath begins, Friday night: "We children, too, felt the holiness of this hour that elevated us above everyday life. After the prayers the out-of-town beggars gathered at the exit. Father always took one of them home; he was the 'oirach' (guest) for the Sabbath."

(16–17, 19, 125–6, 132–3) Sabbath-afternoon visits with his paternal grandparents:

"Grandfather would then inquire about our lessons in 'cheder' and about the portion of the Bible we had studied that week. Father shone with pride when I knew the correct answers." Their livelihood: "My father's father worked as a manager of the timber-felling grounds in the forest. My father, at the age of twelve, went to work as an assistant to his father in the forest." His grandfather survives until December 1942, and the move from Radziechow to Sokal.

(18) Leon's birthplace, Stojanow, sixty miles east of Lvov, with a population of two thousand, of whom one thousand were Jews who lived in the centre of town, and one thousand were Ukrainians who lived in the outskirts: "Our town had a seven year grammar school, a Roman Catholic church, a Greek Catholic church, a synagogue, a police station with a jail for a maximum of two men, and a post office. There was neither a pharmacy nor a doctor, and until 1945 there was not a single radio in the entire town."

(18–19, 136–8) Abraham Weliczker: "My father was born in 1894. He was tall and slim and had very dark black hair. His large, penetrating brown eyes were deeply set under a high forehead, and he wore a short pointed beard. He walked with a slight stoop. His interest in charitable organizations was great and his support of them constant. And he deeply respected learning. He believed that with schooling we children could get what he had been unable to but wanted so much. He respected knowledge, both religious and secular, for its own sake." He is taken in the 19 November Aktion in Lvov, 1942, to Belzec.

(18–20) Leon's father, Abraham Welizcker, a timber merchant, who: "... also had business associations with a company that exported eggs and was a partner in a cement-pipe company. In Stojanov we were one of the richest families." He was born in 1894, married Chana Reiss in 1919, and they had seven children.

(19–20, 126, 137, 280) Chana Reiss Weliczker: "My mother was considered a comely woman; she had dark hair and eyes, was a little shorter and two years younger than my father, and was slightly plump." In Lvov: "Every Wednesday morning mother would get up earlier than on other days to cook for the poor. Huge cauldrons of soup were cooked, and every beggar received a plateful with some bread. Mother served as many as forty beggars; and, including her own family, she would cook for and serve fifty people on those Wednesdays. ... this was, as she used to say, 'her day'. She, too, had the right to do something for herself." She is killed in Lvov 23 August 1942, on the last day of the Aktion.

(19–20) Mother's family: "Her parents had fourteen children, eleven of whom died in their infancy. Only mother, her sister, and a brother remained alive. Her mother ran a drygoods store while her father spent his life studying the Talmud and Kaballah. He had the reputation of being a great scholar, and people who knew him have told me that his knowledge of Hebrew grammar and the Aramaic language was unsurpassed. ... Yosel Moshe Reiss ... was one of the first orthodox Jews to go as a pioneer to Palestine, taking a group of young people there with him. That was in 1920. But after a short while he had to return to Poland because of sickness, and thus the family never migrated to Palestine as he had hoped."

(21–5) "... most of the Jews in Stojanov belonged to a religious sect called Chasidism. ... Chasidism taught that 'Everything that comes from the heart will reach the heart of other people'." Leon's family were followers of the Belzer Chasidic sect.

(26) Family: "My eldest sister, Ellen Lea, was born in November 1923. She was a sensitive, quiet child, who liked to study and read a lot, and seldom played with us. I was the next one, born on March 10, 1925. My brother Aaron was fourteen months younger than I. He was a timid and weak child and didn't want to study. Three years later came Jacob Michael, the rugged individualist of the group. Later, each about fourteen months apart, came two blonde and blue-eyed girls, Rachela and Judith, and at last delicate Bina."

(26–30) Schooling: "At the age of three, exactly on his birthday, a boy started 'cheder' (religious school). ... I was taught, from three on, how to pray and to read Hebrew. ... When I was five ... my religious schooling started in the afternoons ... . At the age of six I began public school." In 1933, in Lvov, he attends a public school, and in 1938, a gymnasium, a high school: "The school hours were normally from 8:00 a.m. to 2:00 p.m. I also studied in a higher Talmudic school – Yeshiva – from 3:00 to 8:00 p.m., six days a week except Saturdays."

(28–9) Leon's father sells his house in Stojanow and prepares to move his family to Lvov, 1933: "... our next-door neighbor suddenly told us he didn't like these new people. The neighbor took my father to the rabbi, who decided that we must sell the house to people acceptable to the neighbor but that in case the next buyer should pay less than the first one would have, the difference must be equally shared between my father and the neighbor."

The coming of war

(31–3) 11pm, 1 September 1939, the bombs fall on Lvov, continuing nightly for four nights: "Everyone in the house ran down to the basement. ... The house and the ground vibrated, and we heard the cracking of window glass and the crash of collapsing houses. ... When we came upstairs and looked out, it seemed as if the whole town were on fire."

(33) The family returns to Stojanow followed by retreating Polish soldiers: "The Jews knew from past experience that during governmental changeovers, while the city was without law enforcement, there were always pogroms and plunderings. Therefore we started to prepare some shelters and hiding places to survive the 'changeover' period and to bury our valuables, such as silverware, clothing, jewels, and so on."

(33–6) Life under Soviet occupation, September 1939 to June 1941, in Lvov: "Nationalization of private property began. The nationalization was, we were informed 'voluntary'. When the officials came to our house, my father, without a question, signed the house over to the government. ... The time was changed to 'Moscow Time'. All moved their clocks two hours ahead so that no one would say they were counterrevolutionary. The new time didn't fit our geographic location. Very soon ... one couldn't buy anything ... ."

(37–9) "We accepted the economic as well as other limitations by trying to make the best of circumstances... . As for freedom of speech, people stopped talking politics, even pro-Soviet politics, and stopped reading the newspapers. The best thing was to be as ignorant as possible. ... All of us began getting new 'values' in life. Being 'happy' could now mean you had had a successful day in the sugar queue, or that you had not been interrupted by the police during the night. Above all, we were satisfied as long as the family was together."

Life under German occupation

(42–4) 22 June 1941, Lvov is bombed as Germany attacks the Soviet Union: "Everyone was then sure that Hitler would lose the war within two years. Hence one would rather endure real hardship for the present than to be sent to Siberia, to be lost in that wilderness forever. ... The Germans were considered the most civilized people in the world."

(44–5) With the German entry into Lvov, a German patrol stops the looting of the Hazet candy factory: "Two Jews are put to work to get things in order again. In uneasy anticipation, both of them – and indeed others besides them – wait to see what will happen when the work is finished. Finally, the tension ends; they are rewarded with chocolate and sweets that remained over in the factory. Then they leave for home." Monday, 30 June 1941.

(45–7) "On Tuesday ... . persecution of the Jews has begun in the city; they are being beaten, arrested, murdered. ... But news of the formation of a Ukrainian militia removes any further doubt. The persecution is now in full swing and goes on relentlessly all day Wednesday." On Thursday, Leon's brother Aaron is arrested, then Ukrainian militia come to arrest Leon and his sick father. July 1, 2 and 3, 1941.

(53–8) After a night and day of torture in a field, Leon and his father are released to Leon's mother and they return home. Leon is able to hide for three days, but is arrested again and brought to work. After a grueling day: "Within earshot of us the Germans deliberated as to whether they would shoot us now or wait until the following day. I was convinced ... the battered creatures around me who had been stripped of the last vestiges of human dignity shared my thoughts. ... '... to sink slowly into death, to lose all sense of pain and to find relief at last.' ... Then, again miraculously, we were allowed to go home." 8 July 1941, Lvov.

(59–61) Leon hides for five days with a friend in an "Aryan" house. His sister Ella brings him food: "... some could not even bring home the desperately small rations – the Jews received only half the quantity granted to the Aryans – for if a woman in a family could not queue up for some reason, it was too dangerous for a man to do so; a passing German or Ukrainian might seize him and dispatch him to 'work'. ... not even the women could be sure of reaching the shop counters ... they, too, were shoved out of place in line and forced to go to the very end of the queue, so that everything was sold out by the time their turn came." Leon is found, taken to clean a school building and then released to return home. Mid-July 1941.

(62–3, 316–17) Leon gets a job as an apprentice glazier repairing the windows of the Hazet candy company, a position that provides him with security during the more than two months he works there, August to November 1941. A Jewish Council is set up: "Everyone had to register. With the establishment of this 'Jewish community' the occupation forces created an instrument responsible for carrying out their orders regarding the Jewish population."

(123) Stojanow, Summer 1942: "From time to time a certain number of Jews had to be allotted to a concentration camp. The Jewish community leaders usually settled this matter in such a way that as long as it remained possible only one member of each family was chosen to go. In this way the worst hardships were avoided, although the fate of those concerned was very sad." (They were taken to Belzec.)

Creation of the ghetto

(63–4) November 1941, the ghetto is established in Lvov: "... each Jew could be allotted two square meters of living space. Each person ... was given a certificate on which was indicated how much space he was entitled to rent."

(132–3) On 1 December 1942, the Jews in Radziechow are allowed to move to Sokal, Brody or Busk: "There were now fifteen towns in the whole of Galicia where Jews were allowed to remain. Ghettos had been set up in all of these towns."

Daily life in the ghetto

(65) "After November 1941, a German named Weber became head of the employment office. ... each Jew received a registration permit." Leon and his father obtain work permits for road construction: "Both of us had to work sixteen hours a day, doing the heaviest kind of constuction work, building a railway. But for the time being we were safe." Lvov Ghetto.

(68) January 1942, six months after the Germans arrived: "Until now our family had been lucky, or so we felt. Such feelings show how quickly human beings adjust to the most terrifying circumstances, the most grinding tyranny. But our hope sustained us."

(88–9) Fifty men were allowed to leave Janowska slave labour camp to return to the Lvov Ghetto for one day to visit their families; typhoid spread to their relatives, from whom it spread to the Aryan population: "Such a danger had to be countered by strict isolation of the Jewish population. ... The Jewish community leaders were faced with the unenviable choice of putting the whole Jewish population into an unbearable position, that is, exposing them to infection, or, alternately, of depriving the camp workers of the last shafts of light from outside the prison camp." Early winter 1942.

(118–19) June 1942, Leon escapes from Janowska and returns to Lvov: "... the face of Lvov had changed. It seemed overshadowed by silent grief. The streets, formerly vibrant with pulsating traffic at that time of day, were almost empty in the semidarkness. ... I must not allow anyone to see me ... my presence here could cause even greater misfortune to be brought about than my death at the camp would have been." Sick with typhoid fever and double pneumonia, his family take him to the hospital where he remains for three weeks.

(135–9) Late December 1942, Leon returns to the Lvov Ghetto after the November Aktion, and finds the only surviving members of his family: his younger brothers Jacob and Aaron. Leon finds work in the ghetto first as a glazier, then as a driver with a team of horses, then as a pipefitter: "The most important thing for me was to have a full-time job, and through it the greatest security."

(140–3, 144) 19 February 1943, Josef Grzymek, a German national and former Chief of Police in Poland, now with the SS, comes to rule the ghetto: "He used to stop people, who, in his opinion, did not march well enough, or whom he noticed for some other reason. ... These 'rejected' persons were sent to prison, from which they were taken and shot."

(142–3) February 1943, Leon's brothers, too young to be allowed to work, become ill with typhoid fever and dysentery: "The all-important thing was to move them to a good hiding place. I dug a spacious hole in the sewer, where they might lie undisturbed throughout the day. Returning from work at night in a state of exhaustion, I had to wash clothes, to cook and prepare everything for the next day. ... I was often on the point of collapse. But I knew I had to carry on."

Deportation

(91–2) Lvov, beginning 14 March 1942 and continuing for two weeks, a round-up of those to "emigrate" were brought to a school: "Then, when night had fallen, the emigres were brought to the railway station, loaded aboard a train, and the journey began. To what destination no one knew; no one ever saw them again. … It was also used to recruit young able-bodied workers to perform the senseless labor we did at Janowska. … this group consisted of young women and grown boys. Some horrible scenes were witnessed here: young women still carrying children at their breasts were roughly torn away from their children; brother and sister clinging to one another were separated; little children ran about, forlorn and crying in anguish. It seemed as if every human impulse had been banished from the world." (Fifteen thousand, not taken to Janowska, were sent to Belzec to their deaths.)

Death camps

(125–9) The Stojanow Aktion: "The Jews who had been herded together in the marketplace were then forced to walk a distance of twelve kilometeres on foot, and were constantly beaten. Then they were forced to stand at the station for two days and two nights completely naked, without food or drink. Finally they were loaded into cattle trucks and taken to the gas chambers at Belzec, near Lublin." Among them, Leon's four sisters, his Aunt Hannah, her two children, and his grandmother. Thirty Jews were left in Stojanow; they were moved twelve kilometers to Radziechow, the railway station to which Leon refers. October 1942.

Slave labour camps and factories

(68–71) 2 March 1942, to protect his father who had missed work due to illness, Leon reported in his father's place, and is taken instead to the Janowska camp. His body is shaved, he showers in "ice cold" water, and when he dresses, he is told: "'Take one set of underwear, a shirt, suit, hat, one pair of socks and shoes; the rest of your clothes remains here.'" When Leon tries to keep his sweater, he is told: "'When an order in here is not carried out exactly, you hear a shot, and again there is one more in heaven. What I have told you about your clothes is also an order.'" (The Janowska road camp, established in October 1941, was set up as a slave labour camp; it was to become also a transit camp to Belzec, and a camp of mass murder.)

(72–3) Morning in Janowska, 3 March 1942: "Tired, emaciated figures moved slowly through the yard. One could hardly believe that these were people who just a few weeks ago had gone about well dressed, healthy, and full of strength, tending to their respective jobs. Now their feet were wrapped in straw, held in place by pieces of cloth and string, their clothes ragged and torn. Around their waists were cords with dirty eating utensils attached to them. … The bitter-cold weather had driven all humane expression from their faces."

(76–7) The second night in Janowska, two drunk Soviet prisoners of war came into their hut: "They immediately proceeded to run amok, striking out left and right at us with the butts of their rifles. They pursued this amusement for the best part of two hours, then cleared out, locking the door behind them. The prisoners showed not the least sign of anger. They had long since been broken to such treatment, and their fate was clearly so irrevocable that reaction was futile."

(80, 85) Leon views the work scene from the workshop window: "At a distance I saw a column of men bearing a dismantled truck body on their shoulders. Even from where we stood, we could hear the blows that fell on the heads and shoulders of these unfortunate fellows. Without sense of purpose they were forced to carry the truck body around in a circle. The sole object of the work was to make the men suffer. I could see other brigades at work too, and the pattern repeated itself everywhere, wringing out the last drop of energy from the captives, and all to no purpose other than to give our captors pleasure." Janowska, March 1942.

(98, 106–8) "As a result of this Aktion in the province, the number of internees at Janowska soon rose to two thousand." With the overcrowding, the men learn of a new camp being built nearby to which they are transferred: "It would accomodate ten thousand men." Spring 1942.

(103–6) The SS officers who ran the camp: Obersturmführer Fritz Gebauer, 35, who: "... in general seemed to have some kind of inner life." Also, Untersturmführer Wilhaus, a few years younger: "He had nothing to compare with Gebauer's expression of a deep interior nature." His brother-in-law was Gruppenführer Fritz Katzmann, the Police Chief of Galicia. And Untersturmführer Richard Rokita, 40: "With Rokita's arrival in the camp, the situation, in a number of respects, took on less catastrophic proportions."

(105–6) Rokita, an SS officer at the Janowska camp complains to the Jewish Council that the packages the community sends to help the prisoners are too small, and he invites members of the Council to see the prisoners in the camp: "Then he forced us to stone these representatives in order to express our obvious displeasure at their miserliness. ... He leveled the accusation against them that this otherwise excellent worker was in poor health simply because they were so indifferent as to the well-being of the internees. ... Rokita had merely made such a scene in order to impress on the Jewish community his benevolence toward the Jews in the camp to make them accommodating as regards apportioning presents to him."

(315–17) After the war, Leon, working at the Jewish Historical Commission in Munich, hears reports of cruelty by some of the "kapos": "The word 'Kapo' was strange to me – we hadn't used it at Janowska. ... despite these reports that some Kapos had beaten their own Jewish fellows, informed on them, and so on, in my experience, the leaders I had known had been, for the most part, superior men of high moral quality."

Witness to mass murder

(47–9) Leon and his father are taken, with other men, to the Ukrainian militia building. Leon is taken to a room: "A huge heap of men, one lying on top of the other, lay helpless on the floor of the room. ... I reached for the foot of one of them ... . As I did so, a savage blow on the head stunned me, and I toppled among the bodies. ... Many who were buried under the heap were destined to remain there." 3 July 1941, Lvov.

(49–52) Leon and his father are taken with the men to a field: "We were ordered to lie flat like the others. ... We could hear the sound of a man, clearly one of us, stumbling awkwardly around, chased and beaten by another as he went. ... Blows were rained down upon him until he dragged himself to his feet again ... . When the pursuers were at last satisfied that the incessant blows had rendered him unable to stir ... . Now it was the turn of a second victim. ... The Germans, in pursuit of their sport, tramped up and down over our backs as we lay there. No one dared to raise his head." 4 July 1941, Lvov.

(86, 93) At evening roll call, six very sick men are forbidden to pass the night in the hut, and are made to sleep in the open: "Since there was a strict prohibition against any movement in the yard after eight o'clock, these men had to lie down on the ground and remain still the whole night. ... On the following morning we saw six small snow-covered mounds over by the railing." March 1942, Janowska.

(88) Leon's friend Feder reports on the murder of seven "quite healthy and hardy young fellows" who are ordered: "... to undress and to get into a vat of cold water ... . After two hours,

chunks of ice could be broken off the corpses of these unfortunate youngsters." January 1942, Janowska.

(93) Late March 1942, Janowska expands as many more prisoners are brought in from Lvov: "The rate at which prisoners were murdered increased greatly, as we could not disseminate information among the newcomers about the strict camp regulations fast enough."

(94) "When the Ober- or Unterstrumführer wished to practice 'sharpshooting', they stood at the window of the office building and used the workers ... who passed by as targets. ... It was the aim of these Germans to strike the hand, the nape of the neck, the knee, or the nose. Once the practice was ended, the Unterstrumführer went about the camp, seeking out those who had been wounded, and giving them a 'mercy shot' in the head. A wound on the finger sufficed as justification for this treatment." Spring 1942, Janowska.

(95) "About twelve hundred men from Przemysl, a town of some twenty thousand, and about five hundred from Grodek Jagielonski, another town of about ten thousand, came to our camp. ... The prisoners were lined up in a row ... . Then they were told that if anyone moved his hands – which were held across the back of the head – he would be shot. ... they were led out to the ground outside the railing. Here they were forced to remain three days without food ... . Then they were sorted out; the weak ones – the majority of the group – were shot. The rest returned to the camp for work." Spring 1942, Janowska.

(95–6) A group of one hundred people from Stanislawow are brought to Janowska, then taken out of the camp. A "heavy-work brigade" follow them returning later to camp, and are given a double ration at supper. One tells Leon: "'We were brought to a site not far from the cemetery of Janowska. A group of SS men were there, entertaining themselves with schnapps and music. Round about them lay a countless number of corpses. These were the people from Stanislav. We were told to collect the bodies together, dig a mass grave, and bury all of them.'"

(108–10) At the Janowska "Todesplatz" – "Death Grounds", while on the way to work, Leon sees: "A number of prisoners, bloated, practically rotting already, were crouched there, wearing dumb and forlorn expressions and waiting for the end to come. Rokita ordered an Askari to bring them food. ... But the moment the first bite was in their mouths, Rokita winked at the Askari and they both opened fire. After a few minutes, the prisoners lay motionless in a great pool of blood." ("Askaris" were Soviet prisoner-of-war mercenaries.)

(112–13) In an effort to stop the spread of dysentery and typhoid, the huts and prisoners are disinfected, one Thursday, after which: "... we were marched to other grounds, and had to lie, stark naked, flat on the ground. Anyone who raised his head was shot. ... Supported by the most meager rations, we were subjected to this ill-treatment until Monday morning. At that stage there were many lying there who would never again get to their feet." Janowska.

(113–15) With five hundred other sick and near-death prisoners, Leon is taken to the "Todesplatz": "We are led out onto the 'sands' ... . We obey the order to remove all our clothes, and then shovels are distributed to us. We must undergo the last extreme of mental torture that can be inflicted on us – digging our own graves. ... Now the pit is deep enough. The first two must now get into it, must lie properly side by side, and are shot. The next two are made to lay themselves transversely across them. The third pair must do as the first, the fourth as the second, and so on – a gruesome crosshatched pattern."

(123–7) The Stojanow Aktion, a week after Rosh Hashanah 1942, described to Leon by Grandfather, with Uncle Jacob, and Uncle Mordecai: "'Yes, my boy,' he said brokenly, 'we are the only ones here – the only ones to survive.'" He reports on the news from Lvov, received the day before the Aktion: "'Your mother, they took her away nine weeks ago.'"

(131–2) 13 November 1942, the last surviving Jew of Stojanow reports the death of the five who had remained there with him after the Aktion, among them, Leon's Uncle Mordecai. This, followed news of an Aktion in Lvov, and news that Kamionka-Strumilowa: "... had been declared 'free from Jews'."

(138–9) Leon builds a hiding place in a cellar under their room to hide out during the imminent Aktion in Lvov, 2 January 1942: "The cellar measured twelve square meters, and we were fourteen persons. Each of us had brought food for two days. ... We spent two whole days in complete darkness ... . The following day we ventured out into the street again. ... There were bodies everywhere. ... Here and there we saw bodies still in their beds. Those had been people who were ill ... . They had been shot then and there ... ."

(146–8) 1 June 1943, SS round up the remnants of the Lvov Ghetto, transport them to the parade ground at Janowska camp where they are held for two days: "Then an order: 'Grownups over sixty and children under five step out!' ... The victims had to undress and were taken away. Next: 'Grownups over fifty and children under eight step out. The rest will go to the camp.' ... The order was repeated many more times. At last eight hundred Jews were left, out of eight thousand. ... aged from fourteen to thirty years."

(150) "Every male individual in the camp never knew when he woke up in the morning whether he would be going to work or to death that day. Only infants and children, the old, the sick and for the most part, women, could be certain the Germans would kill them as soon as they arrived at Janowska. For these there was for the most part no respite." June 1943.

Resistance, ghetto revolts, individual acts of courage and defiance

(63, 106, 316–17) August 1941, the Germans establish a "Jewish community" council in Lvov, headed by Dr. Parnes: "Shortly thereafter Dr. Parnes was shot by a German officer when he told the officer that he was not to be ordered around." On the community council: "... one must bear in mind that the relationship between it and the Germans was completely a product of the SS. When the community failed to carry out the Germans' strict instructions, members were hanged without mercy." Later, Leon writes of the community leaders: "... because of their high moral standards and moral values, they didn't know how to organize a physical resistance. Physical power may have been too repulsive to them."

(71–2, 89–90) The efforts of Leon's family to get him out of Janowska: "They left no stone unturned to get me out. The boss, a Pole, made promise after promise, but put them off one day after another." March 1942.

(75, 78, 87, 116) At Janowska, a friend, Feder, advises Leon to establish contact with his family by smuggling letters to his family with Aryan workers: "... letter writing was forbidden; anyone found with a letter on his person faced certain death. In spite of that ... letters were in fact written; for what reason had anyone to fear death?" Feder later gives Leon his shirt, after Leon escapes from the "Todesplatz".

(81–4, 119) The Jewish Council sent packages to the prisoners in Janowska who had received little or nothing from home. Leon received a package of food, wrapped in a linen towel, which had been addressed to him: "The writing in blue crayon was that of my mother. The letters were blotted, as if tears had fallen on them. The name of the sender was written below – in my sister's writing. I took it that she had brought the package to the Jewish community, for there the signature had to be applied." Later, Leon learns his mother had sold her gold dental bridgework to buy food to send to him.

(111) Leon's work group is used at night to unload and carry building materials from the train station for new huts in the camp, in addition to their work during the day: "It was too much. As we had nothing more to lose ... small groups banded themselves together and proclaimed that they would no longer carry out these extra duties. As was to be expected, the SS replied by firing in all directions. Many, who could not reach cover in time, were shot down. ... Then everything went on as before, day after day, night after night."

(111–12) "Plans for a revolt were at one timed formed. An organization was created ... . Their object was to achieve freedom by means of a general insurrection. ... it was rejected ... . This sense of responsibility extended, first of all to the families ... and ultimately to those of the Jews in general, who lived in the city. ... The project was therefore scrapped ... . When a considerable time later the last Jews in the city and its neighborhood had been liquidated, and there was no longer any reason for not revolting, insurrection was impossible. Mentally and physically battered ... . There was no one left who was physically or psychologically capable of working out a revolutionary plan."

(143) An early March Aktion: "This was the first time that there were clashes between the SS and the Jews. Shots were fired from 72 Zamarstynowska Street, and two Ukrainian policeman were killed." Lvov, 1943.

(145, 204) "Toward the end of March one of the most evil SS men among the Germans was shot and killed by a Jew in Czwartakow Street. A few hours later scores of SS arrived in the ghetto and called up the Jewish police. They chose twelve policemen at random and hanged them one after another from balconies in Loketka Street. Their bodies remained there for forty-eight hours, dangling above the heads of the passersby." 1943.

Partisan activity

(133–4) The dangers for Jews of hiding in the woods amid the Polish and Ukrainian partsans: "... though both were enemies of the Germans, they fought against each other as well. ... The Ukrainians were fighting for a ... national state, whereas the Poles were fighting for their fatherland, the ancient Poland, to which part of the Ukraine belonged. They were implacable enemies of each other. Both, however, hated the Jews just as much as they hated the Germans."

(259–60, 282) The Ukrainian partisan, Bandera, and his followers, the Banderowcy who realized the Germans would not give them an independant Ukraine and therefore fought the Poles to become a majority in the area: "The Banderowcy would catch an important Pole, cut him to pieces, and place him in a public place for other Poles to see, and take note; they wanted to force the Poles to move out of this part of the country. The Jews were even more afraid of the Banderowcy than of SS men." Fall 1943. Leon writes that Bandera was killed in January 1960 in Munich.

Specific escapes

(98–100) April 1942, Janowska, one of the men escapes: "From the brigade in which the escapee had been employed, five men were ordered to stand forth, and were shot without further ado. ... a fourth man made his escape. When he failed to give himself up after three days, his mother, his sister, her child, his sister-in-law, and a neighbor's child, all of whom happened to be in the house at the time were shot. This vehement reprisal evoked a feeling of horror among the internees that was sufficient to banish all thoughts of escape for a long time."

(100–2) Leon is sent, with other prisoners, to work outside the camp. He arranges to meet his family, and his mother, brother, and older sister come, with others who inquire about their husbands or sons. He returns to work: "Scharführer Kolanko appeared ... and said: 'It doesn't make any difference to me, but if the Untersturmführer was here, you can bet your life that I would have struck you down on the spot!' But nothing could disturb me. I had seen my mother again. It had been the happiest day in my life for a long, long time."

(115–16, 210) Leon is taken from the side of the pit in order to bring a dead body back to it: "'He is to be buried with the rest of you.' ... With a quick glance at the Askari, I drop the body and race back like one possessed into the camp, and mix in with a group of workers. ... the next morning, when my comrades arrive for work, I discover that I am assumed dead." He escapes from camp as one working outside, and returns home. 8 June 1942.

(144–6) Mid-March 1943, Leon survives a selection of one hundred workers from seven hundred, by realizing that a few of the one hundred were missing and he is permitted to join them. Later he is to be transferred to Janowska and he jumps from the truck: "The truck did not turn back, and the bullets they sent after me missed me."

(278–9) A post-war report on the fate of those with whom Leon escaped during the breakout of the Death Brigade, described in his diary, and the fate of twenty who were recaptured together with his friend Widder, and put into a new Death Brigade: "The inmates worked with chains on their feet. The chains were never taken off; they did not even have a lock; they were welded together. ... the Russian Army finally caught up with them. The Germans shot the entire brigade; but one of the members, Widder, was not fatally wounded, and lay between the corpses until the next day, when he was liberated."

In hiding, including Hidden Children

(118–20) Leon returns home from Janowska, is taken to hospital to recover from typhoid fever and double pneumonia where he spends three weeks, and returns to hide at home: "At every minute there was the very real danger that someone might see me and betray me. This would have meant the end, not only for me but for my family as well. Thus we lived in constant fear, made worse by the constantly renewed rumors of an imminent Aktion." Lvov, July 1942.

(120–2) In an effort to avoid detection that would endanger his family, Leon decides to leave Lvov, with the help of his 13-year-old brother Jacob, to hide in Stojanow where his sisters (Rachel, 12, Judith, 10, and Bina, 7) are with their grandparents: "The leave-taking was heartbreaking, and my mother insisted on walking with us for several kilometers. Finally she could go no farther. In tears she gazed after us until we had turned the next corner." July 1942.

(129–30) Leon and three brothers he meets in Radziechow survive the Radziechow Aktion hiding: "We crouched between the doors the whole of that day. ... and remained hidden for two days. On the evening of the second day we crept out timidly and learned that the Aktion had taken place and was now over."

(134) Early to mid-December hiding in the woods near Radziechow: "In the daytime I lay well camouflaged in a hole in the ground; at night I went out to forage for food in the surrounding fields or in a nearby village. My life was animal-like, and I had to exert all my willpower not to become completely demoralized." Leon decides to return to Lvov.

(248–62) After his escape from the Death Brigade, Leon finds a hiding place under a barn in Lvov: "Our hiding place housed twenty-four people, three of whom were children; five were women and the remainder men, sixteen of us, the oldest of whom was sixty-two.... . a tiny space – it was about ten feet wide by thirteen feet long – but somehow we managed." They were to remain there from November, until liberation, May 1944.

(291–2) Tierhaus, Leon's friend from the Death Brigade, organized a group after the war to find Jewish children who had been hidden in Christian homes and return them to the community: "Some of the gentiles were glad to return the children to the Jews; others wanted money to do so; and still others, especially those who had taken in infants, would not give them back at all."

Righteous Gentiles

(78–80) Leon is sent to work as a glazier in the Janowska workshop; the supervisor is an Austrian SS Scharführer named Czekala: "He ... asked me how I had come to be here. He listened to my story with such an open expression of dejection, his head nodding in such sheer regret, that I simply could not regard it as a pose on his part. I learned later that he was a very good sort, and had never been known to strike a man in the workshop."

(244–5, 249–51, 262–3, 310) Joseph Kalwinski's father, the owner of the barn, who hid twenty-two people since the big Aktion in August 1942, and agreed to include Leon and his fellow escapee Korn. They remain under his protection until Lvov is liberated by the Soviets in May 1944.

(259, 279) The Juzeks, who hid thirty-two people, twenty-six of whom had been members of the Death Brigade: "The hideout had been reported to the Germans by Juzek's own brother-in-law. ... Juzek and his wife had been arrested and the next day publicly hanged in the market." While being arrested, they attacked the Germans and twenty-eight of the Jews managed to escape. 6 December 1943, Lvov. They were recaptured in April 1944 and killed.

(260) On the Polish underground, Lvov: "The underground paper and radio never came out with strong condemnation of their fellow Poles for helping in the massacre of Jews, and not even against the Poles who informed on the few Poles who were hiding Jews. Anything would have been of help to us. The few Poles who did hide Jews got no moral support – not even the cold comfort of believing that, if a fellow citizen informed on him, the informer might one day be punished."

(275–7) Beresticky and nine others who hid for fourteen months in a cave which they had carved out in the Lvov sewers, with the help of a Polish friend, who brought them food: "The food had to be kept in iron containers to keep it from the rats. But because the rats ate through the iron containers, they suspended the containers from the top of the sewer pipe and placed heavy glass bottles around them so that the rats would slip off the slippery glass surface. A chief form of entertainment during their stay in the sewer was supplied by the acrobatics of the rats in trying to reach the food." (Leopold Socha and Stefan Wroblewski, the Poles who had hidden the group, were later to be recognized by Yad Vashem as "Righteous Among the Nations".)

(292, 310) After the war, Leon's group takes in a 13-year-old girl who had been saved in hiding: "She had been in a monastery during the war – one that had been under the auspices of the great humanitarian Archbishop Szepticki."

Liberation

(262–3) Soviet troops take Lvov, the people hiding under Kalwinski's barn are forced to leave: "Even now our host asked us not to come back to visit him, or for any other reason; it would go hard for him if it were known that he had hidden Jews. Many of the Poles didn't like the idea that even a few Jews had been saved. These survivors could be witnesses that the Poles had collaborated with the Germans in destroying the Jewish population. Others, who had taken over Jewish houses and belongings, were afraid they might have to return them." May 1944.

(266–71) "The street where I used to live, which was once inhabited by Jews, practically all of whom I once knew, looked completely strange now. ... When, until yesterday, the problem had been to escape being killed, survival dominated one's every thought; today this was not a problem anymore. Today the anguish for those who had been killed flooded over me." Liberation day, Lvov. He returns to his family's apartment, which is occupied by a Polish family, where he remains for two days.

(271–4, 282) He spends the next eight nights on the stairway leading to a neighbour's roof. He befriends a Soviet Jewish soldier Arcadi: "We decided that the people who now lived in Jewish apartments and had taken over our furniture owed us at least a meal a day." With Arcadi in his army coat, they are able to bluff a few meals.

(275) At a school in Lvov where survivors had registered: "People sat around the floor, sorrow and tragedy etched on their faces. Others walked around calling out the names of their near ones, when and where they were last seen. They did so to find out whether someone had seen them at a later date than they themselves had." Leon becomes the 184th survivor, within a radius of sixty miles; Lvov's Jewish population had been 150,000 in 1941. (This figure included thousands of refugees who were fleeing the Germans. By the end of 1944, 3,400 Jewish survivors had registered; 820 had been from the Lvov Ghetto.)

(280–3) Leon finds work managing the office of the Soviet-run Organization of Workers' Supplies, and shares a home with other survivors.

(313) On the work of the Jewish organization "Bricha" ("Exodus") whose goal it was to bring Jewish survivors to Palestine: "... the smuggling was done in steps, transporting individuals from country to country. Owing to the strict English blockade of Palestine, only a negligible number could be smuggled into Palestine, while all the others were directed, for the time being, to the American Zones. The members of Bricha were heroes and idealists comparable to any known in the history of mankind; they were people without compensation, risking their lives, their names never to be known, their work endlessly hard, terribly dangerous."

Displaced Persons camps

(294–5, 306–13) Leon escapes Lvov on a train with other repatriated Poles and joins his friends in Gliwice. Begins studying at the Polytechnic Institute in October 1945. In February 1946, he leaves Gliwice for the American Zone.

Stories of individuals, including family members

(93) "A Jew name Zudyk, a former street singer, stood on the edge of a pit, mixing lime. Convinced that Zudyk was working too slowly, the Obersturmführer went up to him and pushed him into the pit, where the poor wretch burned slowly, agonizingly, to death in the corrosive lime." Janowska, Spring 1942.

(95–7) A boy from Hungary comes into their Janowska workshop. He tells them his story, his father taken off from home, he, his mother and siblings deported with the other inhabitants of his town to the Polish border where the SS put the old people and young children into carts, and herd the others: "... driven along like cattle, forced to keep to the middle of the road ... it was nighttime, and pitch dark, and no one could see one another." His mother and one of his sisters is killed, he is separated from his other sister and brother. He is alone: "The child was twelve years old."

(122–3, 125–8) Situation of the children with the separation of the family: parents and sons in Lvov, sisters, Ella. Rachel, Judith and Bina, with the grandparents in Stojanov: "But the sight of Bina made me feel the separation from my mother more from day to day." The girls are killed in the Stojanow Aktion, Fall 1942.

(136) Leon's brothers Aaron and Jacob, after he finds them in the Lvov Ghetto and asks why they aren't trying to hide themselves, late December 1942: "'We didn't care anymore', answered Aaron. 'Father and Mother were dead; you were gone. Why should we expect a better fate than all the rest? So we sold everything and ate our fill of chocolate and sweets for once, and now all we are waiting for is the next Aktion.' Aaron was 15 years old, Jacob, 13."

(148) 3 June 1943, those left in the Lvov Ghetto are taken to Janowska Camp and held, among them, Leon and his two brothers: "My youngest brother, Jacob, tried to hide, and crept up to the fence. He tried to make himself quite small, hoping the SS men would not notice him. But they did. They shot him. ... I was separated from my brother, Aaron, the last of all my brothers and sisters. ... My brother's group was led away for execution. His eyes turned to me. He gave me a last nod, and was marched off with the others ... . He carried his head high. Then I lost sight of him."

(302–5) Leon describes the fate of those who had been arrested by the Soviets during their occupation and sent to Siberia, and also of the refugees from Western Poland who had been sent to Siberia.

Post-war life and career

(284–5, 319–21) Leon testifies before a Soviet Justice Department inquiry into Nazi crimes in Galicia, which decided that the responsibility for the war crimes lay with Nazi Party members: "Joining the Nazi Party, these Russian jurists held, had been strictly on a voluntary basis. There was no known case where anyone was punished for not joining the Party. Thus a Nazi had chosen evil when not under duress. It is true that by being a member one could derive preferential treatment either in his job or social position – but that could not justify subscribing to genocide. Responsibility for the crimes also fell on those who gave only their moral sanction to the Nazi cause, however indirectly, the jurists concluded." Later he bears witness at the Nuremberg Trials.

(285–6) In Soviet Lvov: "A Russian Jew, a retired officer of the N.K.V.D., was appointed by the Russians to head the Jewish Community. We were also informed that some packages with food and clothing had arrived through an American Jewish philanthropic organization and that if anyone wanted to get in touch with a relative overseas, he should go to speak to the new community head. But few availed themselves of this great opportunity. Who would go to a former N.K.V.D. man to ask for something that could be construed the next day as 'traitorous'?"

(287–301) Leon works as a railroad official sent around the Soviet Union to bring goods back to Lvov: "I always got what I was sent for and delivered the items to the proper authorities."

(311–12) His diary is published: "Because of limited funds and scarcity of paper, only one part, namely, the 'Death Brigade', which constitutes Part V of the present book, was published in the spring of 1946."

(314–15, 327, 332) Leon lives in Munich, studies at the Technische Hochschule, "Engineering School", and works at the Jewish Historical Commission, a subsidiary of the Central Jewish Committee of Liberated Jews: "And, in the summer of 1949, after getting my Ph.D. in Engineering, I left for the United States. In this country I was to dwell among strangers no longer."

(322–32) After the war in Munich, the second in command of the Janowska Death Brigade, Hauptscharführer Rauch, is found and Leon is called to identify him. The American officer leaves Leon alone with him, cautioning Leon not to leave visible injuries: "I didn't know what to do. To beat up anybody, even a murderer like Rauch, was repugnant to me. It then struck me that if I didn't react 'normally', it might later be construed that perhaps Rauch was after all 'not so guilty'."

Personal reflections

(80) "It is said that people get 'hardened' to pain. I believe from my own experience that this is so. ... In time, one began to witness the most brutal and degrading scenes without reacting ... . The same process applied to personal beatings. As the amount of the beatings increased, one consciously felt them far less. Hunger, however, did not diminish so dramatically; it was felt by most as the greatest pain, and in time even twenty-five lashes for a bit of bread did not seem too high a price to pay to assuage one's appetite."

(89) Janowska, Spring 1942: "... I began to observe to my disgust that I, too, was coming very near to developing the indifference and apathy of so many others. I was saved from succumbing to these feelings only by the thought of those at home, and the determination that my mother should see me alive. These ideas kept me from yielding, and gave me a positive ideal to strive for."

(200) Working in the Death Brigade, Janowska: "... we consider the dead the lucky ones; they have it all behind them, while our end still awaits us."

(212–13) "How happy one would be to be free! ... If one should ask that man there, walking with his wife and two children, whether he is happy, he would perhaps say 'no'. He probably would like to have this or that; he doesn't know how happy he should be to have his freedom, and to be with his dear ones. We cannot even hope for that; we've already lost ours."

(226) "But I should like to emphasize again that usually the people undress themselves quickly and go to the fire without protest. Some of them even jump into the fire without a order to do so. They have had enough. The tortures have been going on too long. Most of them have already lost all their near ones, and everyone feels that the world is his enemy; even the children in diapers feel this. We are taught that people sharing common tragedy become friends in sorrow. This didn't happen at Janowska. The word 'tragedy' perhaps is not strong enough to convey what had happened to these people."

(279–80) "... I believe that if the tragedy had been on a much smaller scale it would have been harder to take, for it would have been pain within limits of endurance. Beyond that limit one ceases to feel anything more... .Living with and meeting people who shared a similar fate, it seemed that this was the 'normal' life. The non-Jewish world continued to be strange to us. We lived in our own world. We didn't talk about those we lost or how it happened. One's own family was few among millions."

Places mentioned in Europe (page first mentioned)

Austria/Österreich (23), Belz (23), Bereza–Kartuska (305), Berlin (31), Bielsko–Biala/Bielitz (172), Bobrka (217), Bolechow (185), Brody (132), Brzuchowice (217), Bukovina (297), Busk (132), Byszow (124), Cracow/Krakow/Krakau (312), Czechoslovakia (322), Czernowitz/ Cernauti/Chernovcy (297), Dachau concentration camp (327), Dornfeld (217), Drohobycz (299), Föhrenwald Displaced Persons camp (323), France (312), Galicia (94), Gleiwitz/ Gliwice DP camp (308), Grodek Jagielonski (94), Grzymalow (31), Hungary/ Magyarország (96), Italy/Italia (312), Janowska slave labour camp (69), Jaryczow (217), Kamionka–Strumilowa (121), Katowice/Kattowitz (312), Kiev/Kyjiv (37), Kishinev (297), Krystynopol (20), Krzywicki Woods (Lvov) (205), Kulikow (154), Lublin (230), Lvov/Lemberg/Lwow/Lviv (18), Munich/München (182), Nuremberg (284), Podwoloczyska (228), Poland/Polska (20), Przemysl (94), Radziechow (128), Rawa–Ruska (141), Romania (33), Saarbrücken (103), Sambor (94), Silesia/Schlesien/Slask (104), Sokal (132), Stanislawow/Stanislau (95), Stojanow (18), Tarnopol (189), Ukraine/Ukrajina (124), Vienna/Wien (200), Warsaw/Warszawa/Warschau (219), Westerplatte (32), Winniki (239), Wulka (Lvov) (216), Zhitomir (290), Zloczow (216), Zniesienie (240), Zolkiew (57), Zurich (327)

Places mentioned outside Europe (page first mentioned)

Black Sea (297), China (303), Genqistova (303), Ismail (297), Israel/Yisrael (285), Leningrad/ St. Petersburg (298), Mongolia (303), Moscow/Moskva (37), New York City (317), Novosibirsk (302), Palestine (British Mandate) (20), Semipalatinsk (303), Siberia/Sibir (37), United States of America (285), Vladivostok (297)

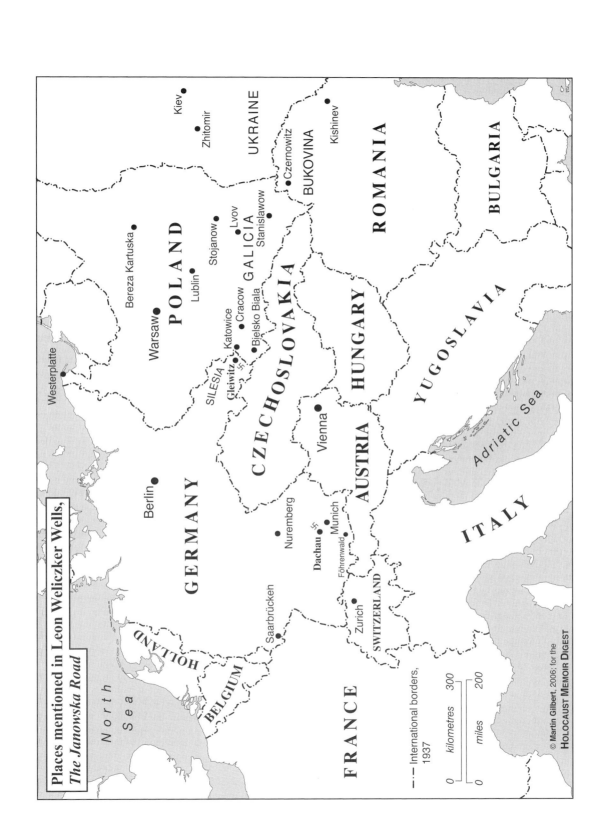

Places mentioned in Leon Weliczker Wells,
The Janowska Road

Kiev ●
Zhitomir ●

UKRAINE

Czernowitz ●
BUKOVINA

Kishinev ●

ROMANIA

BULGARIA

Bereza Kartuska ●

POLAND

Stojanow ●
Lvov ●
Lublin ●
GALICIA
Stanislawow ●

Warsaw ●
Katowice ●
Cracow ●
Bielsko Biala ●
SILESIA
Gleiwitz ●

CZECHOSLOVAKIA

HUNGARY

YUGOSLAVIA

Vienna ●

Adriatic Sea

Berlin ●

GERMANY

Nuremberg ●
Munich ●
Dachau ●
Föhrenwald ●

AUSTRIA

ITALY

Saarbrücken ●

Zurich ●
SWITZERLAND

FRANCE

HOLLAND

BELGIUM

North Sea

Westerplatte ●

─ ─ International borders, 1937

0   kilometres   300
0   miles   200

© Martin Gilbert, 2006; for the
HOLOCAUST MEMOIR DIGEST

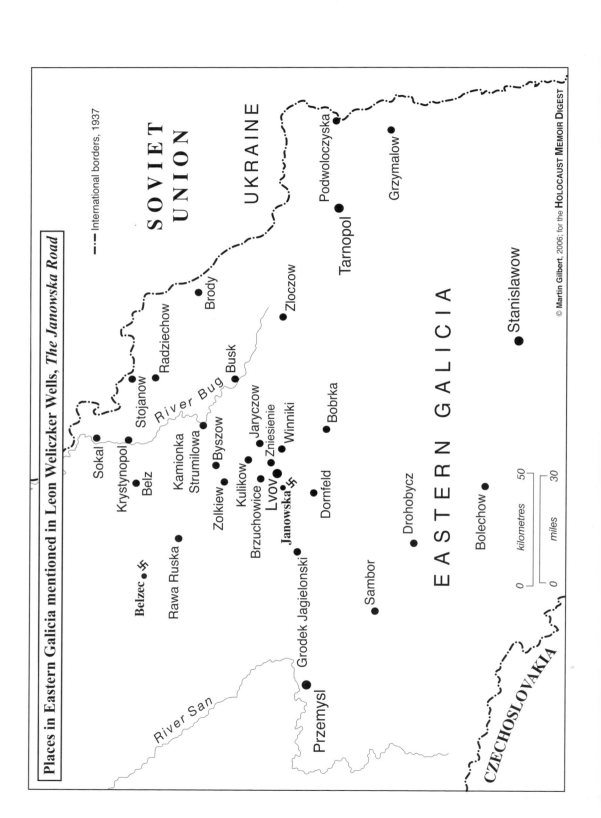

Places in Eastern Galicia mentioned in Leon Weliczker Wells, *The Janowska Road*

International borders, 1937

SOVIET
UNION

UKRAINE

EASTERN GALICIA

CZECHOSLOVAKIA

Grzymalow

Podwoloczyska

Tarnopol

Stanislawow

Brody

Zloczow

Radziechow

Stojanow

Busk

River Bug

Sokal

Krystynopol

Belz

Kamionka
Strumilowa

Byszow

Jaryczow

Zniesienie

Winniki

Bobrka

Zolkiew

Kulikow

Brzuchowice

Lvov

Janowska

Dornfeld

Drohobycz

Bolechow

Belzec

Rawa Ruska

Grodek Jagielonski

Sambor

Przemysl

River San

kilometres   0 ___ 50
miles   0 ___ 30

© Martin Gilbert, 2006; for the HOLOCAUST MEMOIR DIGEST

"When an order in here is not carried out exactly,

you hear a shot,

and again

there is one more in heaven."

Leon Weliczker Wells

Mel Mermelstein, *By Bread Alone*

1927: born in Oroszveg, Munkacs, Eastern Czechoslovakia, to Bernad and Fani Mermelstein, the third of four children, after sister Etu and brother Lajos; sister Magda follows

26 March 1938: sub-Carpathian Russia comes under control of Ukrainian Nationalist Monsignor Augustin Voloshyn

March 1939: area becomes annexed to Hungary, under Regent Miklos Horthy

22 June 1941: Horthy enters war as an ally of Germany

25 June 1941: Mel's father is drafted, and sent to a Ukrainian labour camp; he returns the next spring

March 1944: German troops arrive in Munkacs

10 April 1944: Jews in Munkacs ordered to raise money to ensure their safety.

19 April 1944: Mel and the Jews of Munkacs moved to the Kalus Brickyard transit camp

19/20 May 1944: two transports leave the Kalus Brickyard for "Germany"; Mel and his family leave on the second transport

22 May 1944: arrive Auschwitz

Mid–July 1944: transferred to Gleiwitz slave labour camp

18 January 1945: begins death march from Gleiwitz that ends in Buchenwald in February

11 April 1945: Buchenwald is liberated by United States forces

Summer 1945: returns to Munkacs, finds only his uncle

31 August 1946: arrives by Steamship to New York

20 November 1980: claimed reward offered by Neo-Nazi Institute for Historical Review to prove Jews were gassed

February 1981: he sued the Institute and won

Author: Mel Mermelstein

Title: *By Bread Alone, The Story of A-4685*

Publishing details

Auschwitz Study Foundation, PO Box 2232, Huntington Beach, California 92647. 1979. 255 pages.
ISBN #0-9606534-0-6.
Distributed by the Auschwitz Study Foundation, Inc.

Focus:

Mel, from Munkacs in Hungary, who is 12 in 1939, survives Auschwitz, slave labour, and concentration camps. The events described take place from the German entry into his home town in March 1944 to Mel's arrival in America on 31 August 1946.

Features:

Foreword:	Dedication, written by the author, page iii.
	Acknowledgements, written by the author, page xi.
	Foreword, written by the author, page xii.
	Preface, written by the author, page xiii.
Photographs:	Parents and siblings, wife and children.
	General photographs of Holocaust survivors, victims, and perpetrators.
Documents:	Nuremburg trial documents; his Buchenwald documents; documents and correspondence pertaining to his legal suit; correspondence from the International Tracing Service, International Red Cross; *Los Angeles Times* articles, 16 March 1939 to 14 May 1945, 30 July 1975, 12 March and 10 October 1981; also letters from *The Jerusalem Post*.
Maps:	1939 Europe, by J.F. Horrabin, page iv.
	A partial map depicting major death and concentration camps, page vi.
Afterword:	Epilogue, excerpts from the 23 June 1965 Detroit speech by Dr. Martin Luther King, Jr., page 326.
	"Flight home from the memorial", poem written by David Mermelstein, page 327.

Contents: (by topic, with page numbers)

Pre-war Jewish home and community life

(1–2, 28, 33) In March 1944, Mel (Moishi) is 17, his brother Lajos is 19, sister Magda is 15, sister Etu is 20, his mother Fani turns 44 in April, father, Bernad (Bernard) is 45.

(2–5) Political background to the Carpatho-Ukraine area: "In some regions the Jews were more numerous than all the other religions and creeds combined. ... In the city of Munkacs there were about thirty-six thousand people, of which sixteen thousand were Jews. The majority of the Jewish inhabitants were of the strict Orthodox religious sect ... ."

(253) A post-war recollection: "It was not more than a year before that a Sabbath eve meant a festive table, all the family together, white cloth, our best silver, mother whispering her blessing

as she lit the candles, and father lifting the 'kiddush' cup, as we all stood around and listened to his chant."

The coming of war

(1, 21–6) March 1944, the Germans arrive: "In two short weeks the process of identification and confinement was well under way. ... finally, all Jews were placed under house arrest."

(8, 14, 17, 21) 25 June 1941, his father is conscripted, sent to a Ukraine labour camp: "Jews were conscripted in special battalions; for forced labor, no longer were they trusted with rifle in hand." He returns home the following spring.

(14, 17) Jews fleeing the Nazis come to Munkacs: "They became refugees overnight, and had to be sheltered, fed, and hidden from the 'Arrowcross bandits', who were comparable to the Nazi fascists."

Life under German occupation

(27–8) 10 April 1944, Mel's mother's forty-fourth birthday: "The Nazi-appointed leadership in Munkacs ... was notified by the Gestapo that they would issue a proclamation of safety for all Jews, provided we raised a certain sum of money. ... finally the proclamation ... was posted. All Jews living in towns and villages were to be ready for immediate shipment to camps; all Jews living in cities were to be relocated to ghettos. There was no explanation of what happened to our money or the promise of safety."

Deportation

(33–6) 19 April 1944, they leave their home, with the help of two Hungarian policemen, and are taken to the Kalus Brickyard: "They knew my father well, as they were old friends who had gone to school with him and were members of the same clubs. ... 'Bernard, you must be calm. All shall be well with you and your family. This action is taken for your safety.' ... 'Now', continued my father's friend, 'deposit with us your cash, jewelry – whatever is of value. We'll take care of it until you return.'"

(84, 93–4) 19 and 20 May 1944, two transports leave the Brickyard for "Germany": "The darkness that accompanied the closing of the doors came as a shock, and what arose among us was a collective sigh and a whimpering sound. It was as if the mass within the boxcar had given up hope, as if the sliding door that sealed us in had also sealed our lives forever."

(99–101) The deportation train crosses the Hungarian/Slovak border, the Hungarian guards are replaced by SS, but first: "'Well, there's nothing we can do,' said one soldier to the other. 'At least we can give them some air.' The doors were soon opened, just enough to allow a breath of air in. It was heavenly. ... The soldiers began to talk to us with sympathy. They reached inside for our pails and filled them with water."

(101–2) After three days on the train, it stops, the doors are opened: "It was a scene full of madness. Everyone rose at once and hurriedly began gathering bundles and securing belongings. Shouts and screams for loved ones to stick together filled the air. Mothers hushed their children, frightened by a strange lot of shouting men dressed in blue and white striped uniforms. Their shouts overpowered all others."

Transit camps

(67–9) The Kalus Brickyard in Munkacs becomes their temporary camp: "Soon, we arrived at the brickyard, only to discover that we were not alone. ... For many days, during which time the vigorous fund-raising campaign had been in full swing, men and women and children from nearby villages were already being incarcerated."

(74–7) During the second week in the Brickyard, the able-bodied are weeded out: "'You are the chosen few. I picked you for a special task. As of now, you are the official members of the Camp Police. The following are the six basic orders you will obey.' ... There again: Hebrew foreman over the Hebrew slaves."

(77–80) In the effort to keep outsiders from helping those held in the Brickyard, the SS "Demon" orders the "police" to beat peasants bringing food. Mel is ordered at gun point, then: "... I thought I could get the gun away from him and kill him. But what would happen to my family if I failed, or if I succeeded?"

(80–1) In the Brickyard, the "Demon" puts Mel and other religious "policemen" in charge of the bookburning: "I only felt guilt for the scrolls I helped to burn and for the woman I almost whipped. ... I felt guilty, because 'he' didn't. ... Guilt is a phenomenon that must find a body."

(85–6, 90–1) Bargaining with Eichmann, money and valuables for Jewish lives: "Weeks of waiting in the brickyard turned out to be part of a larger pattern in which hundreds of thousands of us were held in brickyards, in city ghettos, in transit, in camps all over Hungary, waiting for the consummation or the failure of the 'Big Deal'." (This so-called "Big Deal" was a deception by Eichmann intended to lull both the Hungarian Jewish leadership and world Jewry into believing that a deal was in prospect. Even while Eichmann was promising that Hungarian Jews were being kept in safety pending a deal, he was organizing their daily deportation to Auschwitz and their deaths.)

(95) Their train from the Kalus Brickyard continues for a mile to the next stop: "The Ostreicher brickyard had also been converted into a transit camp for Jews, but for Jews from the city ghettos, in preparation for the final journey."

Slave labour camps and factories

(130–1) Tibi and Mel search for their fathers: "He looked at me and broke the terrifying news. 'Both of our fathers were shipped early this morning to a coal mine in Jaworzna!' ... I ran to Lajos feeling totally distraught, barely able to tell what I had heard. ... As it turned out, we spent our last day together. The next day I couldn't find him. A week later, I discovered that he too had been shipped on a transport to the coal mines ... to Jaworzna." (Jaworzno)

(133–7) At Gleiwitz: "The next day we were put to work building the camp. ... I could see a huge mountainous pile of rocks. Without a moment's delay, the Kapos drove us to it. With pick in hand, I cracked the rocks to smithereens and then shoveled them into a wheelbarrow ... . In the afternoon I was switched to the wheelbarrow team, pushing tons of rocks through rough terrain into the camp. Even though I felt exhausted, there was nothing I could do but keep up."

(153–6) Mel becomes a "mussulman", he goes through a selection, the doctor asks him: "'How do you feel?' ... . I took a chance on the truth. Maybe he had a son at home, I prayed, and to him I heard myself saying, 'I am not well enough to go on, Doctor.' He looked at me for a moment and then said, 'You are too young, and can still work.' ... I was at odds; they wouldn't let me live, nor would they let me die."

(163–4) Christmas 1944, Gleiwitz: "The day of Christmas arrived, and to our disbelief we received an extra portion of bread. I clutched it with both hands and wept for joy. We even received a small piece of margarine for a spread; it was truly a feast. ... Suddenly out of the clear, Moll appeared in the middle of the night. ... Why were we driven out in the cold, just as we were promised a restful day?" They spend the rest of the night hauling rocks.

Auschwitz-Birkenau

(109, 112–14) The men are separated from the women and children upon arrival: "Surprisingly, there was no expression of dismay at the separation. ... we told ourselves that this was temporary and that we would be reunited as soon as accommodations were arranged. We were too demoralized by the long journey in the sealed boxcar to do anything but obey."

(118) "They shaved off all our hair so that we looked like peeled onions. From there we were marched to the shower room. ... A sigh of relief hit me as the first batch came running from the building still holding onto their shoes and belts. Our final stop was a clothing storeroom. There each received a pair of pants, a shirt, a jacket and a cap, all striped and made of the same cloth. ... We all looked alike. For the first time I experienced a world with no class distinction. Rich and poor, young and old, shared the same fate as in no way before."

(119, 122–4) They are transferred from Birkenau where they had entered, to the Auschwitz Main Camp: "My first night in Auschwitz was spent in a bed under blankets, in a heated room. It seemed a strange beginning."

(125–7) The "marketplace" at Auschwitz: "I stopped at the marketplace, only to discover that Lajos had traded away his husky pair of shoes for a loaf of bread! I was saddened, since I knew that after bread, shoes were the next necessity for survival. ... It was no use, he would not listen. He just went on his way, contented, not worrying about the next day."

(130) Mel becomes #A4685: "This was to be my prison number, and I soon found it tattooed deep into the skin of my left forearm. For days my arm was painful and swollen from the poisonous ink, which penetrated all my layers of skin, left me feverish for days. ... From that day on I was but a number, not a human being, but simply a number, A-4685. ... The indelible and poisonous ink had hardly sunk into my vein when I ran to tell my brother and father to take note of my new number. I wanted them to know, in case they looked for me later." 22 May 1944.

(131–2) Six weeks after arriving in Auschwitz, Mel is transported to Gleiwitz, a sub-camp of Buna-Monowitz/Auschwitz III: "I was frightened when the convoy began to roll, but I was leaving Auschwitz-Birkenau alive."

Death marches

(165–7) 18 January 1945, two thousand in columns of three evacuate Gleiwitz, marching westward, among them, Mel with his friends Bram, Joey, Meyer, David and Willie.

(169–72) Leaving Gleiwitz on the march, they spend the first night in a civilian labour camp, the second night in a barn, the third night they reach Blechammer: "Camp discipline broke down. There were no more Kapos to be seen. More and more prisoners, inmates of Blechammer, broke through the concrete walls and took to the open roads. ... when I reached the nearest bunk I fell asleep."

Concentration camps

(180) Three weeks after the march began from Gleiwitz, they reach Gross Rosen for one night: "We were driven into barracks without windows or roofs. They had been bombed we were told. There wasn't a dry spot in the area ... I found a board and placed it over the mud ... and fell asleep."

(180–3, 193) February 1945, three days and two nights on a train from Gross Rosen to Buchenwald, where he becomes #130508, which is printed on pieces of cloth that they sew on to their prison clothes: "I learned that the main camp was occupied mostly by political prisoners of different nationalities. The 'Little Camp', as it was known, was an isolation place for the condemned, the hopeless. ... The vicious torture from hunger was total. There wasn't anything to occupy the mind so bread was the only wish ... . It was by bread and by bread alone that we hoped to survive."

(197) February/March 1945 in the "Little Camp" of Buchenwald: "Our only function was to line up, day after day, in front of our barracks, only to be counted as dead or still alive. ... Then the weather changed, and with the change came the sun with its warming rays. ... There were those who felt well enough to lay out in the sun and remove their lice-infested prison garments. I removed mine and spent most of the sunny days outside the barracks sunbathing, coupled with lice picking."

(200–1) April 1945, Buchenwald, Allied airplane raids become the impetus for a complete evacuation of the camp: "The main camp began first. ... Suddenly the typhus barracks and all of the Little Camp became the most sought out hiding place. It was safest because none from the main camp, in particular the SS, would dare enter the area for fear of catching the contagious disease."

(202–3) "On April 8, 1945, the evacuation of the Little Camp began. ... At first we refused to go, but then we had no choice, as we were threatened and then beaten. ... As we started up the hill, we were interrupted by the siren, sounding an air raid. ... I now became certain why everyone was so reluctant to go through the gates. Remaining in camp increased the probability of survival, and beyond the gates was sure death."

(223) 16 April 1945, a photograph taken by: "Private Miller from the U. S. Special Services, who wanted a photo of the liberated prisoners of Buchenwald so he could properly capture and record on film what we looked like. ... That photograph turned out to be one of the most widely circulated and published portraits of the camps. ... Our deep eyes, full of pain and suffering and sickness and fatigue, were already telling the tales of which we could not put into words." The photo appears on page 208 of his memoir.

Witness to mass murder

(114–15, 117) Entering Birkenau: "... a scene right out of Dante's 'Inferno'. Ahead were three huge pits dug deep into the ground. In each a fire was raging. Around the flaming pits naked men were running in an endless circle. All around I could see SS guards and prison 'Kapos' swinging their leather whips and driving the prisoners from behind into the pits. ... I kept pushing myself away from the pit but something kept drawing me back. I was torn between two worlds, the living and the dead."

(127–8) His father Bernard after a day at work in Auschwitz, to his sons: "'This is a place of impending death,' he went on. 'It waits for all, and it will get all of us in the end.' ... We did not understand his utter despondency until it became clear that he had been on a special detail where he could see the corpses as they were being disposed of after gassing."

(133) From the transport truck from Auschwitz to Gleiwitz: "Suddenly I heard machine gun fire ... . They were prisoners of war in bunches. Russians, from the far reaches of Mongolia. They were bunched in small groups of about ten each, lined up against a pile of rocks and then machine gunned to death."

(146) At Gleiwitz, nine Poles and two Russians escape; the Russians are found and hung, in further retaliation: "All the Jews were confined to the barracks while the Poles, Ukrainians and Russian prisoners were ordered to assemble for roll call. ... All of the Poles, Ukrainians and Russians were going to Auschwitz – to the gas chambers."

(146, 152–3) SS Oberscharführer Otto Moll, the new commandant at Gleiwitz: "Moll had been in Auschwitz since 1941, and had steadily risen in rank, recognition and responsibility throughout his years there. No one, even among the SS, remained in Auschwitz for four years without possessing unique talents and abilities, and knowing how to use them to the fullest. The road to 'Oberscharführer' had been paved with the ashes of burnt corpses." His post-war fate is cited.

(172–3, 235) At Blechhammer, Mel watches in disbelief as an SS man unloads a truck of bread: "Why is he bringing us bread? The heap was getting bigger and bigger and the inmates began to gather closer and closer. The SS man, finishing his job of unloading, pulled away, disappearing into the forest. ... A squad of the elite SS emerged from the outskirts of the camp. They watched the inmates gather around the mountain of bread, and then they opened fire, rapid fire. ... Suddenly there was silence – not a sound to be heard. ... They were all dead, piled up on top of each other, covering the heap of bread, soaking it with their blood."

(203–4) April 1945, Buchenwald evacuation: "Realizing their position in the face of the rapidly advancing Allied armies, the SS were afraid to carry out any more executions within the camp itself. But in the forests outside the camp it was a different story. Once they got the prisoners beyond the main gate at the top of the hill, they had no hesitancy in gunning them down. ... As I reached the gate, I was asked to give my number. Since I was a prisoner with two numbers, I asked the recorder which one he wanted. ... 'That will do, since you are not going anywhere from here but to the pits.' At first I did not get the gist of what he said, but it soon hit me as I began to hear the machine gun fire in the background."

(221–2) After liberation: "... the Americans insisted that the German civilians be brought to the area to see with their own eyes what had taken place at Buchenwald. The Germans from nearby towns and villages were dragged in to witness for themselves the atrocities committed by their masters. ... As they were led around the camp I could see them bow their heads as if in prayer. They were visibly shaken ... ."

Resistance, ghetto revolts, individual acts of courage and defiance

(69–71) Hungarian army recruit Bram, in the Kalus Brickyard, April 1944: "'Unless the

Russians speed up their campaign and rescue us, we are doomed,' he began realistically. 'Our task is to see that we live long enough to enable them to save us.'" He organizes the building of shelter, an area for medical treatment, and: "A rude mess hall was set up, where we distributed the food and supplies we received from the ghetto in the city, some donated by friends and some a contribution from the Jewish community there."

(82–3) In the Brickyard, a young girl pleads for her mother to be allowed to stay inside and not be forced out into the rain: "The girl's choice had been cruelly thrust upon her – to spit in the face of this dumpy, petty despot, or to try to win his favor. ... He glanced at his men and saw his own lasciviousness reflected in them. He turned viciously and slapped his whip across her face."

(84) The Rabbi reacts to the order for men to shave their heads, beards and side-locks, in the Brickyard: "We watched as, quietly and with dignity, he approached the Commandant to make his simple request for exemption from cutting for the pious Jews. ... The Rabbi gently lifted himself off the ground, wiping the mud mixed with blood off his face. He stood erect, unmoved and without pain. ... The Demon, surprised at the Rabbi's courage, made a brisk about-face and returned to the guardhouse."

(97) Yom Kippur 1943 before the German invasion, a film 'Jud Suess' is shown in Munkacs: "The movie depicted the Jews as exploiters, and the heroic Nazis came in and rounded them up." When Lajos protests, he is arrested: "Then they took him to headquarters, where he was beaten severely before being released. He wore his wounds with pride."

(97–8) "'There was resistance in Munkacs at the railsidings... . A whole transport refused to embark. But soon the SS, in cahoots with the Hungarian Arrowcross bandits, came to the scene and opened fire, killing the resisters in full view of women and little children. The remainder were shoved into the boxcars. ... If we had had outside help, that would have been the beginning of a successful uprising.'" As reported by Lajos to his family.

(182, 203) Buchenwald, of the camp secretary: "What I couldn't have known at the time was that this man was one of a large group of political activists – socialist and communist prisoners who had banded into a large and efficient underground organization within the camp society. They were able to give aid to the ill and save the dying, and at the same time prepare themselves for the day of resistance and liberation."

Partisan activity

(29–30) His friend Tibi tries to get the children in Mel's family to find the partisans in the woods and join with them to fight. Mel's father dissuades him: "' I beg you – don't do this thing. It's not meant for a Jew.' ... What I saw in my father's eyes was not cowardice; nor was it fear. Instead it was a hopelessness in the odds of this world, curiously mixed with a faith and a hope in the odds of the next."

Specific escapes

(125) "... we discovered that while fortified and electrified, Auschwitz was vulnerable to escape. As we soon learned, two inmates of Auschwitz had escaped just prior to our arrival. A Slovakian Jew named Rosenberg and his buddy broke out. ... But they had escaped on April the 7th, and here we were, toward the end of May, when the gas chambers were hard at work. ... 'They must not have made it,' I thought. 'Otherwise, help would have come long ago.' Again I was

dreaming." (He refers to the escape of Rudolf Vrba and Alfred Wetzler, which is described with its aftermath, in Vrba's memoir "I Cannot Forgive", included in the *Holocaust Memoir Digest*, Volume 1.)

(140–2, 146) 11 August 1944, nine Poles and two Russians escape from Gleiwitz, two, Ivan and Fedor, are caught and hung: "I stood close to the gallows and I could see clearly the life drain from the faces of Ivan and Fedor. ... The escape was a success; nine of the eleven had made it."

Righteous Gentiles

(31–2) Friend Ana gives them food as they leave home: "My mother went to comfort her. 'You'll pray for our safety and perhaps the Lord will hear you.'" April 1944.

(72–3) Wilmos, his boss, sends a package of food to the Brickyard, and an offer: "'Escape to the mountains. Go to the vineyard in the hills. The gates to the cellar are open. We shall care for you in hiding.' The note was signed 'Master Wilmos.' ... My mother and father were united in their desire that I take the offer. ... In the end I chose to stay with my family ... .'"

(136–7, 139, 157, 173–6) Bosnian Pista, a Yugoslav Magyar who had joined the SS, a guard at Gleiwitz who speaks to Mel in Hungarian: "He was convinced that the Nazis were through. For him the war was over and he wanted me on his side. Suddenly I felt I was human once again. ... As I was about to leave, Pista reached into his pack and handed me a small piece of his bread."

(138–9, 159–61) Hans Wagner, in charge of the machine shop at Gleiwitz, asks Mel: "'You seem too young to be here. Where is your home? Do your mother and father know where you are?' He was asking me questions I could not comprehend. I was lost for words. Doesn't he know what's going on around, I thought? I shook my head and pointed to my insignia. 'I am a Jew. Don't you know what they do to Jews?'"

(159–60) "Irena, a frail Polish civilian slavegirl, was part of our team." In the machine shop at Gleiwitz she leaves food for Mel: "She was like an angel from heaven and she was aware of the chances she took by helping the 'Katzetnicks', as the camp inmates were called. ... Around Christmas time Irena was caught by the Nazis ... . She was accused of being involved in an attempted escape; she was brutally beaten by a special SS killing squad and shot against the wall in Block 11, at Auschwitz."

(160–1) Kapo Newman at Gleiwitz; "He was a political prisoner of German origin. A refined individual who hardly lifted a hand to hurt a fellow inmate. He was well known to all as the only human Kapo in the camp, a rare sight in a concentration camp."

(178–9) As the death marchers pass through the village of Manstein, the villagers call out in greeting and then throw bread from their tables to the men: "More important than the pieces of bread we snatched, was the unexpected surge of hope within us. ... In a face-to-face, people-to-people experience there had been a shower of bread that carried the rain of compassion."

Liberation

(204–6) 11 April 1945, Buchenwald: "Then we were told to stay in the barracks and remain still and orderly. Soon a well-dressed and obviously well-fed inmate entered. 'Men,' he said, 'you must be very quiet, not a whisper or a sound. I bring you good news, we may soon be liberated.' ... First we were told that an Allied plane had dropped a message that read: 'Hold on; the Allies will soon be in the camp to liberate you.' The message was stuffed in a loaf of bread, and I felt that the bread itself was the message. ... For me it seemed an inspiration that a loaf of bread from the skies – manna from heaven – should proclaim our imminent liberation."

(207, 218) "Allied planes flew low over the heads of the fleeing SS men, firing at them. The planes ... flew over the tower in which two SS guards were manning a heavy caliber machine gun. As long as they were there, any movement in camp was extremely dangerous. ... Soon after, I saw two inmates with rifles in their hands crawling toward the guard tower. A shouted order went up to the two SS men to lay down their arms. One of them pulled a white handkerchief from his pocket, tied it on the end of a stick and waved it in the air. That simple sign marked the end of Nazi power in Buchenwald!"

(219–20) 11 April 1945: "Slowly the sun set and the moon rose but even with the stars in the sky, they could not dissipate the darkness of Buchenwald. Many continued to die from neglect and diseases which were taking a toll that even 'liberation' could not reverse."

(225–8, 234) Mel regains his health as the war ends; he begins the journey home, hoping to find his mother, sisters Etu and Magda, and his brother Lajos. In Czechoslovakia, he meets up with his friends Bram and Joey: "I heard Bram's voice yell, 'I told you we'd live through it.' It was a moment of real joy."

(236–7) In Bratislava on his way home, Mel finds and tries to help a boyhood friend Joncsi, a former SS man, now running from the Soviets: "Later ... I noticed a group of prisoners being escorted by two Russian soldiers. Among them was Joncsi. ... He had been my playmate, my friend. I grew up with him. But I could not save him. It was no use. The Russian guards would not listen. They were brutal."

(237–9, 242) Mel returns to Munkacs, finds his Uncle Moshe Aaron, returns to the family home: "A young woman, with a child by her side, stood there, in the middle of the main room. ... Shocked and with tears in my eyes, I sat down upon the grass and covered my face with my hands. My uncle placed his hand upon my head ... . 'Listen, before you ask, before you question, repeat after me: "Boruch dayen emess".' ... 'Blessed is the Righteous Judge.' The traditional words on learning of a death seemed harshly inappropriate. But even as I said them, a softening set in."

(243–8) Mel goes to Bucharest, where there are Jewish relief agencies. He is caught as a Soviet deserter and released. Facing the chance of illegal entry to Palestine and the very real possibility of being interred in a concentration camp in Cyprus, he decides to return home. Facing the reality of living under the new Communist system, he sneaks across the border to Prague: "To survive Auschwitz and then die in my own country, shot down by the Russians! ... I now fully realized that I had made my second escape from slavery to freedom."

(249–50) Czechoslovakia and the Soviet Army expel former Nazis and Germans: "I couldn't stand the thought of the formerly persecuted engaging in similar acts of persecution against their fellow men. ... But then I saw it: rows and rows of women, the young and the elderly, heads shaven, clad in blue and white prison garb, wooden clogs on their still frostbitten feet, marching along the street, guarded by special camp guards. ... 'We're repaying our debts to them.'"

(251–3) Mel travels to Munich to say goodbye to his friends. Near the rail station in Munich he meets a Jewish American soldier and spends the Sabbath evening with him and his friends: "I blushed as the company asked me to chant the 'kiddush'. It was an honor to be asked to say the prayers … ."

(255) 20 August 1946, Mel sails on the Steamship Marine Perch from Bremerhaven, he arrives in New York, 31 August 1946.

Displaced Persons camps

(251, 254) Mel arrives at the Eschwege camp near Kassel in Germany; he contacts his aunt in New Jersey, and arranges to leave for America.

Stories of individuals, including family members

(95–6) At the Ostreicher Brickyard, Mel sees his mother's youngest sister Hana, his brother Lajos who joins them on the train, and his grandfather: "Gaunt and hungry looking, weak and stumbling, 'Zeide' was led by both hands, puffing and dazed. I could not believe my eyes."

(97–8) Lajos' attempts to escape, first to join the partisans: "'… the plan didn't work. … They shot Zalman the tailor, because he tried to hide. And they clubbed Ben-Zion the radio man to death because he tried to escape … .'" On the train, he and friend Tibi plot escape: "His plan was to break out, to lift a few boards off the floor and sneak through. It was an attractive plan but no one would buy it."

(109, 113, 119, 129) His mother and sisters: separated from the men at the Birkenau ramp, the realization of their fate, a chance sighting: "'On second thought,' I said to myself, 'that could not have been my mother. That lady had a little baby in her arms. She just resembled my mother, and there are many girls that look like Etu and Magda.' I made peace with myself; I had seen it all wrong." His father confirms their fears: "'Your mother and sisters are …' He paused a moment, unable to go on. 'And you must not torture your minds about their fate. …' And he pointed to the flaming chimneys."

(128–9) Father's advice in Auschwitz that he and his two sons do not remain together, "'… to see … would be the greatest suffering of all.' … My perception of him gained a new maturity; I began to understand the wisdom and sheer courage in what he was asking us to do. … Then more firmly he said, 'But if we stay apart, at least one of us will live to tell.'"

(128–9) In Auschwitz at a roll call, Pinchus and his son Lief: "'It's my son,' he pleaded. 'You can't kill him – it's my son.' The SS turned viciously on Pinchus and beat him too. Both were sent to the gas chambers in the next selection."

(129) Zalman the Pole at Auschwitz: "He wanted to hang himself, but Zalman had neither the stamina nor the strength to tie the rope and noose and go through with all the macabre details. His friend refused. All night long he begged and cried and pleaded for mercy, till finally the assistance he needed was given. His assistant – his friend, his bunkmate, his 'buddy' – was his father."

(156–7) Cleaning the latrines at Gleiwitz, Kapo Fritz in charge: "… in the end Fritz always managed to capture the last one out. Simon, the shoemaker, was caught. Fritz had beaten Simon mercilessly and chased him into the pit filled with manure. He was left there to drown. We were not allowed to rescue Simon."

(161–2) Mel's friend Meyer, #A-4684, is caught "looting" the storehouse at Gleiwitz, the punishment is twenty-five lashes: "There were cries for mercy and help, but not from Meyer: he was too far gone. He no longer felt pain. He had lost his senses. He was a 'mussulman'. ... henceforth anyone looting or breaking into a storeroom or a warehouse would be shot. ... The choice was to die of starvation or of execution. There was no choice."

(171) On the death march from Gleiwitz to Blechhammer: "Liebel the Glazier, as we knew him, lost the wooden part of his shoes and was forced to march that way. The SS guards amused themselves watching Liebel until he collapsed. They pulled him to the wayside to be shot."

(177) After two weeks of the death march, fewer than 200 remain from the 2,000 who had set off; of those who do not survive, Mel's friends Joshua and Chelm, Mojse and Yankel are caught trying to escape, Willie, killed perhaps at Blechhammer, and Hershel the watchmaker, is shot along the road.

(194–5) At Buchenwald, Mel learns from Shimshe Friedman of the death of his father, "Hersh-Ber", Bernard, at Jaworzno on 18 December 1944: "'Your father was a hard worker. ... He tried to stay out of trouble by working himself to death. ... Then one morning, he simply didn't wake up. The effort proved too much for him. ... Be proud Moishele, that he was your father.' ... I was too overcome to clamber to my shelf that night, and slept on the floor beside those who had died during the day. For me, my father was among them."

(195–6, 201) At Buchenwald, Mel finds his friend Elijah, "a frail, bent youngster from Sighet", together they mourn the deaths of their fathers: "Elijah was a sensitive boy, with a strong nose and haunting eyes. There was pain and suffering in his eyes. Elijah cried for his father every time I saw him thereafter."

(195–6, 202) Berry Spitz from Munkacs, who had played soccer with Mel at home: "I remember him as the left striker and I the right striker. We played well as a team. I couldn't believe my eyes when I saw Berry lying near death inside the rack. ... He told me about many of our friends who were with him at the coal mines in Jaworzna."

(200) Ben "the dreamer of Galicia", dies at Buchenwald: "He was describing in minute detail his favorite Sabbath dish, a common topic of discussion. ... He built himself up to a feverish pitch, and then suddenly took a deep breath and fell to the side with his eyes and mouth wide open. ... As often as I had seen death, I had never learned to accept it calmly. I rushed to Ben's side and tried to revive him. It was no use."

(235–6) Willie Bacsi, liberated from Blechhammer, reunited with Mel in Budapest: "'It's all over. We've made it,' Willie would announce from time to time, as if he didn't actually believe it."

(240–1) His Uncle Moshe Aaron tells Mel the fate of his family: "'There was a mother with many little children and an infant in her arms. ... Your mother wanted to help. She took the babe in her arms to hold and keep her safe. ... She wanted desperately to save it from the SS when they demanded it from her. ... But then they took your mother, bearing the other woman's baby in her arms, and together they were led into the gas chambers. ... Etu and Magda went to the left. They were selected for slave labor. ... Seconds later Etu once again leaped across the way to join your mother, to be with her. Followed by Magda, all three were led to the gas chambers at Birkenau.' ... 'Lajos?' ... 'He was shot on the road to Blechhammer from Camp Jaworzna.'"

(248) Brothers Bennet, Kalvin and Steve, three childhood friends, hidden in Buchenwald with Mel during the last days of evacuation, reunited in Usti Nad Labem, Czechoslovakia, January 1946: "I was no longer alone; I had found a family, and I became their brother."

Post-war life and career

(272) He claimed the 20 November 1980 reward, offered by the Neo-Nazi Institute for Historical Review, to prove Jews were gassed. In February 1981, he sued the Institute and won. The court documents are included.

Personal reflections

(Foreword p.xii) "... never before in recorded history has man revealed himself more than during this period. The mask of mankind had dropped and we must therefore take the opportunity to learn what it is in man that makes it possible for such a Holocaust to occur."

(128) Father's advice, Auschwitz: "There is only one way for us to survive. We must stay apart ... each away from the other. At least one of us will live to tell what they've done to us, to our children, to our people. If we remain together, in one place, there'll be agony for us – to feel each other's suffering, to witness each other's pain and experience each other's hunger and starvation. In this place of death and evil, it is better to stay apart."

(170–1) On the death march from Gleiwitz to Buchenwald, an "old-looking" man asks for assistance to keep up the pace but, at a steep hill, he stumbles and pulls Mel down. Mel tries to help him, but with an SS man pointing his rifle at the two, Mel manages to scramble away. The old man is shot: "'God,' I thought, 'how could I leave him like that?' And then, unbidden, another voice sobbed silently at me: 'What would you do if that old man was your father?' ... Pounded from the outside by monstrous taskmasters, racked from the inside by an aware and feeling soul, I felt my youth slip away from me and knew that the question would never go away."

(239–40) Mel confronts his Uncle Moshe Aaron: "'Do you want me to bless God for this unbearable pain? Do you want me to call "just" this hideous unrighteousness?' ... My uncle was crying now. 'Your questions "are" just, but you're not the first to ask them. "As we bless God for the good, so must we bless Him for the evil." Those are the words of the Talmud. They're words beyond understanding; but if we cannot say them, we cannot hope. ... The Jewish way is to bless and to hope ... until hope and blessing surmount the pain and even the bitterness, and the living learn how to go on.'"

Places mentioned in Europe (page first mentioned)

Auschwitz Main Camp/Auschwitz I (86), Birkenau/Brzezinka/Auschwitz II (86), Blechhammer slave labour camp (Blachownia Slaska) (172), Bosnia/Bosna Herzegovina (136), Bratislava/Posony/Pressburg (236), Bremen (255), Bremerhaven (255), Bucharest/Bucuresti (243), Buchenwald concentration camp (181), Budapest (71), Buna-Monowitz/Monowice/Auschwitz III (132), Carpathian Mountains (2), Czechoslovakia (2), Eschwege Displaced Persons camp (251), Frankfurt-on-Main (152), Galicia (200), Germany/Deutschland (2), Gleiwitz/Gliwice slave labour camp (132), Gross Rosen/Rogoznica concentration camp (180), Hungary/Magyarország (5), Hust/Chust (3),

Jaworzno slave labour camp (130), Kalus Brickyard (Munkacs) (67), Kassel (251), Kosice/Kassa/Kaschau (100), Latorca River (29), Manstein (178), Munich/München (252), Munkacs/Mukacevo (5), Natzweiler/Strutthof concentration camp (132), Oroszveg (28), Ostreicher Brickyard (Munkacs) (95), Plzen/Pilsen (228), Poland/Polska (2), Prague/Praha (248), Romania (243), Ruthenia/Sub-Carpathia (2), Sighet/Maramarossziget/Sighetul Marmatiei (195), Slovakia/Slovenska Republic (100), Sudetenland (249), Switzerland/Schweiz/Suisse/Swizzeria (90), Ukraine/Ukrajina (2), Usti Nad Labem/Aussig (248), Uzhgorod/Ungvar/Uzhorod (3), Vistula River (131), Weimar (220)

Places mentioned outside Europe (page first mentioned)

Boston (90), Cairo (91), Cyprus/Kypros/Kibris (246), Dominican Republic (90), Ecuador (90), Israel/Yisrael (30), Los Angeles (90), Mongolia (133), Moscow/Moskva (8), New York City (90), Palestine (British Mandate) (90), Russia/Rossija (2), San Francisco (90), Siberia/Sibir (244), Turkey/Turkiye (91), United States of America (222)

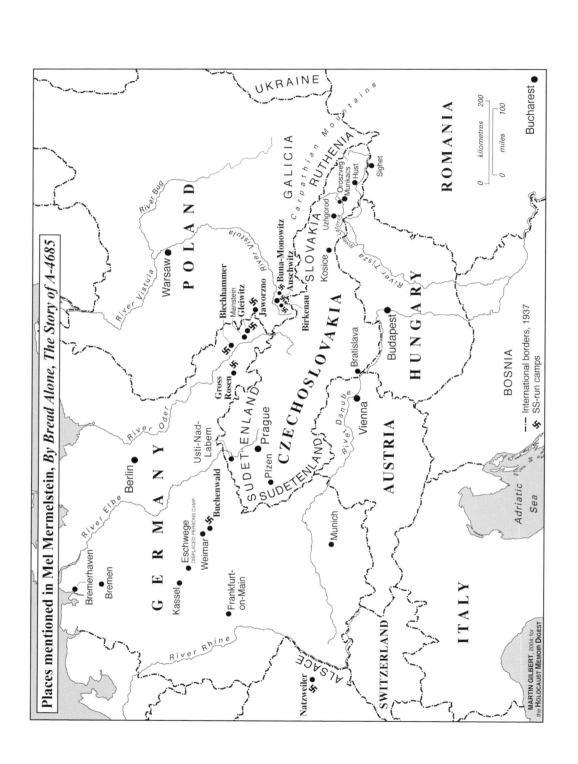

Places mentioned in Mel Mermelstein, *By Bread Alone, The Story of A-4685*

UKRAINE

POLAND

River Bug

River Vistula

Warsaw

GALICIA

RUTHENIA

Carpathian Mountains

Oroszveg
Munkacs
Uzhgorod
Hust
Sighet

ROMANIA

Bucharest

0   kilometres   200
0   miles   100

River Latorca

Blechhammer
Manstein
Gleiwitz
Jaworzno
Buna-Monowitz
Auschwitz
Birkenau

SLOVAKIA

Kosice

River Tisza

River Vistula

Gross
Rosen

Bratislava

Budapest

HUNGARY

BOSNIA

SUDETENLAND

Usti-Nad-
Labem

Prague

Plzen

CZECHOSLOVAKIA

SUDETENLAND

River Danube

Vienna

AUSTRIA

International borders, 1937
SS-run camps

River Oder

GERMANY

Berlin

River Elbe

Eschwege
DISPLACED PERSONS CAMP
Weimar   Buchenwald

Kassel

Bremerhaven
Bremen

Frankfurt-
on-Main

Munich

River Rhine

Natzweiler

ALSACE

SWITZERLAND

ITALY

Adriatic
Sea

MARTIN GILBERT, 2004: for
the HOLOCAUST MEMOIR DIGEST

"… I thought I could get the gun away from him and kill him.

But what would happen to my family

if I failed,

or if I succeeded?"

Mel Mermelstein

Hana Greenfield, *Fragments of Memory*

1926: born in Kolin, Czechoslovakia

13 June 1942: deported with her mother, Marie Lustig, and her sister Irena on the (third) final transport from Kolin, to Theresienstadt

July 1942: Hana's father is deported to Theresienstadt

September 1942: Hana's father is deported from Theresienstadt to Maly Trostenets and killed on arrival

24 August 1943: child survivors of the Bialystok Ghetto arrive in Theresienstadt

7 October 1943: the Bialystok children and 53 care-givers from Theresienstadt, Hana's mother among them, are deported from Theresienstadt to Auschwitz and killed on arrival

15 May 1944: deported to Auschwitz, to the Czech Family Camp (Camp BIIb) in Birkenau

4 July 1944: deported to slave labour camps in the Hamburg area: Freihafen, Neugraben, and Tiefstak

5 April 1945: transferred to Bergen-Belsen

15 April 1945: liberated at Bergen-Belsen

1946: Hana comes to England, to her uncle, and eventually to Israel

Author: Hana Greenfield

Title: *Fragments of Memory, From Kolin To Jerusalem*

Publishing details

Gefen Publishing House Ltd., POB 36004, Jerusalem 91360, Israel. 1998. 110 pages.
ISBN #965-229-185-4.
Originally published in Czech in Prague, under the title "From Kolin to Jerusalem".

Focus:

Hana, from Kolin, Czechoslovakia, who is 13 in 1939, is deported with her sister and mother to Theresienstadt for two years, then she is deported to Auschwitz, and to slave labour camps in Germany. She becomes a Holocaust scholar and lecturer. The events described take place between 1941 and her post-war work as a Holocaust scholar and teacher.

Features:

Foreword:	Written by Vaclav Havel, President of Czech Republic, preliminary pages.
	In Appreciation written by the Author, preliminary pages.
Photographs:	Hana's grandfather, page 19.
	Esti, Hana's friend at Terezin and Auschwitz, page 31.
	Bergen-Belsen 15 April 1945, "The Living Among The Dead", page 45.
	Hana, "Upon arrival in England", 1946, page 49.
	"Monument erected in Kolin Jewish cemetery after the war", page 55.
	Rabbi Dr. Richard Feder, page 58.
	The Treblinka memorial stones, page 68; the railway sign "Treblinka", page 69.
	"The author with her mother", page 77.
	Four care-givers who were taken with the Bialystok children to Auschwitz, Emilie Reinwald, Hana's mother Marie Lustig, Dr. Leo Gach, and Otla Kafka-David, page 92.
	Michael Mahler, 1941, page 96.
Documents:	The German Transport List, from Yad Vashem Archives, showing the name of Hana's friend Alice Ehrlich, along with her parents Hugo and Olga Ehrlich, deported from Kolin on 13 June 1942, page 11.
	Vera Kraus's letter, with a copy of her "Ustredni Kartoteka" showing her transport of 15 May 1942, Au-1 to Lublin, page 15.
Artwork:	Otto Ungar's painting "Deportation to an unknown destination", page 16.
	Pavel Fantel's "The Last Journey", page 25.
	Mieczyslaw Koscielniak's "Appell", page 27.
	Jerzy Potrezebowsky's "Selection of Women", page 28.
	Dina Gottlieb's "Barrel of Soup", page 33.
	"Painting by German pupil from the town of Neugraben" from the Helms Museum, page 36.
	Dina Gottlieb's painting "Returning From Work", page 38.
	Three paintings by Pavel Fantel depicting life in Theresienstadt, pages 63, 64, 66.

Dina Gottlieb's painting "Auschwitz", page 74.

Rosh Hashanah greeting made by Mojzse Treszczanski, one of the Bialystok children, for Emilie Reinwald, one of the care-givers in Theresienstadt, 1943, page 89.

Dr. Pavel Fantel's self-portrait, 28 August 1943, Terezin, page 94.

Five Terezin artists showing the "Children's Transport, Terezin 1943": Pavel Fantel and Ernest Morgan, page 98, Otto Unger and Leo Haas, page 99, and 14-year-old Helga Hoskova, page 101.

"Pencil Drawing by an Unknown Artist" dated 1945, page 108.

Afterword: Epilogue, written by the Author, pages 94–110.

Works cited: Zdenek Lederer, "Ghetto Theresienstadt", Edward Goldston and Son, London, 1953, referred to on pages 81–2.

H.G. Adler, "Theresienstadt 1941–1945" J.C.B. Mohr, Tubingen, 1955, referred to on page 82.

Berl Mark, article in "Biuletin Ludowskiego Instytutu Historycznego", Kwiecien-Wrzesien Publishers, 1953, #2–3, referred to on page 82.

"Zeszyty Oswiecimske", published by the Auschwitz Museum, referred to on pages 82–3.

Josef Lanik (Alfred Wetzler), "Co Dante Nevidel" ("What Dante Didn't See"), published by Osveta-Bratislava, Czechoslovakia, 1964, referred to on page 83.

Dr. Tuvia Citron, testimony, Yad Vashem Archives, M.M./B 165, referred to on pages 83–4.

Andrew Steiner, testimony about Tatranska Lomnice, Czechoslovakia, Yad Vashem Archives M5-165, referred to on pages 84–5.

Dieter Wisliceny, testimony to the Nuremburg Trial, 15 July 1946, referred to on pages 85–6.

Hadassa Lefkowitz, interview with Hana Greenfield, 23 October 1987, referred to on page 86.

Transport Dn/a list from Theresienstadt, Yad Vashem Archives, referred to on page 86.

Contents: (by topic, with page numbers)

Pre-war Jewish home and community life

(22) In a wartime correspondence with Michael Mahler, a Czech Zionist pen pal, Hana decribes her pre-war life and background: "As a child of patriotic, assimilated Czech Jews, I looked with suspicion at somebody who was ready to abandon his country. ... I wrote about my family, about my town which was built in the time of Charles IV, about the river Labe that made its way through the town, where I would go swimming in the summer and ice-skating in the winter."

(53–7, 59) In a post-war visit to Kolin, Hana revisits the scenes of her happy childhood, where Jews had lived since 1376: "... I suddenly heard the rich voice of our cantor, Mr. Reichner, the sermon of my teacher and esteemed Rabbi, Dr. Richard Feder, and the chanting of prayers by the congregants, the children, of whom I was one, running in and out of the synagogue, visiting parents and grandparents and playing outside."

Pre-war anti-Semitism

(59) "In 1913 a young woman, made pregnant by a Roman Catholic priest, committed suicide. The young priest, named Hrachovsky, tried to implicate the Jews in a blood libel, but fortunately they were ultimately exonerated." Kolin.

Life under German occupation

(9–10) Resticted from school, youth clubs, and all forms of recreation, Hana becomes friendly with Alice Ehrlich, a girl she had known previously from synagogue: "... we would meet in different private homes, where clandestine activities for Jewish youth were organized, away from the watchful eye of the Gestapo agents. ... Our dreams of a brighter future boosted our morale, while a yellow star shone from our clothing and our former classmates avoided looking at us whenever they would pass us in town." Kolin.

(22–3) "... Jewish women were forced to work in factories, men on the roads. Food was very scarce. We were left without means to buy the little food that was available, as our possessions were systematically confiscated and our bank accounts blocked." Hana's pen pal Michael Mahler receives permission to travel from his home in Hradec Kralove to Kolin to meet Hana, 1941; she is 15.

(59) "As early as January 1940, Jewish shops had already been confiscated and Jewish women – including my sister and I – were forced to work in the local soap factory, Hellada." Hana is 13.

(63) Hana is summoned to Gestapo headquarters in Kolin, 1941, to work for Dr. Pavel Fantel: "We worked at the Gestapo in an index card complex, where every Jew from the whole district was identified by his particulars, a photograph, and a complete background history of his life and all of his activities to date. These were gathered by the many collaborators that the Germans recruited among the Czech population, many of them with greedy eyes on prospective Jewish property."

Deportation

(10–11, 23) "On the 13th of June 1942, the third and last transport left our town with a cargo of 750 Jews ... . It was frightening leaving with just one suitcase containing so little of our possessions, leaving everything behind in our homes as though we were coming back the next day." (The two previous transports had left Kolin on the 5th and the 9th of June. The total number of Jews deported on the three transports was 2,202.)

(10–12, 102) Hana boards the train with her mother, sister, grandmother and aunt. At Bohusovice, near Terezin: "There, fifty people were taken off the train. ... among them my mother, sister and I. The remainder of the transport was sent on to the East ... . No one returned and no one knows how they perished." 13 June 1942.

(70) From Theresienstadt to Auschwitz, 15 May 1944: "Alone, without my mother and father, I traveled with strangers in a sealed cattle-wagon. So close physically, yet lonely among so many."

Death camps

(67) "On October 7, 1942, while in Terezin, my mother, sister and I were scheduled to be included in a transport of 1,000 inmates leaving the ghetto for some unknown place in the East. Expecting the worst, my mother, who worked as a nurse in the ghetto, injected herself

and became deathly ill. In that way, she managed to get the three of us out of that particular transport. This saved our lives temporarily. That transport was sent to Treblinka … ."

(102) Hana's father, who had married her mother in 1922, and divorced in 1937, was deported from Prague to Theresienstadt in July 1942, and then deported to Maly Trostenets death camp in September 1942.

Slave labour camps and factories

(34–6, 44, 104) As slave labourers in Hamburg, Hana and her friend Erna are among 500 women sent from Auschwitz, 4 July 1944, to stay in storage buildings in Freihafen: "We women prisoners were sent to different parts of the city, which was under daily bombing, to clean up the rubble so that civilian life could contine in Hamburg." When their buildings are bombed out, they are transferred to Neugraben, and then later to Tiefstak.

(37, 39–40) Their days and work in the slave labour camps of Hamburg, late December 1944: "It is beginning to get dark when we return to camp through Hamburg's suburbs. Through the windows of the houses we can see decorated Christmas trees in every living room. It all looks so inviting, so warm and so beautiful. It all seems so abnormal in our dreary prisoners' life. … I become lost in my thoughts: 'It would be nice to be a Christian just for one evening. To warm up my frozen feet in that cosy lit living room, to fill my hungry, shrunken stomach with some warm food and maybe fall asleep in a real bed?'"

Theresienstadt

(18, 20, 30) "Soon after my arrival in Ghetto Terezin in 1942, it was my good fortune to find work in a kitchen that prepared food for 10,000 people from the meagre supplies allocated to the ghetto prisoners by the Germans. To work in any place near food was everyone's dream in the camps." She is able to smuggle out two potatoes which she takes to her grandfather whom she finds there, and he shares with her: "We looked at each other with a smile and felt like conspirators. That was a moment of happiness we shared amidst the sad realities of our daily life in the ghetto."

(24) Late December 1942, Jews from Hradec Kralove arrive in Theresienstadt, among them Hana's pen pal Michael Mahler and his parents. Hana brings them food she has stolen from the kitchen: "They were embarrassed by my gift. They did not yet know what hunger was, and I no longer knew what it meant not to be hungry."

(24–5, 96) Michael develops a high fever: "It took a couple of days until a doctor was found and brought to see Michael, who was diagnosed as having an inflamed appendix. With a little stolen sugar I bribed someone to have Michael transferred to one of the ill-equipped hospitals in the ghetto." Two days later she hears he is to be operated on; the next day she hears he has died from a ruptured appendix: "Michael's mother and I walked together behind the hearse, piled with wooden coffins, pulled by prisoners up to the gate, from where only the dead had the privilege to leave the ghetto." 7 January 1943.

(29–30) "I found a small room in an old house, No. 112, which I shared with twenty other women. Here we put down our mattresses and our few belongings on the bare floor and enjoyed relative privacy in comparison to the halls we had lived in, where 300–400 people were packed in together." Here, she becomes close with a girl named Esti. October 1942.

Auschwitz-Birkenau

(13–14, 26–8, 30, 71, 103–4) Auschwitz: "No matter how conditioned we were to suffering in the previous camps, nobody was prepared for the visual horrors and harsh treatment that greeted us there. ... Here, time was measured by endless 'Appells' (roll calls), the inmates having to stand twice a day to be counted over and over again, because by the time the counting was finished, there were always a few dead bodies confusing the SS, so intent to be exact in their task." (Hana's transport from Theresienstadt was taken, without selection, to the Czech Family Camp, BIIb, in Birkenau, arriving 16 May 1944.)

(30, 32) Hana discovers that her friend Esti from Theresienstadt is in the hospital at Auschwitz: "It was a large building with three-tiered bunkbeds filled with half-dead human beings, without medicine, sheets or any comfort one would associate with the concept hospital." Hana visits Esti in the hospital; the last time, she finds Esti's mother there: "When her mother returned with the soup, she realized that Esti had left us. She sat down on the edge of the bed, ate Esti's last soup ration, got up, closed Esti's eyes, covering her face with the thin grey blanket. Then she sat down and cried ... ." 1944, Esti was 18.

(70–3) Hana's two post-war visits to Auschwitz, the first, with her husband: "Driven by a force that would not let me rest, I wanted to revisit and reconstruct the nightmares that had haunted me ... . I wanted to see for myself what I had lived through then ... ." Her second visit, organized by Yad Vashem; among her group, two other survivors of Auschwitz: "Everyone had come from a different place, arrived at a different time, lived in a different camp. Yet all three of us lived through the same Auschwitz experience, which played havoc with our lives for the rest of our days."

Death marches

(45–6) From Hamburg to Bergen by train: "From Bergen we were forced to walk to Belsen. The road was full of dead bodies, thrown to the side, of those who had gone before us on their last walk. Some dropped dead, some were shot when they could no longer continue the death march. No sooner did we reach the camp than the panicked Germans loaded onto us, like donkeys, the contents of their warehouses and, prodding us with guns and blows, forced us to march back to Bergen. More trains were arriving with similar human cargo, under the same inhumane conditions, from other camps in Germany." 5 April 1945.

Concentration camps

(45–6) At Bergen-Belsen: "Death was everywhere. It stared at us from everyone's eyes. The pitiful 'Muselmänner', the walking dead bodies, no longer knew where they were walking to or why. Everyone was searching for non-existent food. Our tongues were swollen from lack of water. The little water that was available was contaminated with typhoid bacilli. Some drank from it, no longer caring." April 1945.

(50–2) "A small piece of black bread meant another day of remaining alive. When one is very hungry, it isn't luxury one desires, it is that basic piece of bread which dominates the craving to fill the hole in one's stomach. To ease the pain that crawls into every crevice of the body when food is denied for an extended period of time."

Witness to mass murder

(54–5) A post-war realization: "... when in reprisal for the assassination of Reinhard Heydrich,

Hitler's chief officer of the Protectorate of Bohemia and Moravia, not only the village of Lidice was eliminated, but also 750 Jews of Kolin were sent to Trawniki, Poland, where they were all murdererd upon arrival ... ." (On 10 June 1942, in response to Heydrich's death on 4 June, the village of Lidice was destroyed in the belief the village had harboured the Czech assassins.)

(75–6, 78–80, 97–101) 24 August 1943, a transport of children from Bialystok, arrives in Theresienstadt under utmost secrecy: "A column of marching ghosts, with wet rags clinging to their emaciated bodies, accompanied by a large number of SS men." The children are housed in "Kreta" , new barracks outside the Ghetto walls. Doctors and nurses from among the inmates are moved to Kreta to take care of the children, among them, Hana's mother. It was thought they were being sent to Switzerland in exchange for German prisoners of war, instead: "... on Erev Yom Kippur, October 7, 1943, 1,196 children from Bialystok Ghetto in Poland, and 53 doctors and nurses from the Terezin Ghetto in Czechoslovakia, who accompanied them to the end, said their last 'Shema' in the gas chambers of Auschwitz."

Resistance, ghetto revolts, individual acts of courage and defiance

(13) Hana travels from Kolin to visit her friend Vera in Prague in 1941; she is 14: "It was also risky as I bravely took off my yellow Star of David, bought myself a ticket and boarded a train, at a time when Jews could no longer travel on public transportation without a Gestapo permit."

(16–17) In a letter, dated 13 May 1942, Hana's friend Vera from Prague passes on a cryptic message she had received: "A postcard from our friends who left a month ago arrived from Izbica in Poland. They described Izbica as follows: 'We eat like on Yom Kippur, we sleep like on Sukkot and we dress like on Purim. Everybody who arrives in Terezin Ghetto leaves for Poland.'" (Izbica Lubelska was a transit camp for those taken to the death camp of Belzec.)

(20) "With the same penknife he had used only a day before to peel the stolen potatoes, my grandfather had cut the veins on his wrist to end his unbearable existence. When the past becomes a dim memory and the future holds no hope, his was the only free choice. Heroism demonstrates itself not only when we fight with guns; there is also heroism in fighting with what is left to us. I will always remember my grandfather as one of the unknown heroes of the Terezin Ghetto." 1942.

(21–2) "When the war started and we, the Jewish children, could no longer attend school, partake in extracurricular activities or travel freely, because of the anti-Jewish laws, the Jewish community arranged for pen-pals. That gave us an outlet for pent-up frustrations, a chance to get to know how other youngsters fared under similar circumstances, and provided information on what was happening in other Jewish communities in Czechoslovakia." 1941. Hana begins a correspondance with Michael Mahler from the Czech town of Hradec Kralove.

(35–6) While in Neugraben, in Hamburg, Erna is able to send a message to her sister who, with her non-Jewish husband, had remained in Hamburg. The sister sends a package which is discovered: "The 500 women, her co-sufferers, were forced to watch her punishment. Our Lagercommandant Spiez ... forced Erna to bend down and started whipping this defenceless girl. We, the unwilling witnesses, were frozen to the ground by fear, humiliation and the shame of not being able to help. We listened in silence to the swishes of the whip and the screams that never left Erna's lips. ... Erna never revealed the name of her sister nor the man who helped her. She slowly recovered." 1944.

(65) Working for Dr. Pavel Fantel at Gestapo headquarters in Kolin, 1941: "Dr. Fantel taught me how to destroy a card of a Jew who succeeded in escaping, so that no trace could be found. He taught me how to smuggle notes or a little food to Jews who were held at the Gestapo, how to get messages transmitted to people who had been arrested and had not been heard from since." Hana is 15.

(62, 66, 94–5, 100) On Dr. Pavel Fantel's paintings of scenes "depicting with sarcastic humor the daily life" of Theresienstadt which: "... were smuggled out of Ghetto Terezin prior to Fantel's departure for Auschwitz. They were hidden and kept by a Czech friend, who returned them, after the war, to Fantel's mother." They are now among the archives of Yad Vashem's art museum. "Dr. Pavel Fantel, his wife, and his son Tomy did not return from the camps. But his paintings are a reminder of the bravery of the individual and the spirit that could not be crushed under the horrible persecution by the Germans." Pavel Fantel was shot on a death march near Hirschberg, Silesia, on his 42nd birthday, 7 January 1945.

Righteous Gentiles

(41–3) While working in the open countryside in Hamburg, Hana, under the pretext of running to the trees to relieve herself, finds a house, knocks on the door and asks for something to eat. The woman invites her in and serves her some warm soup, and tells her to come back when it is possible. Hana is able to return: "After serving me a bowl of sweet thick porridge, she murmured something to her husband and handed me an old pair of men's shoes with new soles that her husband had prepared for me. ... I never learned the names of those good people nor their address, but for the rest of the winter I blessed them, while my frozen feet recovered thanks to their kindness and humanity." December 1944.

Liberation

(14) "After my liberation from Bergen–Belsen, I returned home where I was reunited with my sister and found the last few articles I had left with her. These were the only possessions tying me to my past."

(46) "And then it happened. The first British tank rolled inside the camp, opened the gates of this indescribable hell, and a bull horn sounded the sweet words we had waited for, for so long: 'You Are Free ... You Are Free ... You Are Free ...'." Bergen–Belsen, 15 April 1945.

(47, 49, 105–10) Hana's uncle in England finds Hana's name on the list of survivors from Bergen–Belsen. He brings her to England: "Life became very difficult for me in his home. In spite of my outside appearance, I was a raped child. I was robbed of my mother and my father, of my home and of the love and warmth to which every child is entitled. I ached with pain and I wanted to talk about it. I wanted to cry and I wanted to scream, and I wanted to be comforted and hugged and understood. Instead I was told to be silent and forget. FORGET?" 1946, Hana is 20. She emigrates to Israel, and later designs a seminar to help survivors teach about their experiences.

Stories of individuals, including family members

(9–12) Alice Ehrlich, "a quiet, shy girl", Hana's friend during the German occupation of Kolin, deported with Hana on 13 June 1942, but not taken off at Terezin: "The only thing that remains of Alice is my memory of her and the number "AAd 55" next to her name on the transport list ... ." She was not yet 16.

(12–17) Vera Kraus, Hana's "blue-eyed black-haired" friend from Prague who wrote a letter to Hana on 13 May 1942 in which she described receiving the news that she and her family will be leaving on Transport Au-1, two days later, on the 15th of May. Vera wrote: "'I went to say good-bye to my teacher. She could not grasp that we were being deported. ... We don't know what awaits us, but I am not painting a rosy picture for myself. ... I am getting used to the thought of leaving, even looking forward to see all my friends and family, who are already there, including my boyfriend Harry.'" Vera was just 16. Her transport went to Lublin. (From Lublin, they were transferred to Izbica Lubelska transit camp, and from there to Belzec death camp where they were killed on arrival.)

(49) Hana's uncle in England: "He was a product of a typical Czech Jewish intellectual family, assimilated to the point where being a Jew was the last thing to play a role in his life, until the day Hitler marched into Czechoslovakia in 1939. He was caught unprepared, lecturing at Cambridge University at that time, while his wife and child were left in Prague."

(54–5, 58, 59) "The Jewish community of Kolin (including the surrounding villages), under the leadership of Rabbi Dr. Richard Feder since 1917, numbered close to 3,000 Jews. ... Only a handful ... returned ... . Dr. Richard Feder, who later became Chief Rabbi of Czechoslovakia, was among them." (Rabbi Feder was born in 1875, survived Theresienstadt, and died in 1970.)

(78–9) While her mother is helping with the Bialystok children in Theresienstadt, Hana slips through to see her, and calls from the distance to her: "As she sat down in the grass in her white nurse's outfit, the children around her, her black hair framing her face, she was beautiful. That is the picture I carry of her in my mind." Her mother was deported with the children to Auschwitz on 7 October 1943, and all were killed upon arrival.

(102–3) Rudi Ehrlich, from Vienna, Hana's mother's friend in Theresienstadt, gave Hana and her sister power of attorney over his assets before he was deported. When Hana was deported, her sister continued to receive the parcels his friend in Vienna sent.

Post-war life and career

(60, 94) At a symposium at the Northwood Pinner Synagogue in London, Hana chaired a session on the history of the Kolin Jewish community. One of the torah scrolls from the Kolin synagogue, collected among the 1,564 scrolls taken by the Germans to Prague, refurbished at the Westminster Synagogue in London, was presented to the Northwood Pinner Synagogue at that ceremony: "And so the 25 scrolls from Kolin are scattered today among synagogues from Australia to Israel as the last remnant of that community." The fourteen synagogues are listed.

(67–9) In Israel, Hana attends the trial of Ivan Demjanjuk: "Inside the packed courtroom, I listened to the proceedings. I pondered, as I had many times before, how the world is divided into two kinds of people: those who were there and those who were not."

(71) Hana researches the Holocaust, speaks and works at Yad Vashem.

(81–7) Hana's attempts to discover and document the history of the Bialystok children who were brought to Theresienstadt in August 1943 for "intensive rehabilitation", and deported with their care-givers to Auschwitz that October. The results of her research was a paper she presented in a 1988 Oxford conference "Remembering for the Future". (Her sources appear in the Works Cited section of the *Digest*.)

(87–91, 93) Hana's book is published in Prague; as a result, she is contacted by the children of three of the care-givers who, along with her mother, accompanied the Bialystok children to Auschwitz. Until Hana was able to tell them of the details of their parents' deaths: "There was no finality, no precise knowledge, no place of burial and no answers to their questions. ... Because of my research, the ... people have found solace ... ."

Personal reflections

(43) "In the difficult days I lived through in Hamburg during the war, I found two good people who restored my faith in humanity and made it possible for me to return there again, many years later, at the invitation of the Mayor of Hamburg."

(46) "Whoever lived through the experience of Bergen-Belsen lived through his own death."

(47) "Nobody realized in those days that we, the survivors were ravaged in our souls, our emotions, that we were one great pain filling every crevice of our guts. The outside was a camouflage, a protective cover that enabled us to live among normal people. Had the outside resembled the inside, we would have looked like lepers among the others."

(56) After a recent visit to Kolin: "... I wondered how different our fate might have been if the Czech people had stood up for the Jews who for centuries had thought they were an integral part of that nation."

(67) At the Demjanjuk trial: "The prosecutor could not understand what he was asking, and the words of the witnesses could not describe what they had lived through."

Places mentioned in Europe (page first mentioned)

Auschwitz Main Camp/Auschwitz I (13), Austria/Österreich (102), Belsen/Bergen-Belsen concentration camp (14), Belzec death camp (71), Berlin (34), Bialystok Ghetto (71), Birkenau/Brzezinka/Auschwitz II (71), Bohusovice (12), Bremen (46), Brno/Brunn (97), Chelmno/Kulmhof death camp (71), Cracow/Krakow/Krakau (71), Czechoslovakia (9), Denmark/Danmark (23), Elbe River/Labe River (10), Freihafen (Hamburg) (35), Germany/Deutschland (23), Gross Rosen/Rogoznica concentration camp (18), Hamburg (18), Hirschberg (95), Hradec Kralove (24), Izbica Lubelska transit camp (16), Kolin (11), Lidice (54), Lodz Ghetto (71), Majdanek concentration camp (71), Maly Trostenets death camp (102), Moravia (23), Netherlands/Nederland (Holland) (23), Neugraben (Hamburg) (35), Norway/Norge (23), Poland/Polska (16), Prague/Praha (13), Silesia/Schlesien/Slask (95), Slovakia/Slovenska Republic (23), Sudetenland (9), Sweden/Sverige (81), Switzerland/Schweiz/Suisse/Swizzeria (79), Theresienstadt/Terezin-Ghetto/concentration camp (12), Tiefstak (Hamburg) (36), Trawniki slave labour camp (55), Treblinka death camp (67), Vienna/Wien (102), Warsaw Ghetto (71), Warsaw/Warszawa/Warschau (71)

Places mentioned outside Europe (page first mentioned)

Australia (60), Britain (14), Cambridge (England) (49), Eilat (95), Galilee (96), Israel/Yisrael (14), Jerusalem/Yerushalayim (12), Kibbutz Neot Mordechai (96), London (England) (60), New Caledonia (59), Palestine (British Mandate) (21), United States of America (81), Yad Vashem

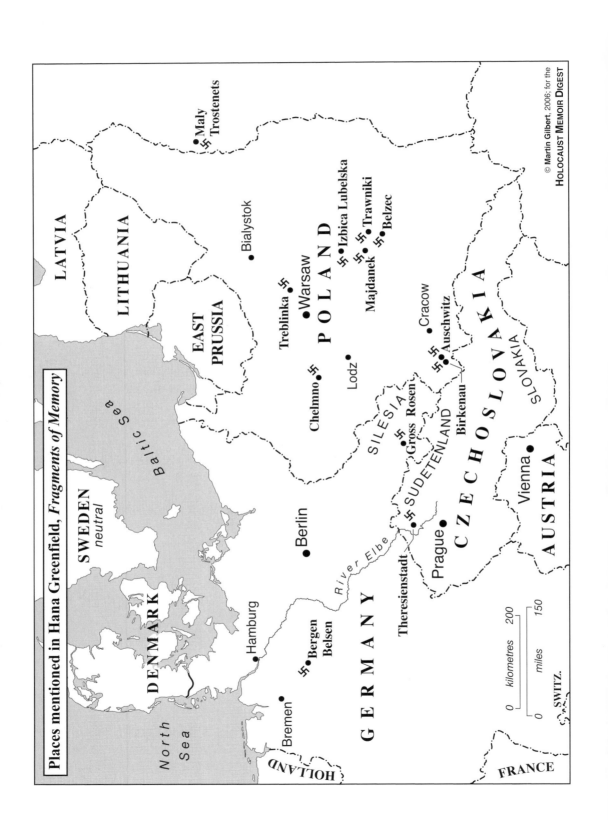

Places mentioned in Hana Greenfield, *Fragments of Memory*

© Martin Gilbert, 2006; for the HOLOCAUST MEMOIR DIGEST

LATVIA

LITHUANIA

Maly Trostenets

SWEDEN
neutral

Baltic Sea

Bialystok

EAST PRUSSIA

Warsaw

Treblinka

POLAND

Izbica Lubelska

Trawniki

Majdanek

Belzec

DENMARK

Berlin

Chelmno

Lodz

Cracow

Auschwitz

North Sea

Hamburg

Bremen

River Elbe

Birkenau

Gross Rosen

SILESIA

SUDETENLAND

Theresienstadt

Prague

CZECHOSLOVAKIA

SLOVAKIA

GERMANY

Vienna

AUSTRIA

HOLLAND

FRANCE

SWITZ.

0   kilometres   200

0   miles   150

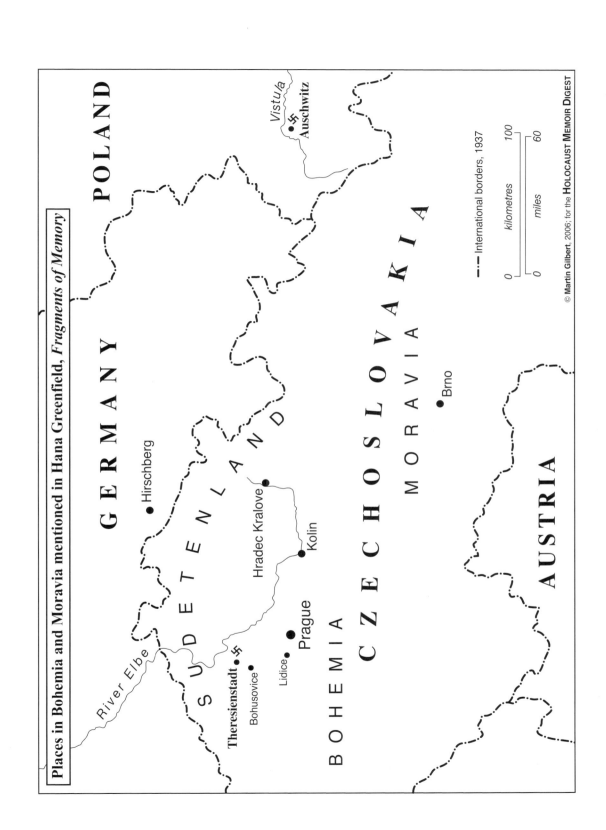

Places in Bohemia and Moravia mentioned in Hana Greenfield, *Fragments of Memory*

POLAND

GERMANY

Vistula

• Auschwitz

Hirschberg •

SUDETENLAND

River Elbe

Hradec Kralove •

Kolin •

Theresienstadt •

Bohusovice •

Lidice •

Prague •

BOHEMIA

CZECHOSLOVAKIA

MORAVIA

• Brno

AUSTRIA

-·-·- International borders, 1937

kilometres   100

0

miles   60

0

© **Martin Gilbert**, 2006; for the **Holocaust Memoir Digest**

Eva Gossman, *Good Beyond Evil*

1931: born in Presov, Czechoslovakia to Salomon Reinitz and Rachel Reinitzova, the second of three children, after Alexander, and sister Gabriela follows

14 March 1939: Czechoslovakia is divided; Father Jozef Tiso becomes head of Slovakia, independent after Sudetenland and Moravia become a German Protectorate; Ruthenia and Sub-Carpathia become part of Hungary; independent Slovakia is allied to Germany

August 1940: Dieter Wislicsny arrives in Bratislava; September: "UZ" established

21 June 1941: Slovakia enters the war, allied to Germany

September 1941: political, economic, social and legal isolation of Jews complete

March to October 1942; summer 1943; fall 1944: three waves of deportations of Slovak Jews

December 1942: with brother, sent across the border to Hungary to relatives in Tolscva; arrested at border

December to mid-February 1943: with brother, spends six weeks in an orphanage, Kassa, Hungary

Mid-February to 1 April 1943: with brother, interned at Ricse internment camp

1 April 1943 to early April 1944: with brother, live with uncle and family in Tolcsva, Hungary

March 1944: German occupation of Hungary; Jews of Tolcsva taken to Satoraljaujhely Ghetto

13 May 1944: along with brother, allowed out of the ghetto; they return over the border to Presov

15 May 1944: the remaining Jews of Presov are deported to central Slovakia, Eva and her family move to Nitra

15 May to mid-September 1944: family moves next door to mother's family in the Jewish Quarter of Nitra

Summer 1944 to March 1945: first Eva and her brother, and then parents, sister and cousin, are in hiding with Maria Krescankova ("Teta") and her daughter Vlasta in Nitra

March 1945: with brother, helps to construct an underground hiding place with the family next door, Pan Laco and Pani Lacova

Last week in March 1945: the eight people in Teta's house move into the underground bunker with nine others, until after Nitra is liberated by Soviet troops; they emerge from the bunker the last days of Passover

Late spring 1945: the family moves to Kosice, now in Czechoslovakia

2 November 1948: mother, accepted to America on German quota, takes three children to America; father, unable to get visa, goes to Israel

December 1991: Vlasta comes to visit them in America

June 1993: Eva and her husband visit Vlasta in Kosice

3 July 1997: Teta and Vlasta are honoured at Yad Vashem as among the Righteous of the Nations

May 1998: Vlasta gets a life pension from the Foundation for the Righteous

Author: Eva Gossman

Title: *Good Beyond Evil, Ordinary People in Extraordinary Times*

Publishing details

Vallentine Mitchell, Premier House, Suite 314, 112–114 Station Road, Edgware, Middlesex HA8 7BJ, England. 2002. 129 pages.
ISBN #0-85303-446-X.

Focus:

Eva, from Presov in Slovakia, who was 8 years old in 1939, survives in hiding with her parents and siblings; they are hidden by a Slovak woman and her young daughter, who were later honoured by Yad Vashem. The author became a philosopher, and focuses her memoir on the moral implications of those who saved and those who were saved. The events described take place between 1939 when Slovakia signed a Treaty of Protection with Germany, and 1977.

Features:

Foreword: Dedication, page vi–vii,
                   Acknowledgements, page ix, written by the Author.
                   The Library of Holocaust Testimonies, written by Sir Martin Gilbert, page x.
                   Foreword written by Colin Richmond, pages xi–xiii.
Photographs: Eleven photographs of Eva, her family and friends, and her family's rescuers.
                   Photograph of the author, back cover.
Afterword: Epilogue, page 130, and Postscript, page 131, written by the Author.
Appendix: Chronological Table, pages 132–4.
Works cited: A quotation from the charges of the 1952 Slansky trial in Czechoslovakia, quoted from Mir Cotic, "The Prague Trial", Herzl Press, New York, 1987.
                   Statistics of countries who took in Jews before 1938, from "Atlas of the Holocaust", Martin Gilbert, Routledge, London and New York, 2002.

Contents: (by topic, with page numbers)

Pre-war Jewish home and community life

(8) "The Presov of my childhood was a pleasant and prosperous city of 60,000 inhabitants. A lively commercial centre with broad avenues, countless city squares, handsome architecture and an active cultural life, its 6,000 Jews participated in the life of the city as well as in their own communal and religious affairs." (The figure of 6,000 dates from 1940 and includes 2,000 refugees.)

(18–19) "My father, after working briefly in his family's lumber business, was appointed, at the ageof thirty-one, 'Notar' of the 'Kehilla': the legally incorporated Jewish community in Presov. ... the focus for the interactions of the various institutions under the Jewish community umbrella – the synagogues, schools, ritual bath, burial society, etc. The 'Notar' also represented the Jewish community in its interactions with state and local officials. My father was the last 'Notar' of the Jewish community of Presov." Her father, Salomon Reinitz, was appointed in 1932.

(19–20) "We were not an assimilated family, and our lives were governed by religious traditions, rituals and learning. ... My mother's father, although an orthodox rabbi in Hamburg, Germany, had earned a doctorate in philosophy ... . My father attended business school in Berlin and many of my uncles entered the professions. We lived our lives both as Jews and as citizens of Czechoslovakia."

(123) A memory of Eva's paternal grandparents and of their walnut grove: "As children we were not allowed to shake the trees to coax them into yielding their nuts. Instead we had to wait until they fell on the ground, a sign that they were ripe enough to crack and eat. But it was a catch twenty-two situation. My paternal grandmother, always exceedingly frugal, would gather the walnuts as soon as they fell off the trees and store them for later use."

Pre-war anti-Semitism

(8–9) March 1939, Bohemia and Moravia became a German Protectorate; Slovakia became independent, headed by the Catholic priest, Monsignor Jozef Tiso. Ruthenia was ceded to Hungary: "... Tiso and his government ordered the forceful removal of most of the Jews who lived in the territories adjoining the readjusted borders with Hungary, along with those who claimed Hungarian citizenship.... . The expulsion, carried out under inhuman conditions, left a large number of people stranded without adequate food or shelter. Some were sent off to labour camps, others were eventually absorbed in Hungary and Romania ... ."

(9–10) "... persecutions and harassment started almost immediately after the declaration of Slovak independence. Decrees excluding Jews from business, the professions and government service came in rapid succession. We felt besieged; outcasts in our own country and among our own people." March 1939.

(11–12) "Tiso's chief qualifications for the presidency came from his position as head of the Hlinka Slovak Peoples' Party, a strongly nationalistic and rabidly anti-Semitic political party established by a Cathoic priest, Andrej Hlinka, in 1918 to oppose the newly created Czechoslovak Republic. Tiso's political platform ... had two major planks: political independence from the Czech Republic and the elimination of Jews from all aspects of Slovak life. Anti-Semitism and nationalism were deeply intertwined, both in the minds of the majority of the population and in the new laws of the land. Jews, dangerous and implacable enemies of the newly created Slovak state, had to be dealt with harshly and decisively."

(12–13) "Because of the deep religious roots of the Hlinka party (about 70 per cent of the population of Slovakia was Roman Catholic), the Jews were also portrayed as the killers of Christ, with frequent references to the ritual killings perpetrated by them on young Christian boys and girls. The myth of ritual murder was deeply embedded in the minds of the citizens ... often supported by the teachings of the Church ... . The Tiso government did not have to invent the charge – only to resurrect it. Doctrinal anti-Semitism nourished the secular anti-Semitism of the state." ("Ritual murder" was also known as the "Blood Libel".)

(12–13) "One of the staunchest defenders of Jews against the ritual murder accusations was the first President of Czechoslovakia, Thomas Garrigue Masaryk. ... He now had the moral authority, the power and the platform to work for the establishment of institutional and legal safeguards against persecution and discrimination, which became the cornerstone of the fledgling republic." He died in 1937.

The coming of war

(14–16) Measures taken by the new Slovak government to isolate Jews: "Jews' monthly incomes were limited to a set amount; ownership of Jewish businesses had to be passed to 'Aryans'; Jewish children could not attend public schools; Jews were forbidden to participate in any civic activities or to attend public functions. Law did not guarantee their physical safety and their property could be expropriated on the flimsiest excuse. The confiscated property was often distributed to the citizens as a gesture of 'good will'. ... Thus, two years after it came into existence, the Slovak state was fully equipped for the persecution of the Jews. It had an ideology that demanded it, a government agency that oversaw it, a legal framework that justified it and an internal military force that, with the blessing of the German Government, would enforce it." Autumn 1941.

Life under German occupation

(15, 20–1) September 1940, Slovakia was formally independent but effectively under German control: Eichmann's deputy Dieter Wisliceny established an "Ustredna Zidow (UZ)", a Jewish Council in Bratislava, and in February 1942, in Presov: "With the creation of the 'UZ', Jewish communal life in Presov was fundamentally transformed and its primary focus shifted from religious and spiritual concerns to concerns for the physical, economic, psychological and social survival of the community. The head of the 'UZ' no longer represented the interests and concerns of the 'Kehilla', made up of fully fledged citizens, to the government, but unhappily became the messenger, the negotiator, and at times even the enforcer, of government edicts. Perhaps because he was the executive director of the Jewish community of Presov, my father was asked to become the head of the newly created 'UZ' branch in Presov."

(22–4) On the moral choices one must make in an immoral world: "There is an extensive rabbinical literature dealing with the circumstances under which one is permitted, or even obliged, to meet the demands of a tyrant, a murderer or an enemy. This literature continued to provide moral guidance for the Jews, even in times of their most brutal oppression – in overcrowded ghettos, decimated communities and labour camps." (In fact far more than one in ten were destroyed.)

(25–6) The SS deport unmarried Jewish men and women. Eva's family's Jewish maid hides under a bed during a raid: "But we knew that the search would be repeated on another day and that Fanny would not be lucky twice. That evening she left for a safer place. But safety in our circumstances was relative and temporary. We never saw her again, and I do not believe that she survived the war." March 1942.

(48) "Over the years, many of the edicts against the Jews came suddenly and were put into effect immediately. This strategy accomplished two things: it caught the victims unaware and unprepared and, perhaps even more important, it was a terrifying and concrete manifestation of the absolute power of the state and the helplessness of the intended victims."

Creation of the ghetto

(34–5) March 1944, with the German occupation of Hungary: "... all the Jews of Tolcsva were taken to a ghetto in Satoraljaujhely, the provincial town in the Tokaj region ... . We were frightened and disoriented. With infinite dignity and calm, my uncle, who had no illusions about the fate that awaited us, comforted his family and his congregation."

Deportation

(18) "Massive deportations of the Jews of Slovakia occurred in three waves. Between March and October 1942, nearly 75 per cent of the Jews living in Slovakia were deported, some to labour camps, most to the Auschwitz concentration camp. By the winter of 1942, fewer than 1,000 Jews were left in Presov. The second wave occurred in the summer of 1943, when every few weeks Jews were rounded up randomly and transported to concentration camps. The final roundup of Slovak Jews (when none were left in Presov) occurred in the late fall of 1944... ."

(27) "... in the late spring of 1942, the Germans and their Slovak allies started the deportations of all families who were not deemed economically essential to the state. Friends, relatives, neighbours and schoolmates disappeared from one day to the next, without warning and often without goodbyes. The transports were public, the grief private, the destination unknown."

(37–8, 123) Fate of her father's family who had been deported from the Satoraljaujhely Ghetto in May 1944: "Upon arrival in Auschwitz, my grandmother and Aunt Ancsi, who had a club-foot, were immediately marked for annihilation. Aunt Rozsi, Alice, and Marica were sent to the Plaszow labour camp near Cracow ... . As the Russian Army approached Cracow, Plaszow was evacuated and Rozsi, Alice and Marica were sent back to Auschwitz. In September 1944, Alice was separated from her mother and sister, and never saw them again. ... When the inmates of Auschwitz were evacuated, Alice was sent to a work camp near Leipzig, and when that city came under seige, she, together with thousands of others, was forced to go on the twenty-three-day death march to Theresienstadt. She was liberated on 9 May 1945. Uncle Kive survived until a few weeks before liberation. He was shot in the Flossenbürg camp in March 1945. The fate of my cousin, Ocsi, is unclear." Eva's grandfather had died before the war.

(40–1) 15 May 1944, the remaining Jews in Presov are deported by train to Nitra: "What we left behind were our remaining possessions, our decimated communal life and whatever hope we had retained that no matter how difficult our situation might be, it would not get worse and we would survive the war." (The communal life was in fact destroyed, not merely decimated, as far more than one in ten were killed.)

Transit camps

(31–3) Eva and her brother are taken to the internment camp of Ricse, a Hungarian camp for political prisoners and Jewish refugees, where they remain for a few weeks and are then released to the care of their aunt and uncle: "... my brother and I were the only children in the camp. I was housed with the women and my brother with the men. We could cross from one section to another easily, and we were used as couriers for notes from husbands to wives and from young women to their boyfriends." Mid-February to April 1943.

Resistance, ghetto revolts, individual acts of courage and defiance

(22–3, 49) She refers to the "'Bratislava Working Group', headed by the Orthodox Rabbi Chaim Weismandl, and his socialist Zionist cousin, Gisi Fleishmann ... . Their efforts to protect the small remaining Jewish community of Slovakia from further deportations may have been partially successful." (The rabbi was Michael Dov Weissmandel.)

(38–40) Winter 1942 to spring 1944, Presov, and her father's position as head of the "UZ": "He used whatever protection his official position offered him to help not only the remaining members of his community by warning them of new edicts or roundups, but also the small trickle of Jews who had managed to escape from labour camps and from the ghettos of Poland to Slovakia on their way, by underground railroad, to Hungary."

(66–9, 75) Their neighbours next door in Nitra, the grocer Pan Michael Laco and his wife Pani Margareta Lacova, a brother-in-law Rudolf Valent and his friend William Koenig: "… Rudolf and William would ask us to drop off a written message at some appointed place … . We did what we were asked to do, and did not inquire … . We were also convinced that we were participating in something that was larger than our own lives, and that what we were asked to do was in some way related to our hopes for liberation."

(67–8) "For many who went into hiding, every day was a fight for survival, motivated not only by the will to live, but also a will to defy the enemy and to deprive him of his bounty. Viewed from a historical perspective, it may be hard to understand how much courage it took to keep on inventing adequate defences for living another day or another week."

(107–8) Vlasta's memories of Eva's mother: "What she recalled most vividly about her were her scrupulous religious observances, even while we were in hiding, and her refusal to touch non-kosher meat or break the laws of the Sabbath."

Partisan activity

(18, 53–4) September and October 1944, Slovak partisans revolt: "At the height of the uprising, close to 16,000 soldiers and civilians, of whom roughly 10 percent were Jews, fought fiercely against the forces loyal to Tiso and the SS units that joined them." The German Army defeated the partisan forces by the end of October, and proceeded to deport the remaining Jews from Slovakia.

Specific escapes

(27–8) Eva and her brother are smuggled across the border to Hungary to stay with her Aunt Rozsi and Uncle Kive. With them is another boy: "As we approached the border and were saying goodbye to our fathers, he refused to let go of his and to come with us. In great agitation his father, who was eager for us to leave under cover of darkness, slapped him and pushed him away. That was the last contact between father and son. … his father returned. It was very painful to see him after the war – my brother and I knew that we were constant reminders of the circumstances under which he and his thirteen-year-old son had parted." Winter 1942.

(29–30) Captured by Hungarian police after crossing into Hungary, Eva and her brother are interrogated, and also their companion: "When asked whether he knew where he was he answered, truthfully, 'Kosice'. His mistake was that he identified the town by its Slovak name rather than by its Hungarian designation, Kassa. He was yelled at and slapped hard. No one was ready to make allowance for a child whose vocabulary could not keep up with the rapid changes in European geography." The three children are taken to a Jewish orphanage; they remain there for six weeks. Late December 1942 to mid-February 1943.

(33) Eva is among those selected to be sent from Ricse to a work camp: "Then I heard one of the soldiers whisper to the other, 'I cannot take this one, she has such sad eyes!' And so, having touched momentarily the heart of a man who undoubtedly was hardened to much human suffering, I was temporarily saved. … Ironically having sad eyes could be very dangerous. … Not infrequently, Jews who … looked Aryan … were given away by the sad and hunted look in their eyes."

(36–7) "Five days before the start of the deportations from the ghetto, a policeman appeared in our quarters with fake orders to take my brother and me to headquarters for interrogation, claiming that there was evidence that we had been used as couriers for the Hungarian Underground. The ploy worked for us, but it was too late to save the rest of my father's family. Once the deportations started, the Germans were in total control and there was no exit." Eva and her brother are smuggled back over the border and return home to Presov. May 1944.

(63–4, 74) The family in hiding with Teta escapes discovery during a visit from the landlady who came to dispel rumours that Jews were hiding there: "Her search was accompanied by loud and profuse cursing of the whole tribe of Israel. Teta joined her in her diatribe and egged her on. We were mesmerized by the performance of the two furies, but we were absolutely convinced that the play would soon be over and that all would be lost. ... To our great astonishment, the landlady ... neglected to climb up the steps that led to the attic."

(64–6) The family in hiding with Teta listens to the BBC broadcasts on their clandestine radio: "... a voice that would connect us to another world; a world in which humanity and decency were the norm, a world which reminded us of our past and, for a brief moment, liberated us from the oppression of the present."

In hiding, including Hidden Children

(27, 34) April 1943 to April 1944, Eva and her brother, having escaped the deportations from Slovakia, live with their Aunt Rozsi and Uncle Kive Kornitzer, the rabbi in Tolcsva: "We did not hear from our parents and knew little about their condition, although at one point my father succeeded in sending some money to help my uncle in his strained financial situation."

(50–2) Eva and her brother, with false birth certificates, becomes Magda Kasprisinova, and her brother Alexander becomes Toni Kasprisin, cousins to each other, and niece and nephew to Teta: "It takes a certain maturity and considerable cunning to maintain the fiction of a false persona – to both be, and not be, the person you appear to be." June/July 1944 to March 1945.

(54–5) Eva hears from a neighbour who reports "quite gleefully" of the deportation orders for the Jews of Nitra: "I wanted to run, to scream, to bang my fists against the counter, but I remained mute. Instead, I picked up an onion ... and, as if in a trance, I started to slice it. Tears were now rolling down my cheeks ... ."

(55–6) As the Jews are about to be deported from Nitra, Teta moves the rest of Eva's family into the dwelling she had taken for herself and her daughter, for Eva and her brother, who had acquired Aryan identities; Teta takes in Eva's parents and sister, and 15-year-old cousin Greta: "We were now all together – three adults and five children; four ration cards and three beds; two people with their own birth certificates; two people with false birth certificates; and four people without any papers."

(57–63) The practical difficulties of eight people in hiding, when only four people were thought to be living there: eliminating human waste, obtaining food and fuel, caring for those who became ill, containing movement and noise, managing their meagre financial resources, and containing the fear that Eva's mother had of mice: "There was no way we could win the war against the mice. They bred more quickly than we could catch them, and they lived in the attic. The thought of being betrayed by a mouse was both grotesque and real."

Righteous Gentiles

(6–7) On those who helped and saved Jews: "They never thought of themselves as heroes, and they certainly were not heroes in their own communities. During the war, they were enemies of the 'law' and of the 'state', subject to harassment by neighbours, betrayal by informers, and death at the hands of the Nazi collaborators and the local police. At best they were unpatriotic, at worst they were traitors. After the war, they were commonly viewed with suspicion, either because they were thought to have obtained material rewards from those they saved (greed being more comprehensible than altruism) or, even more perniciously, because they robbed the Final Solution of its ultimate success."

(7, 81, 82–9, 96–8) The five people who saved her, her parents, her brother, sister, and a cousin: "... a young woman we called 'Teta' (aunt in Slovak) and her eleven-year-old daughter; a grocer and his wife ... and a chambermaid in a local hotel." Five others who helped them: a Jewish officer in the Soviet Army, "... a military doctor; an adventurer of uncertain nationality; a crazed survivor of a concentration camp; and a Carmelite nun. ... we would have survived without their interventions. Nevertheless, their actions brought light and kindness into our otherwise bleak existence."

(27, 36) "... an official in the Hungarian police...", a contact of Eva's Aunt Ancsi, arranges for Eva and her brother to be smuggled over the border into Hungary and taken to Aunt Rocsi and Uncle Kive, in December 1942, and again makes arrangements for the two children to be taken out of the Satoraljaujhely Ghetto before the deportations begin, May 1944.

(43–7, 127, 131) 7 July 1997, Maria Goblova Krescankova, and her daughter Vlastimila Krescancova are honoured at Yad Vashem as the "Righteous Among the Nations"; fifteen members of the family are there, among them Eva, her brother and sister who were saved, and Vlasta. In May 1998, Vlasta is granted a life-long pension from the Jewish Foundation for the Righteous, which is supported by the American Jewish community: "The Foundation currently provides pensions to about 1,300 rescuers in 25 countries. A few of them live in Slovakia."

(47–8) "Never a conformist, Teta's moral code was not built on religious faith, political commitments or social approbation. Hers came from an internal command. What is more surprising is that out of her sense of marginality she developed a great capacity for love and a sense of unswerving loyalty to the people who put her trust in her." Born 2 January 1915, she died in 1982.

(48–51) "Teta", who worked as the cashier at the Presov "mikvah", the Jewish ritual bath, and her efforts to help the Reinitz family in Presov: May 1944, she takes in Eva's parents and sister for a few days; during the relocation to Nitra, she also moves there to arrange a hiding place for the family there: "She was brave to offer a temporary shelter to my family during an unexpected roundup of Jews. But it was a giant leap to go from there to uprooting herself and her child, leaving everything that was familiar and secure behind, riding a train into darkness."

(49) The risks for helping Jews: "The carefully drawn racial and legal boundaries between Jews and non-Jews disappeared instantaneously when Gentiles proffered a helping hand."

(69–70) Teta appeals to the grocer next door, Pan Laco and his wife Pani Lacova, for extra food: "We still had in our possession a large gold bracelet, dating back to times we could hardly remember, and we were ready to offer it in exchange for food. I do not now what the Lacos response to Teta was, or whether they registered a great deal of surprise when they were told that a large family lived next door to them. I know that they did not accept the bracelet, since it remains the only piece of family jewellery that survived the war. I also know that without our revelation and their willingness to help, we might not have survived."

(70–2, 89) Pan Laco and Pani Lacova: "They told us that if, for whatever reason, we had to leave our house, and if we could escape unnoticed, we could move into their air raid shelter. … Whoever we might be, we were shown kindness and acceptance, with no questions asked." Eva and Alexander help with digging and preparing the hiding place: "It is hard to describe the sense of freedom and satisfaction we derived from building the bunker and stocking it with items we needed for survival. … By enlarging the circle of our saviours we felt less vulnerable and less alone."

(73–5) The landlady of the house Teta had rented, Pani Eperjesova, came with a Jewish family of three whom she had been hiding to the bunker at Pan Lacos: "In the evening, when sixteen people were assembled in the bunker (the eight of us, our hosts, Pan Valent and Pan Koenig and Pani Eperjesova with her three 'guests'), it seemed to us that all the good people of the town, and all the Jews who had thus far survived in Nitra, were in the same place."

(74) Pani Eperjesova, the landlady of Teta's house, had hidden a Jewish dentist, his wife and teenage son, from October 1944 to March 1945: "Even if she was the only chambermaid living in the attic of the hotel with no immediate next-door neighbours, it is difficult to fathom how the dentist and his family managed to escape detection."

(79–80) Eva's maternal great-grandfather, deported and killed at age 93 in Auschwitz: "… the Christian inhabitants of Nove Zamky presented a petition to save him from deportation (he was the rabbi of the town), but the Gestapo paid no attention."

Liberation

(67–8) Their fears as the battles neared – that their financial resources would not last, and that Nitra would be bombed and: "… we would be forced out of our house and thus fall prey to hostile neighbours and whatever local militia was still around. … Thus, on one side we saw the promise of life, on the other side the real threat of extreme hunger and violent death." Spring 1945.

(76–8, 80) 31 March 1945, Soviet troops liberate Nitra: "I remember a sense of relief, but not of triumph. We were out of danger, but also rootless and homeless. … we found ourselves disoriented, devastated by our gradual discovery of the enormity of the destruction of our community and our extended family … fearful of the present and uncertain about the future. … Our neighbours were not pleased that we had survived – and our liberators treated us as citizens of a conquered country." They, together with Teta and Vlasta, move to Kosice, which had been returned to Czechoslovakia in 1945, and her father: "… was invited to take a leadership role in rebuilding the Jewish community."

(81–3) A Jewish-Soviet officer befriends them after they emerge from their bunker. His wife and children had been murdered in the Ukraine in 1941; his war was of personal vengeance. He brings a piano into their house, throws open the doors and windows and plays and sings Yiddish songs: "For months we had lived, both literally and figuratively, with closed doors and windows, hiding our Jewishness. Now the neighbours were gathered outside ... listening to the words and melodies of a world that had been destroyed, and yet had, at least momentarily, survived in their midst." He leaves telling them, "... he would never forget that he spent the last day of Passover in the spring of 1945 in Slovakia, with an intact Jewish family of five."

(83–5) Eva seeks the help of a Soviet military physician who treats her and then comes to visit her in her convalescence: "Perhaps he found comfort in his ability to be a physician in the full sense of the word once more; to tend to the patient as a person, even in the absence of a grave physical threat."

(85–7) An unknown stranger brings food to the family and a sense of concern for Eva: "Dropping unexpectedly into our midst, he helped awaken in me the belief that life might have another side – where generosity, beauty and abundance were the norm." Nitra, spring 1945.

(87–90) Pani Trattnerova, who shares their apartment in Nitra, protects Vlasta, Greta and Eva from a group of: "... several Russian soldiers, in various states of inebriation. ... Did we survive the war only to be destroyed by our liberators?" Pani Trattnerova, "Like a demented fury ... ." scares them away. The three girls and Eva's younger sister are taken, with the help of Pani Helena Slabejova and Dr. Zavodny, to a mental hospital under the pretext of a stress disorder: "We were play-acting again, but this time our 'secret' was that we were sane and that we were confined for our physical safety."

Stories of individuals, including family members

(33) Eva's bunkmate at Ricse, 20-year-old Magda: "She taught me some of the survival skills my brother thought were essential, and she helped me fight bed bugs, hunger, loneliness and fear. She was later deported to a concentration camp but survived the war."

(34) With her Aunt Rozsi and Uncle Kive Kornitzer in the town of Tolcsva where her uncle was the rabbi for the three hundred Jews there: "My brother and I became part of an extended family that included my aunt and uncle and their three children, Alice, Ocsi and Marica, all about the same age as we were, as well as my Aunt Ancsi who had arrived from Presov before us, and my paternal grandmother. Only three of us survived the war: Alice, my brother and I."

(41–3, 55–6, 124) The fate of Eva's mother's family, Aunt Ida, Uncle David, their children Arthur, Greta and Immy who had been deported from Bratislava to Nitra in 1941: Arthur had been deported in 1944; Uncle David shot in the October 1944 round-up; Aunt Ida and Immy deported; Greta went into hiding with Eva's family. She survived and moved to England after the war.

(79–80) The fate of Eva's extended family: "Almost all our relatives on my father's side, and most of our friends, young and old, were dead ... ." Her mother's five siblings survived, her two sisters emigrated with their husbands and children to America, and of her three brothers: "... one went to England, where he was interned on the Isle of Man as an enemy alien; one spent the war in hiding in the mountains of Italy; and one served in the Palestinian brigade of the British Army. Her mother was sheltered by successive Dutch families and moved to America after the war." Her mother's grandfather and her aunt Sari were killed in Auschwitz.

(87–8) Pani Trattnerova, the woman with whom the family shares their apartment in Nitra after liberation, the only survivor of her family to return home: "Her despair was profound and total. Skeletal in appearance, she talked little, ate even less, and walked with the gait of a sleepwalker, barely conscious of her surroundings. She was a constant reminder of the deep divide between those very few of us who, regardless of the hardships we endured, had spent some part of the war in hiding and who emerged as a family, and those who had been sent to concentration camps and came back alone."

(108–9) Eva's family in America, as of Vlasta's visit in 1991: her mother had become a Hebrew teacher; Eva's sister Gabriela, married, with two children and two grandchildren had become a Hebrew teacher and an innovative teacher of the Holocaust; her brother Alexander had enlisted in the United States Air Force, had studied engineering, and was living in Israel. Eva, married, with a daughter, had studied in night school while being a secretary, and had a graduate degree in philosophy, and a: "… deep interest in moral philosophy, professional ethics and public policy which … have their roots in the chaotic world in which we both grew up."

(122) On Eva's 1993 visit to Slovakia, where she met the head of the Presov Jewish community of "52 registered Jews": "… Mr Desire Landa, who … . remembered my father and he showed me the book about the history of the Jews of Presov, which my father had written in 1940. Mr. Landa has himself written several historical and commemorative pieces about the Jewish community of Presov, as well as an account of his survival in Auschwitz."

Post-war life and career

(35, 43, 47, 99–102) February 1948, Communists seize control, the family decides to emigrate. They leave Prague in October by train to Naples, and then sail for America on board the "Vulcania". Eva's mother, a German national, is able to enter the United States, on the German quota: "My mother and her three children (aged twelve, seventeen, and eighteen) arrived in the United States on 2 November 1948. My father left for Israel in the spring of 1949." Her father lived in Israel until his death in 1970.

(91–95) 1945–48 in Kosice, Eva attends school: "By the time we left in the fall of 1948, my brother and I were within a year, or at most a year and a half, of graduation from the Gymnasium. We both finished our secondary schooling at night at McKinley High School in Washington, D.C."

(95–8) Spring 1948, The government of Eduard Benes is overthrown; parochial schools are abolished and nuns are brought in to teach in the public schools: "One teacher in particular, Sestra Smutna (Sister Sad), who taught science and mathematics, took a great interest in me. … I sensed that her attachment to me was in some way related to my being a Jewish child who had survived the war. … She wanted me to succeed, not only in a worldly, but also in a moral, sense, as if my success could, in a very small way, right a very big wrong in which her Church was complicit."

(103–12) Teta died in 1982, Eva kept in touch with Vlasta, who came to visit the family in 1991: "… we talked with an ease and a love that belied our very different life experiences." On reconnecting with Vlasta: "… she was loved and honoured not for building bridges, but for the person she was, as a child and as a mature woman, and for the memory of her mother that she brought with her."

(113–29) June 1993, Eva goes with her husband to visit Vlasta in Slovakia "I was neither a native nor a tourist. I felt trapped and claustrophobic, yet no longer regretting my decision to come." Vlasta was their guide: "When she asked people on the street to show us the way to a synagogue or a monument and they told us that they did not know, she chastised them. 'You should know', was one of her constant refrains. The subtext was clear and urgent ... .'"

Personal reflections

(1) Why she writes: "What I wanted to preserve was not the horror of the war, the enormity of our individual and collective losses, or the pain of survival. Rather, I struggled to save from oblivion the deeds of a handful of people without whose help neither my family nor I would have survived."

(3) "Will the focus on those who saved us blur the pain and suffering that was the harsh reality of our daily lives? ... It is impossible to remember the good without the evil, and it is impossible accurately to render the depth of the evil when it is illuminated by the good."

(5) "The major theme of the period has to be the evil master plan executed on an unprecedented scale with fanatical zeal, bureaucratic efficiency and industrial might; the minor theme has to include the presence of those who defied evil and who, through their acts, affirmed not only the humanity of those they saved, but the humanity of all of us. ... The standard they set for what is possible should inform our assessment of the past and our expectations of the future."

(5) "Our claim to being human is based on our willingness to take responsibility for our acts – even as we recognize that our lives have boundaries and that our freedom has limits. To say that we cannot choose the circumstances under which we are compelled to act does not mean that we have no choice about how we act in the circumstances in which we find ourselves."

(6) "Our choices have consequences – good or bad, intended or unintended, foreseen or unforeseen. ... our choices do not only define the quality of our individual lives, they also have an effect, minuscule as it may be, on the course of history. However much we might believe that vast impersonal forces determine historical events, it is impossible to make sense out of the past without giving weight to the intervention of individual actors – some performing on the world stage, most toiling in their private and communal worlds."

(11) "Assessing the gradual unfolding of events from the secure position of the present, we may have to accept the fact that we suffered from a lack of imagination about the depth of depravity and inhumanity with which a legitimately-constituted government could act against its own citizens. The Jews of Slovakia, and those in most other countries occupied or allied with the Reich, paid a high price for living with hope."

(23) "During the war we were reluctant to face the future; after the war, we avoided the past. We paid a price for these chronological interruptions – but they were the ransom we offered for our survival, first physically, by carrying out our daily tasks despite enormous pressures to give up, then psychologically, by creating a new life out of ashes."

(46) On the silence of survivors with their children: "We fear that by sharing our experiences we may kill their optimism, their joy in life, their confidence that the world is a hospitable place and above all, that we can and will protect them from evil. If there were times within our own memories when parents could not protect their children, can we protect them?"

(55–6) Rachel Reinitz refuses to join her family in hiding with Teta without taking along one of her young cousins, Greta or Immy: "To hide another person presented grave risks to all of us, both by increasing the likelihood that we would be discovered and by obliging us to feed another person who did not have a ration card. ... How do we weigh the claims of saving one additional life against the claims of seven others ... to create the safest possible conditions for survival? Was my mother's stand ethically justified, or was she creating irresponsible roadblocks in a moment of extreme crisis? On what basis do we choose between saving the brother or the sister? Why not both? What claim does any single individual have to being saved, while others, through no fault of their own, are being killed?"

(80) After liberation: "For the Russians we were Slovaks and for the Slovaks we remained Jews."

(83) "By the end of the war, we had so completely lost our trust in human decency and benevolence that every act of kindness and concern had a powerfully healing effect on us. Our moral order was still reversed: we expected evil and were surprised by the good."

(115) On Germany today: "... I began to understand the efforts of the younger generation, particularly those who came to adulthood after the war, to accept the historical, moral and psychological burden imposed on them by the acts of their fathers and mothers, and their own commitment to building a just and democratic society. They seemed willing to take responsibility for events in which they had not participated, to confront their recent history and to live with knowledge of it without becoming paralyzed by it. ... Understanding does not bring forgiveness, and forgiveness does not bring forgetfulness."

(125) "... a question I have asked myself often over the years, and which came back to me with full force during our visit – how would I have acted had I been an ordinary citizen of Slovakia? It has always been easy to dismiss the possibility of active collaboration; it has been more difficult to dismiss the possibility of remaining an uninvolved and therefore complicit bystander. It has been, and remains to this day, impossible to claim that I would have become a rescuer. Perhaps I was judging others by standards that were harsher than the ones that, in similar circumstances, I would have accepted for myself."

Places mentioned in Europe (page first mentioned)

Auschwitz Main Camp/Auschwitz I (9), Banska Bystrica (18), Bardejov (118), Bardejovske Kupele (118), Belzec death camp (9), Berlin (19), Berne (113), Bohemia (9), Bratislava/Posony/Pressburg (15), Budapest (28), Chelmno/Kulmhof death camp (9), Cracow/Krakow/Krakau (37), Crman (Nitra) (51), Czech Republic/Ceska Republic (11), Czechoslovakia (8), Danube River (127), Denmark/Danmark (113), Flossenbürg concentration camp (37), Germany/Deutschland (9), Hamburg (19), Hungary/ Magyarország (8), Italy/Italia (79), Kiev/Kyjiv (13), Kosice/Kassa/Kaschau (22), Leipzig (37), Majdanek concentration camp (9), Moravia (9), Naples/Napoli (35), Netherlands/ Nederland (Holland) (113), Nitra (41), Nove Zamky/Ersekujvar (80), Paris (104), Plaszow slave labour camp (37), Poland/Polska (36), Prague/Praha (12), Presov/Eperjes (8), Ricse camp (31), Romania (8), Ruthenia/Sub-Carpathia (8), Satoraljaujhely (32), Satoraljaujhely Ghetto (34), Slovakia/Slovenska Republic (1), Sobibor death camp (9), Sudetenland (9), Tabor (Nitra) (122), Tatra Mountains (Eastern) (118), Theresienstadt/Terezin- Ghetto/concentration camp (37), Tokaj (27), Tolscva (27), Treblinka (9)

Places mentioned outside Europe (page first mentioned)

Baltimore (109), Beer Yaacov, Israel (22), Britain (79), Brooklyn (110), Isle of Man (79), Israel/Yisrael (22), Jerusalem/Yerushalayim (82), London (England) (99), Moscow/Moskva (110), New Hope (Pennsylvania) (110), New Jersey (110), New York City (104), Philadelphia (109), Princeton (New Jersey) (105), United States of America (23), Washington (DC) (95), Yad Vashem (Israel) (43)

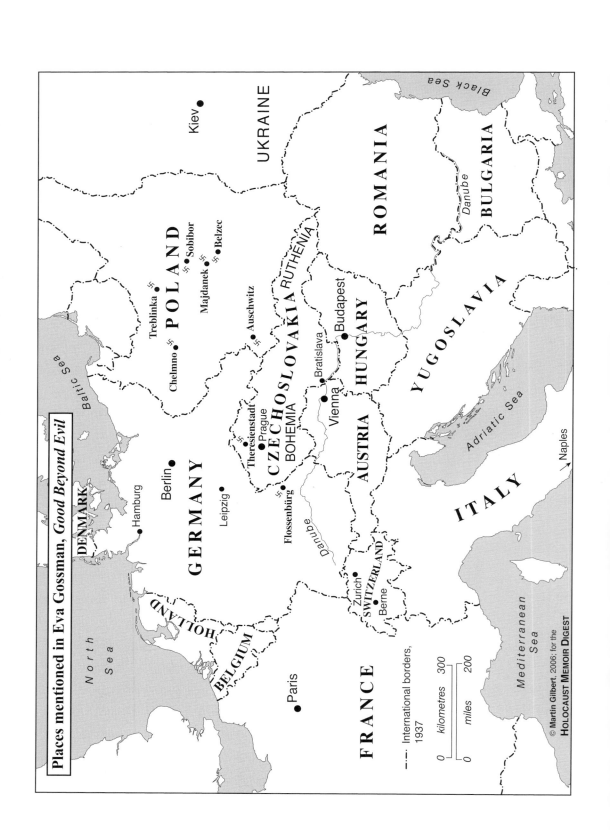

Places mentioned in Eva Gossman, *Good Beyond Evil*

- - - International borders, 1937

0 _____ kilometres _____ 300
0 _____ miles _____ 200

© Martin Gilbert, 2006; for the
HOLOCAUST MEMOIR DIGEST

Black Sea
UKRAINE
Kiev •
ROMANIA
BULGARIA
Danube
POLAND
Treblinka •
Sobibor •
Majdanek •
• Belzec
Chelmno •
• Auschwitz
RUTHENIA
CZECHOSLOVAKIA
Bratislava
Budapest
HUNGARY
Theresienstadt •
• Prague
BOHEMIA
Vienna •
AUSTRIA
YUGOSLAVIA
Baltic Sea
Hamburg •
Berlin •
GERMANY
Leipzig •
Flossenburg •
DENMARK
Adriatic Sea
Naples
Zurich •
SWITZERLAND
Berne •
Danube
ITALY
HOLLAND
BELGIUM
North Sea
Paris •
FRANCE
Mediterranean Sea

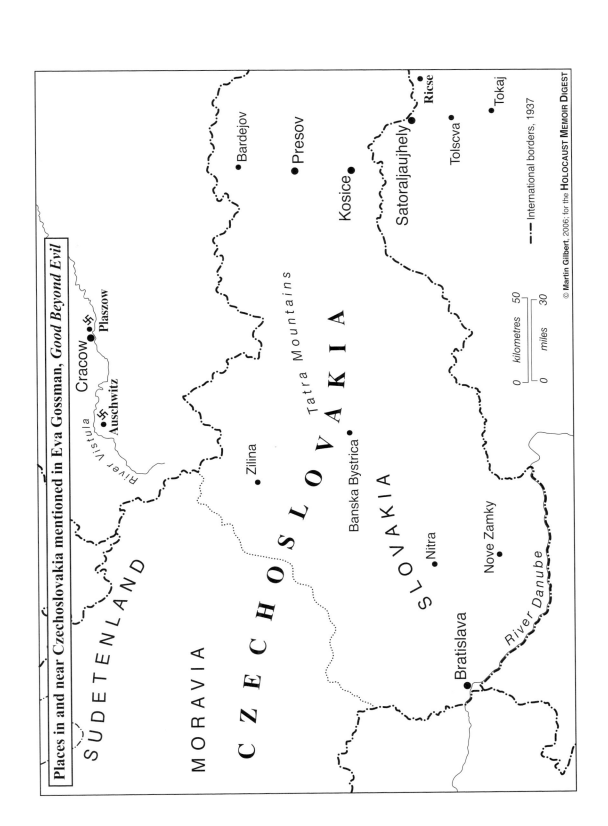

Places in and near Czechoslovakia mentioned in Eva Gossman, *Good Beyond Evil*

SUDETENLAND

MORAVIA

C Z E C H O S L O V A K I A

SLOVAKIA

Tatra Mountains

River Vistula

Cracow
Plaszow
Auschwitz

Zilina

Banska Bystrica

Nitra

Nove Zamky

Bratislava

River Danube

Bardejov

Presov

Kosice

Satoraljaujhely

Ricse

Tolscva

Tokaj

International borders, 1937

0   kilometres   50
0   miles   30

© **Martin Gilbert**, 2006: for the **HOLOCAUST MEMOIR DIGEST**

Study Guide

INTRODUCTION

This Study Guide accompanies the *Holocaust Memoir Digest*, and is intended to serve as a Lesson Plan for the *Digest*.

The term "Holocaust", which has entered into common usage in the past few decades, comes from classical Greek and means "consumed by fire: a burnt offering" . In Hebrew, which is both the language of prayer among Jews, and also the language of the State of Israel, the Holocaust is called "Shoah": "catastrophe", and in Yiddish, the traditional language of East European Jews, it is "Hurban": "destruction".

Since 1945, the Holocaust has come to refer to the planned, systematic murder of Jews who were living in European lands occupied or dominated by Germany during the Second World War. The war began with the German invasion of Poland on 1 September 1939. What had started as the random killing of Jews became, with the German invasion of the Soviet Union in June 1941, the mass murder of Jews on a daily basis. The surrender of Germany on 8 May 1945 brought the war in Europe to an end; six million Jewish men, women and children had been killed.

From the first days of their liberation in 1945, many survivors felt the need to record their eyewitness accounts, to memorialize their destroyed families, to remember their pre-war way of life. The first such memoirs, written soon after the war, introduced the Holocaust to the public consciousness. In recent years, the passage of time and a growing interest in their experiences during that traumatic time have been the impetus for many other survivors to record their memories for posterity.

The will to live, to maintain hope, to survive and to rebuild – this gives the Holocaust its universality. Jews are known as the People of the Book, that book being the Bible, the narrative of their origins, laws and early history. The need to write and record, to document, and to remember are an integral part of Jewish tradition. This makes the Holocaust a window into both the best and the worst of human behaviour. The Holocaust was not the only genocide of the twentieth century; it was almost certainly the most documented one.

Each survivor's experiences are unique; each memoir contains aspects of the Holocaust that add to our knowledge of that terrible time. The *Holocaust Memoir Digest*, by reviewing the published memoirs of Jews who survived the Holocaust, provides a guide and reference for the teaching, not only of the Holocaust, but also of recent history, human relations, the pattern of genocide and the psychology of good and evil.

TOPICS

The entry for each memoir in the *Holocaust Memoir Digest* consists of the following six parts:

1. The **author, title**, and **publishing details**;
2. A one-sentence **focus** which sets the geographic area and time;
3. A list of **features** that are not part of the memoir itself but added to it;
4. The **contents** of the memoir, divided into twenty-six categories;
5. A list of **places** mentioned in the memoir, both in Europe and beyond;
6. A **map** or **maps** showing each place in Europe mentioned in that memoir.

The first two of the twenty-six categories are **Pre-war Jewish home and community life,** and **Pre-war anti-Semitism.** These describe what life was like throughout Europe for Jews, some of whose ancestors had lived in these countries for many hundreds of years. In **Pre-war Jewish home and community life,** survivors write about the culture, education, traditions, community structure and the life Jews led as they struggled to grapple with changing twentieth-century values: Should they maintain family and religious traditions, or seek assimilation? Should they work toward a better economic situation where they lived, or would they find better opportunities elsewhere? Should they seek to fulfil their Zionist aspirations, or was carving out a life in the "desert" of Palestine too difficult?

One of the main factors that determined how pre-war European Jewish families faced these questions is that many of them lived amidst an all-pervasive **Pre-war anti-Semitism,** the second category of the *Digest.* They lived in a Christian world that was in many ways foreign to them or had alienated them.

The segregation and humiliation of Jews, legalized under the Nuremberg Laws of 1935, had begun in Germany when Hitler came to power in 1933. Hitler separated the Jews from the general population by making them into a scapegoat – by taking advantage of latent anti-Semitism and blaming Jews for Germany's ills. He then removed Jews from their positions in government, the law, universities, schools and hospitals. German colleagues took over their positions; those who had been under them moved up the ladder. Jewish businesses were confiscated, or "sold" for a fraction of their worth to local people who were loyal to the Nazi Party.

By the time Jews were separated physically from the larger German community, those of Hitler's compatriots who had accepted his plan, and benefited from this exclusion of the Jews, were not particularly interested in helping the Jews when persecution intensified. This segregation and humiliation extended to Austria in March 1938, when it became part of the German Reich, and to the Sudetenland region of Czechoslovakia in October 1938.

The coming of war and **Life under German occupation** categories describe how the beginning of the war in September 1939, the sudden violent imposition of Nazi rule, and the constant struggle for survival affected the memoir writer. In each country that Germany conquered between September 1939 and June 1941 – Poland in September 1939, Denmark and Norway in April 1940, Holland, Belgium, France and Luxembourg in May 1940, Yugoslavia and

Greece in April 1941 – anti-Jewish legislation was put in place, often upheld by the local collaborationist regime. Jewish businesses and possessions were confiscated.

In Poland, from the first days of the German conquest, Jews were rounded up, beaten, and several thousand were murdered. Later the Jews were forcibly removed from their homes and crowded into ghettos.

Ghettos were established in Poland in many towns in which Jews were confined amid considerable hardship and privation. Some ghettos existed for only a short time. Others lasted up to four years. This is described in the two categories **Creation of the ghetto,** and **Daily life in the ghetto.** Having lost their property and livelihood, the only further value Jews represented to the Nazi occupier was in their labour. Thus the struggle by Jews for survival in the ghettos centred on trying to find food and obtain valid work permits, both of which were tightly controlled and restricted.

Those Jews deemed by the Nazis no longer "essential" were rounded up and removed from the ghettos. The category of **Deportation** describes the physical movement of Jews from their home towns or ghettos, in most cases to their deaths. Usually deportations took place by train, and were undertaken with deliberate deception, and promises that were recognized as false only when it was too late. The destination of the deportation trains was a tightly guarded secret. Only a few deportees returned.

Starting in June 1941, when Germany invaded the Soviet Union, four "commandos" of specially-trained SS killing squads, the *Einsatzgruppen*, rounded up Jews in hundreds of towns and villages, and took them by force to nearby ditches, ravines and forests where they were shot. The largest of these **Mass murder sites** were located near cities which had large Jewish populations. These sites include Babi Yar outside Kiev, Rumbuli outside Riga, Ponar outside Vilnius, and the Ninth Fort outside Kaunas, at each of which tens of thousands of Jews were killed. Also included in this *Digest* category are smaller sites where thousands of Jews were murdered by shooting.

Transit camps: Drancy in France, Malines in Belgium, Westerbork in Holland, Fossoli in Italy, were among the principal transit camps where Jews were taken for short periods of time and then deported to an "unknown destination in the East" – in most cases, to their deaths. Other transit camps were to be found throughout Europe.

December 1941 saw the first systematic gassing of Jews. This took place in German-occupied Poland, near the village of Chelmno (in German "Kulmhof"), which became the first death camp. Belzec (pronounced Belzhets), Sobibor, and Treblinka were also **Death camps** in German-occupied Poland to which, with Chelmno, as many as two million Jews were deported and killed. A fifth death camp, Maly Trostenets, was situated near Minsk in German-occupied Byelorussia.

The only Jews who survived for more than a few days in the death camps were a small group of slave labourers forced to dispose of the bodies, usually in mass graves where the bodies were then burned. These labourers were also used to sort the clothing and belongings of the victims:

material that was later redistributed among the SS, the German armed forces and the German people. Almost none of the slave labourers in the death camps survived.

Many German factory owners took advantage of the plentiful labour supply and built factories and labour camps close to the ghettos and camps, as described in the category **Slave labour camps and factories**. Those Jews who were able to work had a better chance of survival, despite the harsh conditions in those camps which ensured a high turnover of labourers. Many memoir writers survived as slave labourers.

The deception practiced by the SS in their killing operations depended on secrecy and the complete control of information. Northwest of Prague, the SS established a ghetto in the former Czechoslovak garrison town of **Theresienstadt**, (**Terezin** in Czech). It was here that the Red Cross was shown what was "happening" to the Jews during a massive deception operation, complete with Jewish children at play. Much of the art, poetry and music created by the Jews during the Holocaust came from those who were interned in Theresienstadt. Most of those who did not succumb to the privations in Theresienstadt were deported to Auschwitz and Maly Trostenets and killed.

While mass murder by shooting continued in the East throughout the last six months of 1941 and for all of 1942, experimental means were being investigated in German-occupied Poland to make killing more "efficient". What had begun at Chelmno with exhaust fumes was "perfected" at **Auschwitz-Birkenau,** where Zyclon B gas pellets were thrown into sealed "shower" rooms. The bodies were then burned in crematoria. This method of killing began in the summer of 1942. By the autumn of 1944, five crematoria were operating.

Although "Auschwitz" has come to refer to the whole facility, it consisted of three large camps in close proximity. The original and Main Camp, with its single crematorium, was known as Auschwitz I. Birkenau, where four of the five crematoria were located, was known as Auschwitz II. Auschwitz also contained several satellite slave labour camps in the vicinity, the largest of which was attached to the Buna synthetic rubber and oil factory at the nearby town of Monowitz, and was known as Buna-Monowitz, or Auschwitz III. Descriptions of Buna-Monowitz and the other slave labour camps in the Auschwitz region are to be found in the *Digest* in the category of **Slave labour camps and factories**.

In January 1945, as Soviet forces approached the Auschwitz region, the SS evacuated the camp and the surrounding slave labour camps, and moved the surviving Jews westward, initially on foot. Those who were sent westward by rail were put in open railway wagons in mid-winter. Amid terrible brutality by their guards, many of the deportees were to "march" with little food, water or shelter, until April. The toll from these **Death marches** was high.

When the Nazi Party came to power in Germany in 1933, it immediately established concentration camps for political prisoners. These camps were run by the SS. Dachau, outside Munich and Sachsenhausen, north of Berlin, date from this period. These concentration camps, located on German soil, were used for German political prisoners, opponents of the Nazi regime, writers, artists, teachers, religious leaders, pastors, priests, homosexuals, common criminals, and later, prisoners of war, particularly Soviet soldiers. Towards the end of the war, tens of thousands of Jews on death marches were brought to the **Concentration camps** in Germany, among them Dachau, Bergen-Belsen, Buchenwald and Mauthausen, and their many sub-camps.

Also included in the *Digest* category of **Concentration camps** is Majdanek, although this camp had many different aspects. Located in Poland near the city of Lublin, Majdanek initially served as a concentration camp for Soviet prisoners of war, who were held there in horrific conditions, and for Polish political prisoners. For the thousands of Jews who were taken to Majdanek and were later sent to Auschwitz, it was a transit camp. In addition, thousands of Jews from as close as Lublin and as far as Holland and Greece were brought to Majdanek and killed. After the defeat of the Warsaw Ghetto Revolt and the destruction of the Warsaw Ghetto, and later the revolt in Bialystok, many thousands of survivors of those revolts were taken to Majdanek and murdered during the notorious "Harvest Festival" in November 1943.

One of the main reasons that survivors have written their memoirs of the Holocaust is to bear witness, to describe what they lived through, what they saw, and what the people whom they knew had witnessed. The category of **Witness to mass murder** makes it possible to begin to understand the scale of what happened.

As well as recording the details of the places to which Jews were taken, survivors also sought to chronicle the events and to write about the people who inspired them to continue, the people who helped them, and the ways they were able to evade death. The category **Resistance, ghetto revolts, individual acts of courage and defiance** includes acts of physical resistance, armed revolts, and also acts of "spiritual resistance": dignity in the face of inhumanity, the will to rise above the circumstances, the determination to live through the time of torment, the will to live.

Again and again, Jews fled to forests and outlying areas where they could fight the Nazi occupier. The category of **Partisan activity** refers to armed resistance against the German Army and German occupation, either by Jews, or by non-Jewish resistance fighters. Unfortunately, Jews who were able to escape to the forests and fight the Germans as Partisans also had to fear some Polish and Soviet Partisan groups who did not consider the Jews to be allies. One of the tragedies of the Holocaust is that some of those who were fighting the Nazi occupier were also fighting the Jews.

The category of **Specific escapes** refers to those few Jews who were able to escape from the deportation trains, or from those who would betray them, or from other situations of grave danger; or to find a brief respite from the constant terror.

In order to survive, many Jews went into hiding, as described in the category, **In hiding, including Hidden Children**. This could involve a physical hiding place: often a cellar or an attic, a cupboard, or a cavity in a wall, or under the floor, or in a barn. For those who did not have "typically Jewish" features and were able to pass as Christians, it also involved a psychological hiding. In such cases, along with the false identity papers, a whole new persona and demeanour had to emerge. In the struggle to find safety, families were split up; children were often hidden separately from their parents. Of those children who survived, many lost their families; nearly all lost their childhood.

Many Jews were fortunate to receive kindness and help from non-Jews. Many of these **Righteous Gentiles**, as they have become known, risked, and some even lost, their lives for helping Jews. Showing great humanity, they shared food, shelter and risk. It is to their credit that thousands of Jews survived.

The category of **Liberation** denotes the time when Soviet, American, British, Canadian and other Allied troops liberated the camps and the areas in which many Jews had been in hiding. For the Jews, liberation meant an end to their physical suffering, and the beginning of their quest to try to find family members, and to try to find a country that would give them safe haven. Many eventually made their way to Palestine (later Israel); many went to Britain, the United States, Canada, Australia, South Africa and Argentina.

The category of **Displaced Persons camps**, describes the refugee camps where survivors lived after they had been liberated. These camps were also used as a base for those who travelled to find relatives. Most survivors began to rebuild their lives while in DP camps; some spent several years there while waiting to find a country that would take them.

The category of **Stories of individuals, including family members** identifies the lives and fate of individuals mentioned by the memoir writer, as well as the fate of family members if known. Each survivor identifies extended family, neighbours, friends, colleagues and many of those individuals with whom he or she came into contact.

The category of **Post-war life and career** focuses not only on the achievements of the survivors after liberation, but on their search to explore their past. The final category of **Personal reflections** provides an understanding of how the survivors view the world, and gives the reader the opportunity to learn – through the survivors' own words – their philosophy, their psychology, their connection to religion, and what is important to them.

Because the borders of many countries in Europe have changed so much in the twentieth century, the names of **Places** also changed. For example, the capital of Slovakia is today Bratislava. When it was part of the Austro-Hungarian Empire, the Germans called it Pressburg, and the Hungarians knew it as Posony. The capital of Lithuania is today Vilnius. It was a part of Poland between the two world wars when Poles called it Wilno; to the Jews it was Vilna.

Many towns in the East had a Yiddish as well as a local name. Thus Brest-Litovsk was Brisk, and Wlodzimierz Wolynski (Vladimir Volynski) was Ludmir. The *Digest* shows these various spellings of towns and cities. Also, by locating each place on **Maps**, specially prepared by the *Digest* for each memoir, we can follow the memoir writer's travels, experiences, and torments.

The following is a series of questions within each category, with a key indicating which memoirs address these particular issues in that category.

Pre-war Jewish home and community life

How was a Jewish religious life observed?
The Janowska Road, Leon Weliczker Wells
By Bread Alone, Mel Mermelstein
Fragments of Memory, Hana Greenfield
Good Beyond Evil, Eva Gossman

What were the discussions among members of the author's family about following Zionist dreams and moving to Palestine?
Fragments of Memory, Hana Greenfield

What cultural aspects created a sense of community?
The Janowska Road, Leon Weliczker Wells
Good Beyond Evil, Eva Gossman

Pre-war anti-Semitism

How did the annexation of Austria and parts of Czechoslovakia affect Jews living in those areas?
Good Beyond Evil, Eva Gossman

What was the "Blood Libel" and how was it used against Jews?
Fragments of Memory, Hana Greenfield
Good Beyond Evil, Eva Gossman

The coming of war

What was it like to experience the bombing raids?
The Janowska Road, Leon Weliczker Wells

What was the situation for Jewish refugees?
By Bread Alone, Mel Mermelstein

What were the first encounters with the Germans like?
The Janowska Road, Leon Weliczker Wells

How did Soviet occupation affect Jewish life?
The Janowska Road, Leon Weliczker Wells

Life under German occupation

How did life change for Jews under German occupation?
Survival in Auschwitz, Primo Levi
The Janowska Road, Leon Weliczker Wells
By Bread Alone, Mel Mermelstein
Fragments of Memory, Hana Greenfield
Good Beyond Evil, Eva Gossman

What was the economic impact of German occupation?
The Janowska Road, Leon Weliczker Wells
By Bread Alone, Mel Mermelstein
Fragments of Memory, Hana Greenfield
Good Beyond Evil, Eva Gossman

How was the German chain of command established?
The Janowska Road, Leon Weliczker Wells
By Bread Alone, Mel Mermelstein
Fragments of Memory, Hana Greenfield
Good Beyond Evil, Eva Gossman

How did the Germans use local sentiment to further their goals?
The Janowska Road, Leon Weliczker Wells

Creation of the ghetto

How were the smaller ghettos established?
The Janowska Road, Leon Weliczker Wells
Good Beyond Evil, Eva Gossman

How were the larger ghettos formed?
The Janowska Road, Leon Weliczker Wells

Daily life in the ghetto

What was the day-to-day existence like in the larger ghettos?
The Janowska Road, Leon Weliczker Wells

Deportations

What were conditions like on the deportation trains?
Survival in Auschwitz, Primo Levi
By Bread Alone, Mel Mermelstein
Fragments of Memory, Hana Greenfield
Good Beyond Evil, Eva Gossman

Which deportations came to Auschwitz?
Survival in Auschwitz, Primo Levi
By Bread Alone, Mel Mermelstein
Fragments of Memory, Hana Greenfield
Good Beyond Evil, Eva Gossman

Which deportations came to death camps?
The Janowska Road, Leon Weliczker Wells
Fragments of Memory, Hana Greenfield

How were deportations used to move Jews to slave labour camps?
The Janowska Road, Leon Weliczker Wells
Good Beyond Evil, Eva Gossman

Were there eyewitnesses to the deportation trains?
By Bread Alone, Mel Mermelstein

What was known of the destination of the deportation trains?
Survival in Auschwitz, Primo Levi
The Janowska Road, Leon Weliczker Wells
By Bread Alone, Mel Mermelstein
Fragments of Memory, Hana Greenfield

Mass murder sites

No memoirs in this volume.

Transit camps

What were conditions like in transit camps?
Survival in Auschwitz, Primo Levi
By Bread Alone, Mel Mermelstein
Good Beyond Evil, Eva Gossman

Death camps

Who was taken to Belzec?
The Janowska Road, Leon Weliczker Wells

Who was taken to Treblinka?
Fragments of Memory, Hana Greenfield

Who was taken to Maly Trostenets?
Fragments of Memory, Hana Greenfield

Slave labour camps and factories

What were conditions like in the slave labour camps?
Survival in Auschwitz, Primo Levi
The Janowska Road, Leon Weliczker Wells
By Bread Alone, Mel Mermelstein
Fragments of Memory, Hana Greenfield

How were workers enslaved and then moved to different factories and camps?
Survival in Auschwitz, Primo Levi
The Janowska Road, Leon Weliczker Wells
By Bread Alone, Mel Mermelstein
Fragments of Memory, Hana Greenfield

Theresienstadt/Terezin

What were conditions like in Theresienstadt?
Fragments of Memory, Hana Greenfield

Auschwitz-Birkenau

What was the routine upon entry into Auschwitz?
Survival in Auschwitz, Primo Levi
By Bread Alone, Mel Mermelstein
Fragments of Memory, Hana Greenfield

What were conditions like in Auschwitz-Birkenau?
Survival in Auschwitz, Primo Levi
By Bread Alone, Mel Mermelstein
Fragments of Memory, Hana Greenfield

How could the mind help or hinder survival?
Survival in Auschwitz, Primo Levi
By Bread Alone, Mel Mermelstein
Fragments of Memory, Hana Greenfield

How could relationships help or hinder survival?
Survival in Auschwitz, Primo Levi
By Bread Alone, Mel Mermelstein
Fragments of Memory, Hana Greenfield

How did the author convey a sense of the number of people being killed there?
Survival in Auschwitz, Primo Levi
Fragments of Memory, Hana Greenfield

What purposes did the tattoo have?
Survival in Auschwitz, Primo Levi
By Bread Alone, Mel Mermelstein

How were those who came from Theresienstadt treated?
  Fragments of Memory, Hana Greenfield

Death marches

What was the evacuation of Auschwitz like?
  Survival in Auschwitz, Primo Levi

What were conditions like on the road?
  By Bread Alone, Mel Mermelstein
  Fragments of Memory, Hana Greenfield

What period of time elapsed and what distances were covered by those on death marches?
  By Bread Alone, Mel Mermelstein
  Fragments of Memory, Hana Greenfield

Concentration camps

What were conditions like in these camps during the war?
  By Bread Alone, Mel Mermelstein
  Fragments of Memory, Hana Greenfield

What were conditions like for those who came in from death marches?
  By Bread Alone, Mel Mermelstein
  Fragments of Memory, Hana Greenfield

Witness to mass murder

What were the early reports of mass murder?
  The Janowska Road, Leon Weliczker Wells

Which survivors saw mass murder at Auschwitz?
  Survival in Auschwitz, Primo Levi
  By Bread Alone, Mel Mermelstein

What eyewitness accounts of mass murder were there in cities, slave labour camps and other areas?
  The Janowska Road, Leon Weliczker Wells
  By Bread Alone, Mel Mermelstein

Resistance, ghetto revolts, individual acts of courage and defiance

What do we know about organized resistance at Auschwitz, and the crematorium blown up at Birkenau?
  Survival in Auschwitz, Primo Levi

What could individuals do to resist?
Survival in Auschwitz, Primo Levi
The Janowska Road, Leon Weliczker Wells
By Bread Alone, Mel Mermelstein
Fragments of Memory, Hana Greenfield
Good Beyond Evil, Eva Gossman

In what ways could Jewish Councils resist?
The Janowska Road, Leon Weliczker Wells
Good Beyond Evil, Eva Gossman

What secret messages were transmitted through the mail?
Fragments of Memory, Hana Greenfield

What acts of a religious, educational, cultural or artistic nature took place, and how can they be considered resistance?
By Bread Alone, Mel Mermelstein
Fragments of Memory, Hana Greenfield
Good Beyond Evil, Eva Gossman

What was the penalty for resistance?
Survival in Auschwitz, Primo Levi
The Janowska Road, Leon Weliczker Wells
By Bread Alone, Mel Mermelstein
Fragments of Memory, Hana Greenfield

Partisan activity

What were the betrayals, the hazards of Jews forming or joining partisan units?
Survival in Auschwitz, Primo Levi
The Janowska Road, Leon Weliczker Wells

What were the successes in working with the Partisans?
Good Beyond Evil, Eva Gossman

Specific escapes

What were some examples of physical escapes?
The Janowska Road, Leon Weliczker Wells
By Bread Alone, Mel Mermelstein
Good Beyond Evil, Eva Gossman

What were some examples of psychological escape?
Good Beyond Evil, Eva Gossman

In hiding, including Hidden Children

What was involved in the hiding of children?
The Janowska Road, Leon Weliczker Wells
Good Beyond Evil, Eva Gossman

What was involved in taking on a new identity in order to survive?
Good Beyond Evil, Eva Gossman

What was involved in finding a physical hiding place?
The Janowska Road, Leon Weliczker Wells
Good Beyond Evil, Eva Gossman

What were conditions like for those in hiding?
The Janowska Road, Leon Weliczker Wells
Good Beyond Evil, Eva Gossman

What were the risks involved in hiding Jews?
Good Beyond Evil, Eva Gossman

Righteous Gentiles

What kinds of offers were made by non-Jews to help their Jewish friends?
Survival in Auschwitz, Primo Levi
The Janowska Road, Leon Weliczker Wells
By Bread Alone, Mel Mermelstein
Fragments of Memory, Hana Greenfield
Good Beyond Evil, Eva Gossman

Who were to be the beneficiaries of non-Jews who supplied real assistance?
Survival in Auschwitz, Primo Levi
The Janowska Road, Leon Weliczker Wells
By Bread Alone, Mel Mermelstein
Fragments of Memory, Hana Greenfield
Good Beyond Evil, Eva Gossman

How could even kindness be seen as an act of righteousness?
Survival in Auschwitz, Primo Levi
The Janowska Road, Leon Weliczker Wells
By Bread Alone, Mel Mermelstein
Fragments of Memory, Hana Greenfield
Good Beyond Evil, Eva Gossman

What were the risks to non-Jews who helped?
The Janowska Road, Leon Weliczker Wells
By Bread Alone, Mel Mermelstein
Good Beyond Evil, Eva Gossman

In what ways have the Righteous been recognized?
The Janowska Road, Leon Weliczker Wells
Good Beyond Evil, Eva Gossman

Liberation

What evidence did survivors have that the Germans might lose the war?
Survival in Auschwitz, Primo Levi
By Bread Alone, Mel Mermelstein

How did liberation from the Germans not end the threat of death?
Survival in Auschwitz, Primo Levi
The Janowska Road, Leon Weliczker Wells
By Bread Alone, Mel Mermelstein
Good Beyond Evil, Eva Gossman

What was the situation involved in returning home?
The Janowska Road, Leon Weliczker Wells
By Bread Alone, Mel Mermelstein
Good Beyond Evil, Eva Gossman

Displaced Persons camps

Who was able to benefit from the DP camps?
The Janowska Road, Leon Weliczker Wells
By Bread Alone, Mel Mermelstein

Stories of individuals, including family members

What was the fate of parents, siblings, and extended family?
What was the fate of friends, and those met along the way?
Survival in Auschwitz, Primo Levi
The Janowska Road, Leon Weliczker Wells
By Bread Alone, Mel Mermelstein
Fragments of Memory, Hana Greenfield
Good Beyond Evil, Eva Gossman

Post-war life and career

How have survivors continued to seek justice for the perpetrators and the deniers of the Holocaust?
The Janowska Road, Leon Weliczker Wells
By Bread Alone, Mel Mermelstein
Fragments of Memory, Hana Greenfield

Which survivors were able to return home only after an absence of many years?
Good Beyond Evil, Eva Gossman

How have their experiences in the Holocaust inspired survivors to write and teach about the Holocaust?

By Bread Alone, Mel Mermelstein

Fragments of Memory, Hana Greenfield

Personal reflections

Compare Primo Levi's and Leon Wells' views of being hardened to pain. How does Hana Greenfield continue to use that shell?

Compare Primo Levi's and Leon Well's views of happiness.

What does Mel Mermelstein mean by a "just God"?

Compare the influence of Leon Wells' mother and Mel Mermelstein's father.

What does Hana Greenfield mean when she writes: "… the world is divided into two kinds of people: those who were there and those who were not."?
What difficulties of this nature might be encountered at trials like the one for Ivan Demjanjuk?

Eva Gossman writes about the "depth of depravity"; where does Primo Levi find that depth?

Compare Eva Gossman asking how she would have acted, and Mel Mermelstein's guilt at saving himself.

Hana Greenfield calls her grandfather a hero; compare Primo Levi's friend Steinlauf on "the power to refuse our consent'.

Hana Greenfield writes: "The only thing that remains of Alice is my memory of her and the number "AAd 55" next to her name on the transport list … ." In which other cases might this be true?

GENERAL QUESTIONS

How did the following elements help the Germans to carry out their genocide:
Segregation
Restrictions
Confiscations
Control of information
Ruthlessness in dealing with those opposed to Nazism

What part did economics play in the Holocaust and in the German war effort, in terms of confiscated assets, and slave labour?

What is meant by "hunger", as experienced by the Jews?
What is meant by "fear"?
What is meant by "hope"?

In what ways can "courage" and "defiance" comprise very real resistance?

Why were some non-Jews willing to help, and for what reasons did they help?

To what extent has the reality of Auschwitz alerted us to the potential for evil in the world?

What is meant by "crimes against humanity" and why is it important to know what happened during the Holocaust?

GLOSSARY OF TERMS USED BY THE MEMOIR WRITERS

Compiled by Sir Martin Gilbert

Aktion/Aktsia (German: "action"): a raid on the ghetto, the roundup and arrest of Jews, often accompanied by mass slaughter.

Aliyah (Hebrew: "going up"): *Aliyah la-Torah:* going up to the bimah (reader's desk) in synagogue to read from the Torah. *Aliyah le-Regel:* going up to Jerusalem for the pilgrim festivals. A third meaning was immigration to Ottoman and British Mandate Palestine, and (since 1948) to Israel. In the 1930s, as Britain imposed severe restrictions on Jewish immigration, illegal immigration was known as "Aliyah Bet" ("Aliyah B").

Altalena: a ship hired by the *Irgun* in southern France to bring immigrants and arms for its own use into Israel, shortly after the foundation of the State. The Prime Minister, David Ben Gurion, ordered the *Irgun* to hand over the ship to the Israeli army and to give up its arms. When they refused to do so, he instructed the army to open fire. Forty of those on board were killed, and the ship was sunk just off Tel Aviv. The story of the *Altalena* is told in a museum in Tel Aviv.

Amcha (Hebrew: "a Jew", "the Jewish people"): "one of us", used as a form of code word between Jews to ascertain whether the person spoken to was Jewish.

American Jewish Joint Distribution Committee (*the Joint*): an organization set up in 1914 to help Jewish refugees in the Russian-Polish borderlands during the First World War; active to this day in Jewish welfare work worldwide.

Anschluss (German: "unification"): the union of Germany and Austria, forbidden by the Versailles Treaty of 1920, but secured by Hitler in March 1938.

Appel (German: "roll call"): in the slave labour and concentration camps, inmates were lined up and counted, usually both before they went out to work and after their return. It was often a time of torment and danger.

Armia Krajowa (Polish: "Home Army"): Polish underground movement loyal to the Polish government in London.

Armia Ludowa (Polish: "People's Army"): Polish underground movement loyal to Moscow, and predominantly Communist.

Arrow Cross (in Hungarian, "Nyilas-kereszt"): a leading Hungarian fascist political party, led by Ferenc Szalasi, a former army major. In 1939, it numbered almost five hundred thousand members, and won thirty-one seats in the parliamentary election (25 per cent of the total national vote). On 15 October 1944 Szalasi became Prime Minister and Head of State of Hungary. From then until the arrival of the Soviet Army in January 1945, it was responsible for the murder of several thousand Jews in Budapest. After the war, Szalasi and many other Arrow Cross leaders were tried for war crimes and executed.

Aryan side (*Warsaw*): the non-Jewish sections of Warsaw after the creation of the Warsaw Ghetto, which was surrounded by a high brick wall.

Askari (originally, an East-African native soldier or policeman): the name given to Soviet prisoners of war who formed units that worked for the Germans.

Aussiedlung (German: "resettlement"): a euphemism for deportation, usually to a death camp.

Bet Am (Hebrew: "House of the People"): the name often given to a Jewish community house or centre.

Banderowtzi / Banderovtsi: members of a clandestine and violently anti-Jewish paramilitary force, the Ukrainian Insurgent Army (Ukrainska Povstanska Armyia), organized at the end of 1942, and named after the Ukrainian nationalist leader Stefan Bandera.

Bar-Mitzvah (Hebrew: "son of the covenant"): a Jewish boy's coming of age, on his thirteenth birthday, when he is able to assume religious obligations as an adult.

Block (in German "*bloc*"): a barrack in a concentration camp usually designated with a number or a letter.

Blockaltester (German): the barrack leader.

Blood Libel: an accusation levelled against the Jews, especially during the Middle Ages, that they murdered Christian children in order to use their blood in the baking of unleavened bread (*matza*) at Passover. The *Blood Libel*, which persisted throughout the nineteenth century, was revived by the Nazis in their campaign of hatred against the Jews. Also known as "ritual murder".

Boche (French: "a German", plural: *les Boches*): slang word for Germans.

Bread and Salt: the traditional East European offering to newcomer or a stranger, as a sign of friendship.

Bricha (Hebrew: "flight"): the organization set up by Jews from Palestine in September 1944, to smuggle Jewish survivors out of Europe, in defiance of the British Mandate restrictions. It was first active in Vilna and Rovno after the liberation of those two towns, and later was centred on the Displaced Persons camps in southern Germany. The main route led through Austria to Italy, and then by sea to Palestine. Those brought by the *Bricha* who were intercepted by the British were sent to internment camps in Cyprus.

Bund (Yiddish: "union"): the Jewish Social Revolutionary party, founded in Russia in 1898 as an association of Jewish workers worldwide, committed to world revolution and social equality.

Bunker: a hiding place, often in a cellar, or dug underneath a building.

Camps: places where Jews and other opponents of Nazism were confined, under strict guard. See also: *Concentration camps, Death camps* and *Slave labour camps*.

Canada (*Kanada*): a large hutted area at Auschwitz-Birkenau set aside for the sorting of the belongings of Jews deported to the camp from all over Europe. A vast storehouse of clothing and personal possessions.

Centos (Polish acronym): pre-war Polish Jewish welfare organization for orphans.

Chasidism (from the Hebrew word "hasidim", "pietists"): a popular religious movement founded in the eighteenth century in Poland-Lithuania in which ecstasy, mysticism, mass-enthusiasm, close-knit group cohesion and charismatic leadership were the distinguishing marks. An early leader was Israel Ben Eliezer, who took the name Ba'al Shem Tov ("master of the good name"), known by his acronym as The Besht. The movement consists of various "dynasties" each with their own Rebbe (the Yiddish word for "rabbi"), named after their original geographic locations.

Cheder (from the Hebrew word "heder", "a room"): a school for the teaching of Judaism for boys from the age of three. The teacher, called the "rebbe" or "melamed", received his fees from the parents; the class was normally held in a room in the teacher's home. The age groups were from 3 to 5, where the children were taught reading in the prayer book; 6 to 7, where they were taught the Pentateuch (*Torah*) with Rashi's commentary; and 8 to 13, where they were taught *Talmud*. No secular studies were taught. From the *cheder*, the pupil usually proceeded to the *yeshiva*.

Concentration camps: camps where the Nazis incarcerated their opponents behind barbed wire and high walls; places of extreme brutality by the guards, who were often common criminals; places to which Jews were deported, and where murder was commonplace.

Crematorium/crematoria (*crematory*): places in concentration camps where the corpses of those who had died, or been murdered, were burned. Auschwitz had five, each one attached to a gas chamber where the murders took place.

Death camps: concentration camps in which almost all those deported there were murdered within a few hours, usually by gas.

Decimate (from the Latin "decimare", "to take the tenth man"): a term from classical antiquity meaning to kill one in ten (which the Romans did after conquering), increasingly misused to mean total destruction.

Displaced persons camp (*DP Camp*): post-war camps in which survivors of the Holocaust were gathered, and awaited rehabilitation.

Dowry: the property, movable and immovable, brought into the marriage by the bride. Thus the Biblical Rebecca took maidservants with her, on her way to marry Isaac. By Talmudic times, it was customary for the bride to be endowed by her father. Among ultra-Orthodox Jews, the amount set aside by the bride's parents is often used to enable their new son-in-law to continue his Talmudic studies. Throughout the ages, "dowering the bride" ("*Hakhnasat kallah*") was a communal responsibility, considered especially meritorious, and one of the highest precepts of Judaism.

Dulag (German: abbreviation for *Durchgangslager*): transit camps in the SS concentration camp system.

East (as in "*to the East*", "*somewhere in the East*"): the "unknown destination" of almost all the deportation trains from mid-1942 to mid-1944. As a result of the escape of four Jews from Auschwitz in April and May 1944, the main "unknown destination" was revealed as Auschwitz-Birkenau, a death factory. Another long-kept secret destination "in the East" was the death camp at Maly Trostenets, near Minsk.

Eretz Yisrael (Hebrew: "the Land of Israel"): a phrase used frequently in the Bible. It was used by Jews between 1922 and 1948, before the establishment of the state, to describe the British Mandate of Palestine.

Family Camp (at Auschwitz-Birkenau): also known as the "*Czech Family Camp*", a substantial section of Birkenau in which some 10,000 Jews from the ghetto of Theresienstadt, most of them Czech Jews, were kept together as families and not subjected to the full rigours of the camp. They were even allowed to receive Red Cross parcels, and to send postcards. This device enabled the SS to maintain that Auschwitz was a camp of "protective custody", not extermination. After several months, almost all those in the Czech Family Camp were taken to the gas chambers and murdered.

(FPO) Fareynigte Partizaner Organizatsie (Yiddish: The United Partisan Organization, Vilna Ghetto): a clandestine Jewish partisan organization set up in the Vilna Ghetto at the beginning of 1942. On 1 September 1943 the first clashes took place between the *FPO* and the German occupation authorities. On 23 and 24 September, during the liquidation of the ghetto, and round-ups for deportation to local slave labour camps and to Estonia, a few hundred members of the *FPO* managed to escape to the forests and formed two fighting units. On 13 July 1944 the survivors of these units entered Vilna as liberators alongside the Soviet Red Army.

Folkschul (Yiddish: a Jewish "people's" school): usually a non-religious school.

Gestapo (*Geheime Staatspolizei*, of which "*Gestapo*" is an acronym): the much-feared German Secret State Police.

Häftling (German): prisoner.

Haftorah (Hebrew: "conclusion"): the section of the prophetical books of the Bible that are recited in synagogue after the Reading of the Law (Torah) at morning services on Sabbath and festivals, during the afternoon on fast days, and at both services during the fast of the Ninth of Av (*Tisha b'Av*). In Sephardi and Eastern communities, a minor may be given the privilege of reading the Haftorah.

Haganah (Hebrew: "defence"): Jewish self-defence organization established in Palestine in 1921. In 1938 it set up a clandestine organization (*Aliyah Bet*) to bring Jews to Palestine despite the British restrictions. In 1948 the *Haganah* became the principal component of the Israel Defence Forces.

Hanukah (Hebrew: "dedication"): the Jewish festival commemorating the victory of the Maccabees (between 165 and 163 BC) over the Hellenistic Syrians who had tried to eradicate the Jewish religion. The main observance of *Hanukah* is the kindling of the festival lamp, the "*Hanukiyah*" each night of the eight-day holiday.

Havdalah (Hebrew: "distinction" or "separation"): a blessing recited at the end of Sabbath and festivals in order to emphasize the distinction between the sacred and the ordinary. It is one of the most ancient blessings in Jewish ritual.

High Holy Days: the solemn festivals of the Jewish New Year, *Rosh Hashana* and the Day of Atonement, *Yom Kippur*.

Hitler Youth ("*Hitlerjugend*", "*HJ*"): the National Socialist youth movement, established as the "Adolf Hitler Boys' Storm Troops" in 1922, renamed Hitler Youth in 1926. By 1935 it comprised 60 per cent of German youth between the ages of 10 and 18. The Nazi ideology that the movement took was permeated with hatred of Jews. Many Hitler Youth members were later active in the Final Solution – the plan to murder all of Europe's Jews.

(HKP) Heeres Kraftfahrpark (German: "Army Motor Vehicle Depot"): workshops in Vilna, where several thousand Vilna Ghetto Jews worked and lived in a special labour camp attached to the workshops. The man in charge, Major Karl Plagge, was later recognized as a Righteous Gentile for his efforts to help the Jews while they were working for him, and to warn them of danger.

Hlinka Guard: Slovak militia named after the Slovak nationalist Andrej Hlinka (who died in 1938). When it was established in 1938 it acted against Jews, Czechs, socialists and all opposition to Slovak independence. From 1941 its members were trained in SS camps in Germany. In 1942 it participated in the deportation of Slovak Jews to the death camps in German-occupied Poland. Its members wore black uniforms.

International Brigade: military formation made up largely of volunteers from all over the world who went to Spain between 1936 and 1939 to fight on the Republican side against the Franco nationalists. Several thousand Jews, including many from North America, joined the Brigade in the hope of playing an active part against fascism.

Internment camps: camps, mostly in German-dominated Western Europe, in which Jews were held before being sent to transit camps – and then to death camps.

Irgun (Hebrew: *Irgun Zvai Leumi*, National Military Organization): an anti-British minority organization, established in the mid-1930s in Mandate Palestine. Denounced by mainstream Jewish political figures, it carried out a series of attacks against British targets, and violent reprisal actions against Arabs. In 1949 it became a political party, *Herut*, which later evolved into *Likud*, and was represented in Israel's Parliament. Its leader, Menachem Begin, became Prime Minister of Israel in 1977.

Jewish Brigade: Jewish soldiers in the British Army, who in 1944 were given their own military formation and Star of David insignia within the British forces. After fighting against the Germans in Italy, many of them were active after the war in helping Jews escape from Central and Eastern Europe and to make their way from Austria to Italy – and in due course to Palestine.

Jewish Co-ordinating Committee: a relief organization in the Warsaw Ghetto. After the ghetto uprising it focused its efforts on helping those who had survived, including providing them with false papers. It also tried to help Jews in the Czestochowa Ghetto after it had been destroyed.

Jewish Council ("*Judenrat*"): Jewish administrations established in the ghettos at German insistence. They were responsible for all aspects of Jewish internal life in the ghetto, including health and education. Some collaborated with the Germans, or were forced to do so; most resisted German demands, even taking a lead in helping Jewish resistance. Jewish Council members, including those who had collaborated, suffered the fate of all Jews in the ghetto. The head of the Jewish Council in Warsaw, Adam Czerniakow, committed suicide rather than hand over to the Germans the daily quota of Jews they had demanded for deportation to Treblinka.

Jewish Fighting Organization (*JFO*): see Glossary entry for *ZOB*.

"*Jewish Uncle*": a Christian who committed himself to helping Jews, despite the hostility of his Christian neighbours to this course of action.

Joint, the: see the Glossary entry for *American Jewish Joint Distribution Committee*.

Judenrat (German): see the Glossary entry for *Jewish Council*.

Kabala (also *Kabbalah*): a mystical Jewish system developed in the eleventh and twelfth centuries, which seeks to find an inner meaning to the scriptural writings.

Kapo: a supervisor of concentration camp or slave labour camp inmates, himself a prisoner. Often a common criminal. The word is believed to derive from the Italian word "capo" – "chief". Some kapos were cruel in the extreme; others could act fairly.

Kehilla (Hebrew): a Jewish community residing in a particular place; its leaders were responsible for the welfare of the community, including education, charity and burial.

Kiddush (Hebrew: "sanctification"): the prayer recited over a cup of wine in the synagogue or in the home to consecrate the Sabbath and the festivities to fulfil the Biblical commandment, "Remember the Sabbath day, to keep it holy.'

Kol Nidrei (Hebrew: "All Vows"): the opening prayer of the Day of Atonement. The phrase, based on the first two words of that prayer – which is mostly in Aramaic – has come to mean the whole evening service in synagogue at the opening of the Day of Atonement.

Kristallnacht (German: "night of broken glass"): the night of 9/10 November 1938, when one thousand synagogues throughout Germany and Austria were destroyed, and many Jewish businesses and homes ransacked. Ninety-two Jews were also murdered that night, and tens of thousands of Jewish men sent to concentration camps.

Lagerführer (German): camp chief. If the head was a woman, then "*Lagerführerin*".

Levi: the surname of members of the Biblical tribe who descended from the third son of the patriarch Jacob. Aaron, the High Priest, belonged to the tribe of Levi. The Levites were chosen to carry the Sanctuary during the Israelites' forty years in the wilderness, and later to serve in the Temple. In synagogue, they are called up for an *aliyah* after the *Cohens* (Priests) to the Reading of the Law (*Torah*).

Maftir (Hebrew: "one who concludes"): the honour reserved for the last worshipper summoned for an *aliyah* to the Reading of the Law (*Torah*). It comprises the final verses of the portion being read that Sabbath or Festival from the Torah scroll. On the *Sabbaths* before *Passover* and the *Day of Atonement*, *Maftir* is usually given to a rabbi or a learned and pious layman.

Marshall Plan: United States aid package, introduced in 1947, to rebuild the war-shattered economies of Europe. The Soviet Union rejected the plan and made all its Eastern European Communist satellites do likewise. Named after its founder, General George C. Marshall, Chief of Staff of the United States Army, 1939–45, and Secretary of State, 1947–49. In recognition of the success of his plan, Marshall was awarded the Nobel Peace Prize.

Masada: King Herod's palace and fortress overlooking the Dead Sea. In the final stages of the Jewish revolt against Rome (which lasted from 132 to 135) the surviving rebels held out against a Roman siege until the wall was breached. The Jews committed collective suicide to avoid capture.

Matza (Hebrew, plural *matzot*): unleavened bread, a thin, dry biscuit-type bread eaten by Jews during the eight days of Passover, in memory of the exodus from Egypt, when there had been no time to bake leavened bread.

Megilla (Hebrew: "scroll"): usually refers to the Scroll of the Biblical Book of Esther, which is read in synagogue on the festival of *Purim*.

Melina (Yiddish): a hiding place (a word mostly used in Poland and Lithuania) often in a cellar, or behind a cupboard.

Molotov Cocktail: a crude explosive device, usually a bottle filled with gasoline and ignited through a rag stuffed into the neck of the bottle. First used by the Finns in their defence against the Russians in the Russo–Finnish War (1939–40), and named by them derisively after the Soviet Foreign Minister at that time, Vyacheslav Molotov.

Mussulman/muselmänner: an emaciated concentration camp prisoner who had given up the will to live, and was near death.

Muzhiks (Russian: "a Russian peasant"): used informally to mean a "dude" or "chap".

Nazi-Soviet Non-Aggression Pact (also known as the *Molotov-Ribbentrop Pact*): the agreement between Hitler and Stalin, concluded in August 1939, whereby Nazi Germany and the Soviet Union agreed publicly to cease their public animosity, and agreed secretly to partition Poland. A week later, German forces invaded Poland from the west. Soviet forces then moved in to occupy the eastern half of Poland. Molotov and Ribbentrop were the respective Soviet and German Foreign Ministers who negotiated the pact.

Nebich (Yiddish: "poor thing"): an unfortunate person.

Nyilas: Hungarian fascists who rampaged through Budapest in late 1944, murdering many thousands of Jews. Thousands more Jews were protected from the Nyilas gangs by the Swedish diplomat Raoul Wallenberg and his fellow diplomats in the city (see also Glossary entry for Arrow Cross).

Oberkapo: a senior supervisor in a concentration camp (see "*kapo*").

Palestine Mandate: the governance of Palestine, between the Mediterranean Sea and the River Jordan, granted to Britain by the League of Nations in 1922 as a Mandate. Britain relinquished the Mandate in 1948, when David Ben-Gurion declared a Jewish State (Israel). The West Bank and Gaza Strip areas of the Mandate were occupied by Jordan and Egypt respectively, until occupied by Israel in 1967.

Papal Nuncio: the senior representative of the Pope and the Vatican in foreign capitals. The Papal Nuncio in Budapest – Angelo Rotta – was particularly active in trying to protect Jews.

Pogrom (from the Russian "to demolish"): a violent attack on a particular group, religious, ethnic or other, and the destruction of their homes, businesses and places of worship. Historically used to denote attacks on Jews in Tsarist Russia, the first in Odessa in 1821 when fourteen Jews were killed. The two largest waves of pogroms were from 1881 to 1884, and 1903 to 1906 when an estimated two thousand Jews were killed.

Prominenz (German): a prisoner who was able to organize special privileges and benefits, albiet for a short time.

Purim (Hebrew: "lots"): Jewish festival commemorating the deliverance of Persian Jewry from their intended destruction by the Grand Vizier, Haman. It was one of the King's wives, Esther, a Jewess, who secured the salvation of the Jewish community. The festival is celebrated with the reading of the history of that time, from the *Megillat Esther,* "The Book of Esther". It is a time of enthusiastic jollity, parties and entertainment, in which children participate in costumes.

Quisling: the surname of the head of the wartime Norwegian collaborationist regime in Norway – Vidkun Quisling. The word became synonymous with treachery.

Reichsautobahn Lager (German): slave labour camp run by the German road-building administration, for the construction of the autobahn network. Jews were among those who worked in the camps.

Reparations: money paid by the German government, and by some German companies, in recognition of the personal suffering and material losses suffered by Jews during the Holocaust. The German government initiated this process in 1952, under the Luxembourg Agreement with the State of Israel.

Resettlement: see Glossary entry for *aussiedlung*.

Rosh Hashana: the Jewish New Year, marking the start of the High Holy Days.

SD ("*Sicherheitdienst*", of which *SD* is an abbreviation): "Security Service"; the Intelligence Service of the SS. It was created in 1931 by Reinhard Heydrich; in 1939, it was placed under the authority of the RSHA, "Reichssicherheitshauptamt", the Reich Security Main Office.

SS ("*Schutz Staffeln*", of which *SS* is an abbreviation): "Defence Squad", created in Munich in the 1920s to protect Nazi Party speakers from attacks by their opponents; from 1933, responsible for administering the concentration camps and slave labour camps, and for carrying out the racist policies of the Nazi regime. Following the German invasion of the Soviet Union in June 1941, SS mobile killing squads "*Einsatzgruppen*" murdered at least a million Jews. The SS was headed by Heinrich Himmler.

"*Sad Eyes*": the eyes of a Jewish person who was trying to find safety by pretending to be a Christian; a reference to the way a Jew in hiding or in disguise could be recognized by a non-Jew. These "*sad eyes*" could be the cause of exposure and betrayal.

Selection (*selektsia*): the act of dividing Jews into two groups: those who were to be taken away and murdered, and those who were to return to the ghetto or concentration camp barracks – to work, and await yet another selection. Selections often took place during mass roll calls.

Shabbat (in Hebrew), *Shabbos* (in Yiddish): the Jewish Sabbath, beginning on Friday night at sundown. The Jewish day of rest.

Shanda (Yiddish: a shame, a scandal): to make "a shanda fur die goyim" is to do something embarrassing to Jews in a place where non-Jews can observe it.

Shema (Hebrew "Hear"): the opening of the prayer declaring God's oneness, recited twice daily by religious Jews.

Shtetl (Yiddish: a small town or village): in Eastern Europe, where Jews lived in self-contained and self-sustaining communities, far from the cities, often extremely poor, and largely cut off from the nearby non-Jewish towns, or the non-Jewish parts of the town.

Siberia: Eastern region of the Soviet Union, from the Ural mountains to the Pacific Ocean; the location of many Soviet labour camps and labour camp zones of the utmost severity.

Slave labour camps: SS-run camps, often attached to factories and factory zones, in which large numbers of Jews – and other captive peoples – worked amid extreme severity, and in which many died of the harsh conditions and brutality of the guards.

Smous: a derogatory term for Jews (in Belgium).

Sonderkommando: groups of Jewish prisoners forced by the Germans to work in and around the gas chambers disposing of the corpses. In almost every case the group selected were murdered within a few months, and replaced by others who were also murdered.

Succot: a Jewish festival, celebrated in rooms open to the sky.

Talmud (Hebrew for "study" or "learning"): used to denote the body of rabbinical teaching which comprises the commentary and discussions on the Oral Law (*Mishnah*).

Tarbut (Hebrew for "culture"): a pre-war Jewish educational and cultural system established throughout Eastern Europe. Particularly active in Poland, where, by 1935, there were 183 elementary and nine secondary Tarbut schools, seventy-two kindergartens, four teachers' seminaries, four evening schools, and an agricultural school. In all Tarbut schools, Hebrew was the principal language of instruction. Both biblical and modern Hebrew literature were taught. The education was Zionist oriented, and many pupils went as pioneers to Palestine.

Todesplatz (death square): an area of the Janowska camp where people were brought to be murdered.

Todt Organization: a German organization, originally headed by a Nazi Party engineer, Fritz Todt (who died accidentally in 1942). The Todt Organization, which employed Jewish and non-Jewish slave labour, was responsible for the construction of projects of strategic importance, including the Siegfried Line defence in western Germany, railway facilities for the German Army on the Eastern Front, and the "West Wall" fortifications to protect against an Allied landing in northern France.

Torah: the Five Books of Moses (the Pentateuch).

Transit camps: camps to which Jews were taken, and then held until being deported to a death camp.

Uberleben (Yiddish, German: "to live through"): the hope of Jews during the Holocaust: to live through the time of torment, to survive.

Umschlagplatz (German: "collection place"): a railway siding from which Jews were deported. In Warsaw, they were brought there on a regular basis from all over the ghetto and held until deported by train to Treblinka.

UNESCO: United Nations Educational, Scientific and Cultural Organization: established in 1946 to further "a universal respect for human rights, justice and the rule of law, without distinction of race, sex, language or religion", in accordance with the United Nations charter. Dedicated to the free flow of information, and the preservation of freedom of expression.

UNRRA: *United Nations Relief and Rehabilitation Administration*: set up in the aftermath of the Second World War to help refugees and Displaced Persons. Among its tasks was the distribution of food.

Ustachi: a fascist force in the wartime independent State of Croatia, responsible for the mass murder of Serbs and Jews. The concentration camps under its control were much feared.

UZ Ustredna Zidov (Slovak, "Jewish Centre"): the Jewish Council established by the Slovak government in 1940 to run Jewish affairs. In the summer of 1942, some members of it negotiated with the SS in an ultimately unsuccessful attempt to try to end the deportation of Slovak Jews to the death camps.

Vichy: a town in central France, which, following the German defeat of France in June 1940, became the capital of the "Vichy" government, headed by Marshal Petain, and subservient to Germany. Vichy's police were active in the roundup of Jews for deportation. The word "Vichy" became synonymous with collaboration.

Volksdeutsche (also known as "*ethnic Germans*"): German minorities living outside the German Reich, including the Sudeten Germans in Czechoslovakia and the Volga Germans in the Soviet Union. Some groups had lived many hundreds of miles from Germany for several centuries. Many became strong supporters of Nazism after the German Army occupied the regions in which they lived, and benefited considerably from the German occupation.

Wehrmacht: the German armed forces. In 1939 they consisted of 2,700,000 men, and in 1943 of more than 13 million. Separate from the armed forces of the SS (*Waffen SS*).

Yeshiva (plural, *yeshivot*): an institution of learning in which Jews pursue the study of the Torah. The word comes from the Hebrew verb "*yashav*", "to sit". The system of study is based on the keen debate of Biblical and rabbinical sources. Many famous *yeshivot* were destroyed during the Holocaust. Some were able to renew their existence after the war, mostly in the United States and Israel.

Yom Kippur: the Day of Atonement, the holiest twenty-four hours in the Jewish religious calendar, a time of prayer and fasting, and seeking forgiveness from God.

Zachor (Hebrew "To remember"): a basic Jewish precept.

Zloty: the Polish currency.

ZOB (Polish: *Zydowska Organizacja Bojowa* "*Jewish Fighting Organization*"): established in Warsaw on 28 July 1942, when the mass deportations were taking place to Treblinka. Determined to offer armed resistance against the German occupation forces, it organized two ghetto uprisings in Warsaw, the first in January 1943 and the second – the Warsaw Ghetto Revolt – in April 1943. In August 1944, many of its members who had survived the crushing of the ghetto revolt participated in the Polish Uprising in Warsaw.

Zohar: the classical work of the *Kabala* containing a record of the divine mysteries said to have been granted to a second century Jewish teacher, Rabbi Simeon ben Yohai, and his mystic circle. The word means "illumination" or "brightness".

Zytos (Polish, acronym): a Jewish relief agency in the Warsaw Ghetto.

SS POSITIONS AND RANKS MENTIONED IN THE MEMOIRS

Reichsführer: the head of the SS (Heinrich Himmler)
Oberstgruppenführer: Colonel-General
Obergruppenführer: General
Gruppenführer: Lieutenant-General
Brigadeführer: Major-General
Oberführer: Brigadier
Standartenführer: Colonel
Obersturmbannführer: Lieutenant-Colonel
Sturmbannführer: Major
Haupsturmführer: Captain
Obersturmführer: Lieutenant (UK), First Lieutenant (USA)
Untersturmführer: Second Lieutenant
Oberscharführer: Sergeant-Major
Scharführer: Sergeant
Unterscharführer: Lance-Sergeant
Sturmmann/Rottenführer: Corporal
Obergrenadier: Lance-Corporal
Grenadier/Panzergrenadier: Private

REFERENCE WORKS CONSULTED

Danuta Czech, *Auschwitz Chronicle 1939–1945*, I.B.Tauris, London and New York, 1990.

Martin Gilbert, *Atlas of the Holocaust*, 3rd edition (with gazetteer), Routledge, London and New York, 2002.

Martin Gilbert, *The Holocaust, A History of the Jews of Europe During the Second World War*, Henry Holt, New York, 1985.

Martin Gilbert, *The Righteous, The Unsung Heroes of the Holocaust*, Transworld Publishers, London, 2002.

Israel Gutman, Editor in Chief, *Encyclopedia of the Holocaust*, Macmillan Publishing Company, New York, 1990.

David J. Hogan and David Aretha (eds), *The Holocaust Chronicle*, publisher Louis Weber, Publications International, Ltd. Lincolnwood, Illinois, 2000.

Zdenek Lederer, *Ghetto Theresienstadt*, Edward Goldston & Son Ltd., London, 1953.

Czeslaw Pilichowski, *Obozy hitlerowskie na ziemiach polskich 1939–1945: Informator encyklopedyczny*, Glowna Komisja Badania Zbrodni Hitlerowskich w Polsce, Warsaw, 1979.

Cecil Roth and Geoffrey Wigoder (eds), *Encyclopaedia Judaica*, Keter Publishing House Jerusalem, Ltd., Israel, 1996.

INDEX

Compiled by the editor

Holocaust Memoir Digest

Volume 1

On Both Sides of the Wall, Memoirs from the Warsaw Ghetto
Vladka Meed

Night
Elie Wiesel

I Cannot Forgive
Rudolf Vrba

Of Blood and Hope
Samuel Pisar

And the Sun Kept Shining …
Bertha Ferderber–Salz

Dry Tears, The Story of a Lost Childhood
Nechama Tec

Dottore! Internment in Italy, 1940–1945
Dr. Salim Diamand

Unveiled Shadows, The Witness of a Child
Ingrid Kisliuk

Out of the Ghetto
Jack Klajman

Holocaust Memoir Digest

Volume 2

Study Guide Maps

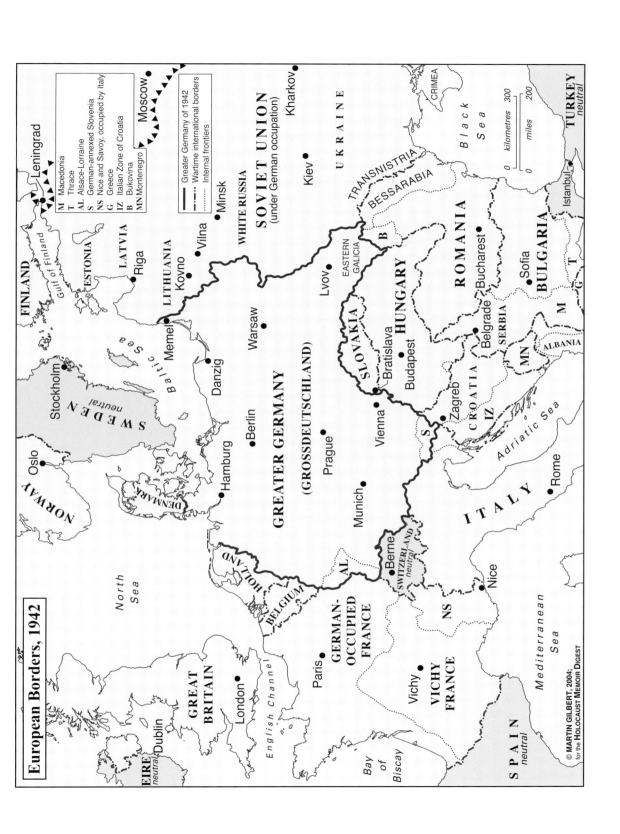

European Borders, 1942

M	Macedonia
T	Thrace
AL	Alsace-Lorraine
S	German-annexed Slovenia
NS	Nice and Savoy, occupied by Italy
G	Greece
IZ	Italian Zone of Croatia
B	Bukovina
MN	Montenegro

——— Greater Germany of 1942
—·—· Wartime international borders
········· Internal frontiers

Moscow

Leningrad

FINLAND

Gulf of Finland

ESTONIA

LATVIA
Riga

LITHUANIA
Kovno •
Memel

Vilna •

Minsk •

WHITE RUSSIA

SOVIET UNION
(under German occupation)

Kharkov •

UKRAINE

Kiev •

TRANSNISTRIA

BESSARABIA

EASTERN
GALICIA

Lvov •

SLOVAKIA
Bratislava •

HUNGARY
Budapest •

B

ROMANIA
Bucharest •

Black
Sea

CRIMEA

0   kilometres   300
0   miles   200

TURKEY
neutral

Istanbul •

BULGARIA
Sofia •

T

G

M

SERBIA
Belgrade •

MN

ALBANIA

CROATIA

Zagreb •

IZ

Adriatic Sea

S

NORWAY
Oslo •

SWEDEN
neutral
Stockholm •

DENMARK

Baltic Sea

Danzig •

Warsaw •

Berlin •

Hamburg •

GREATER GERMANY
(GROSSDEUTSCHLAND)

Prague •

Munich •

Vienna •

ITALY

Rome •

North
Sea

HOLLAND

BELGIUM

AL

GERMAN-
OCCUPIED
FRANCE

Paris •

Berne •
SWITZERLAND
neutral

NS

Nice •

Mediterranean
Sea

EIRE
neutral
Dublin •

GREAT
BRITAIN
London •

English Channel

Bay
of
Biscay

VICHY
FRANCE
Vichy •

SPAIN
neutral

© MARTIN GILBERT, 2004;
for the HOLOCAUST MEMOIR DIGEST

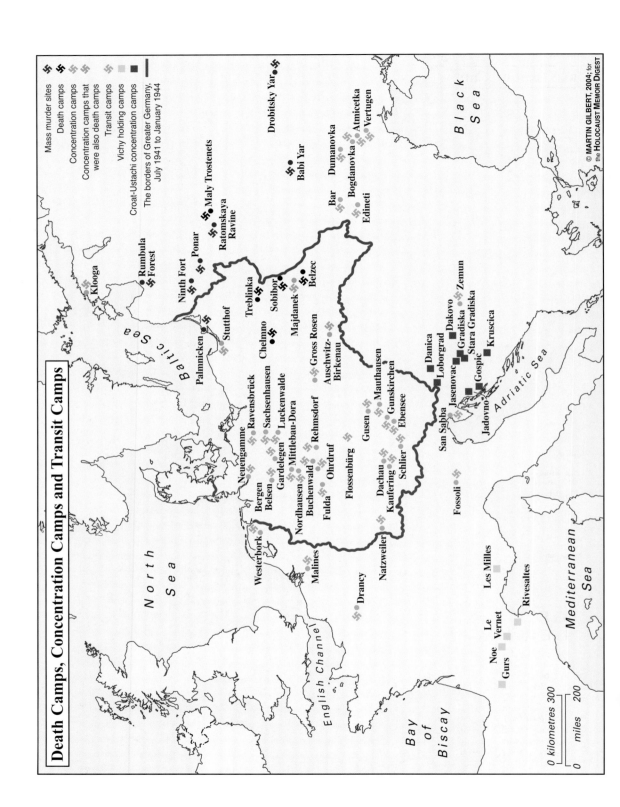

Death Camps, Concentration Camps and Transit Camps

Mass murder sites
Death camps
Concentration camps
Concentration camps that
were also death camps
Transit camps
Vichy holding camps
Croat-Ustachi concentration camps
The borders of Greater Germany,
July 1941 to January 1944

© MARTIN GILBERT, 2004; for
the HOLOCAUST MEMOIR DIGEST

Place names on map:

North Sea
Baltic Sea
Black Sea
Adriatic Sea
Mediterranean Sea
Bay of Biscay
English Channel

Klooga
Rumbula Forest
Ninth Fort
Ponar
Maly Trostenets
Ratomskaya Ravine
Drobitsky Yar
Bar
Dumanovka
Bogdanovka
Atmicetka
Vertugen
Babi Yar
Edineti
Palmnicken
Stutthof
Treblinka
Chelmno
Sobibor
Majdanek
Belzec
Gross Rosen
Auschwitz-Birkenau
Neuengamme
Ravensbrück
Sachsenhausen
Luckenwalde
Bergen Belsen
Gardelegen
Mittlebau-Dora
Rehmsdorf
Nordhausen
Buchenwald
Ohrdruf
Fulda
Flossenbürg
Gusen
Mauthausen
Gunskirchen
Ebensee
Dachau
Kaufering
Schlier
Natzweiler
Westerbork
Malines
Drancy
Fossoli
Danica
Loborgrad
Dakovo
Gradiska
Zemun
Stara Gradiska
Kruscica
Jasenovac
Gospic
Jadovno
San Sabba
Les Milles
Rivesaltes
Le Vernet
Noe
Gurs

0 kilometres 300
0 miles 200

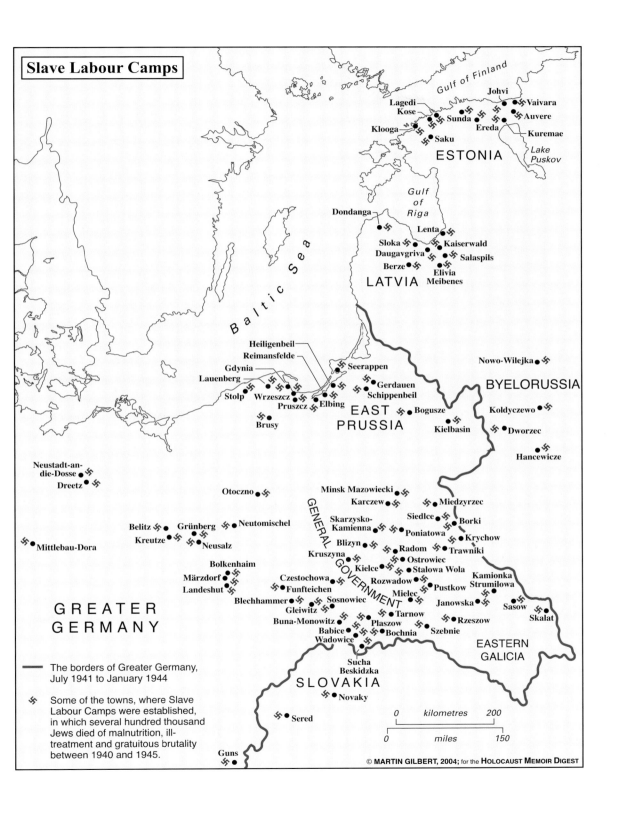

Slave Labour Camps

Gulf of Finland

Lagedi ⚡ Johvi
Kose ⚡ ⚡ Vaivara
Klooga ⚡ Sunda ⚡ ⚡ Auvere
⚡ Ereda ⚡ Kuremae
Saku
Lake Puskov

ESTONIA

Gulf of Riga

Dondanga
Lenta ⚡
Sloka ⚡ ⚡ Kaiserwald
Daugavgriva ⚡ ⚡ Salaspils
Berze ⚡ ⚡
Elivia ⚡
Meibenes

LATVIA

Baltic Sea

Nowo-Wilejka ⚡

Heiligenbeil
Reimansfelde
⚡ Seerappen
Gdynia
Lauenberg ⚡ Gerdauen
Stolp ⚡ Wrzeszcz ⚡ Schippenbeil
Pruszcz ⚡ Elbing
Brusy ⚡ Bogusze **BYELORUSSIA**
EAST
PRUSSIA ⚡ Koldyczewo ⚡
Kielbasin ⚡ Dworzec
⚡ Hancewicze

Neustadt-an-
die-Dosse ⚡
Dreetz ⚡

Otoczno ⚡ Minsk Mazowiecki ⚡
Karczew ⚡ ⚡ Miedzyrzec
Skarzysko- ⚡ Siedlce ⚡ Borki
Belitz ⚡ Grünberg ⚡ Neutomischel Kamienna ⚡ Poniatowa ⚡ Krychow
Kreutze ⚡ Neusalz Blizyn ⚡ Radom ⚡ Trawniki
⚡ Mittlebau-Dora Kruszyna ⚡ Ostrowiec
Kielce ⚡ Stalowa Wola Kamionka
Bolkenheim Rozwadow ⚡ Strumilowa
Märzdorf ⚡ Mielec ⚡
Landeshut ⚡ Czestochowa ⚡ Sosnowiec Pustkow Janowska ⚡ ⚡ Sasow
Blechhammer ⚡ Funfteichen Gleiwitz ⚡ Tarnow Rzeszow ⚡ Skalat
GREATER Buna-Monowitz ⚡ Plaszow Szebnie
GERMANY Babice ⚡ ⚡ Bochnia
Wadowice **EASTERN**
GALICIA

─── The borders of Greater Germany,
July 1941 to January 1944

Sucha
Beskidzka
SLOVAKIA

⚡ Some of the towns, where Slave Novaky
Labour Camps were established,
in which several hundred thousand
Jews died of malnutrition, ill- Sered
treatment and gratuitous brutality
between 1940 and 1945.

kilometres
0   200

0   150
miles

Guns ⚡

© **MARTIN GILBERT**, 2004; for the HOLOCAUST MEMOIR DIGEST

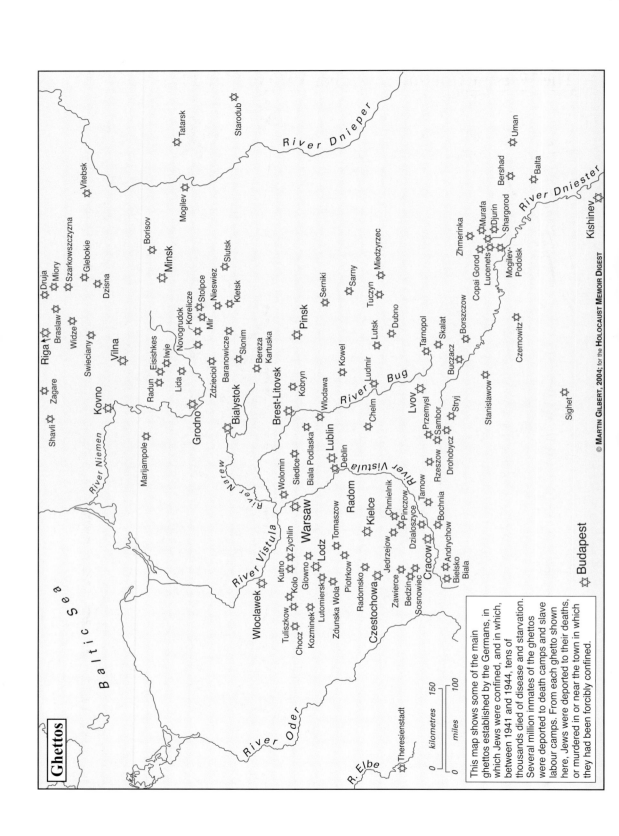

Ghettos

River Dnieper

River Dniester

River Niemen

River Narew

River Bug

River Vistula

River Vistula

Baltic Sea

River Oder

R. Elbe

Starodub
Tatarsk
Uman
Bershad
Vitebsk
Balta
Mogilev
River Dniester
Borisov
Zhmerinka
Kishinev
Druja
Miory
Szarkowszczyzna
Minsk
Murafa
Glebokie
Slutsk
Copai Gorod
Djurin
Shargorod
Braslaw
Dzisna
Korelicze
Nieswiez
Lucenets
Riga
Widze
Stolpce
Kletsk
Mogilev-Podolsk
Swieciany
Novogrudok
Serniki
Czernowitz
Zagare
Vilna
Radun Eisishkes
Ilwje
Mir
Slonim
Pinsk
Sarny
Tuczyn
Miedzyrzec
Shavil
Kovno
Lida
Zdzieciol
Baranowicze
Bereza
Kowel
Lutsk
Dubno
Tarnopol
Skalat
Borszczow
Sighet
Marijampole
Grodno
Bialystok
Kartuska
Wlodawa
River Ludmir
Chelm
Lvov
Buczacz
Brest-Litovsk
Kobryn
Przemysl
Stryj
Stanislawow
Wolomin
Siedlce
Biala Podlaska
Lublin
Rzeszow
Sambor
Drohobycz
Deblin
Tarnow
Wloclawek
Zychlin
Chmielnik
Bochnia
Kutno
Tomaszow
Pinczow
Radom
Glowno
Kielce
Dzialoszyce
Piotrkow
Andrychow
Lodz
Jedrzejow
Cracow
Lutomiersk
Kozminek
Bielsko
Zdunska Wola
Zawierce
Biala
Tuliszkow
Bedzin
Warsaw
Chocz
Kolo
Sosnowiec
Radomsko
Czestochowa
Budapest
Theresienstadt

© MARTIN GILBERT, 2004; for the HOLOCAUST MEMOIR DIGEST

0   150
kilometres
0   100
miles

This map shows some of the main ghettos established by the Germans, in which Jews were confined, and in which, between 1941 and 1944, tens of thousands died of disease and starvation. Several million inmates of the ghettos were deported to death camps and slave labour camps. From each ghetto shown here, Jews were deported to their deaths, or murdered in or near the town in which they had been forcibly confined.

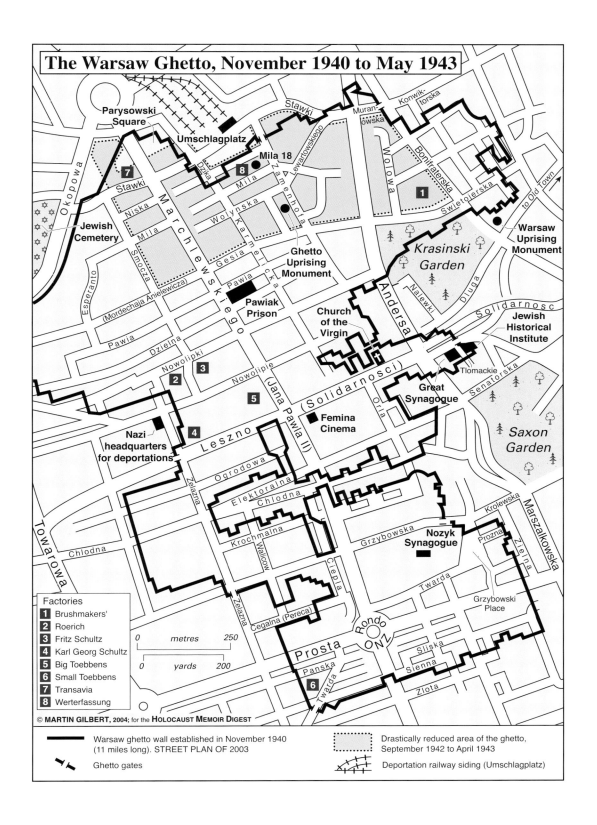

The Warsaw Ghetto, November 1940 to May 1943

Parysowski Square

Umschlagplatz

Mila 18

Stawki

Muran-owska

Konwik-torska

Wolowa

Bonifaterska

1

Swietojerska

to Old Town

Warsaw Uprising Monument

Jewish Cemetery

Okopowa

7

Stawki

Niska

Mila

Smocza

Esperanto

Dzika

Mila

Wolynska

Karmelicka

Gesia

(Mordechaja Anielewicza)

Pawia

8

Zamenhofa

Lewartowskiego

Ghetto Uprising Monument

Krasinski Garden

Nalewki

Dluga

Solidarnosc

Jewish Historical Institute

Pawia

Dzielna

Nowolipki

Marchlewskiego

Pawiak Prison

Pawia

Church of the Virgin

Andersa

Tlomackie

Senatorska

Saxon Garden

2

3

Nowolipie

(Jana Pawla II)

5

(Solidarnosci)

Orla

Great Synagogue

Nazi headquarters for deportations

4

Leszno

Ogrodowa

Femina Cinema

Krolewska

Marszalkowska

Zelazna

Elektoralna

Chlodna

Krochmalna

Walicow

Grzybowska

Nozyk Synagogue

Prozna

Zielna

Towarowa

Chlodna

Ciepla

Twarda

Grzybowski Place

Zelazna

Cegalna (Pereca)

Prosta

Panska

Twarda

Rondo ONZ

Sliska

Sienna

Zlota

Factories

1	Brushmakers'
2	Roerich
3	Fritz Schultz
4	Karl Georg Schultz
5	Big Toebbens
6	Small Toebbens
7	Transavia
8	Werterfassung

6

0 metres 250

0 yards 200

Warsaw ghetto wall established in November 1940 (11 miles long). STREET PLAN OF 2003

Ghetto gates

Drastically reduced area of the ghetto, September 1942 to April 1943

Deportation railway siding (Umschlagplatz)

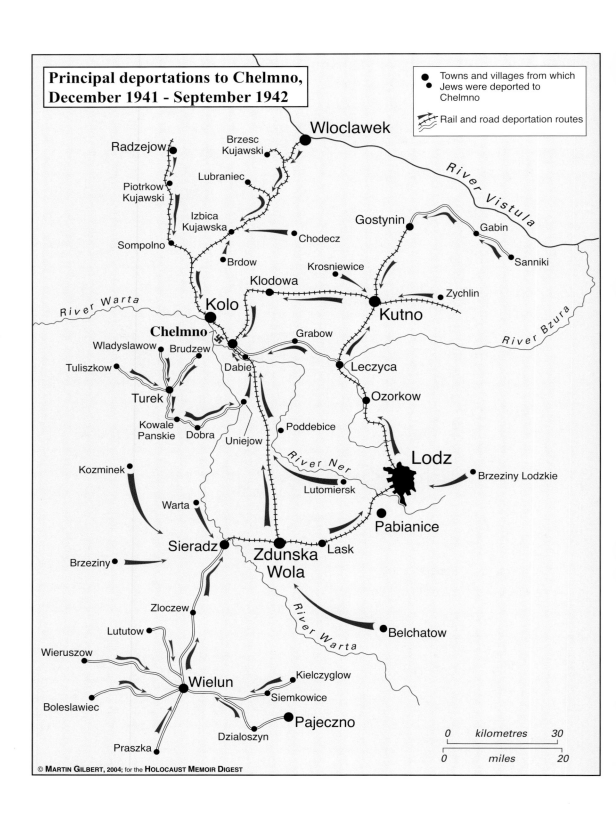

Principal deportations to Chelmno, December 1941 - September 1942

● Towns and villages from which Jews were deported to Chelmno

Rail and road deportation routes

Wloclawek

Radzejow

Brzesc Kujawski

Lubraniec

Piotrkow Kujawski

Izbica Kujawska

Sompolno

Chodecz

Brdow

River Vistula

Gostynin

Gabin

Sanniki

Krosniewice

Klodowa

Kolo

Kutno

Zychlin

River Warta

Chelmno

Grabow

River Bzura

Wladyslawow

Brudzew

Dabie

Leczyca

Tuliszkow

Turek

Ozorkow

Kowale Panskie

Dobra

Uniejow

Poddebice

River Ner

Lodz

Kozminek

Lutomiersk

Brzeziny Lodzkie

Warta

Pabianice

Sieradz

Zdunska Wola

Lask

Brzeziny

Zloczew

River Warta

Belchatow

Lututow

Wieruszow

Wielun

Kielczyglow

Siemkowice

Boleslawiec

Pajeczno

Dzialoszyn

Praszka

0 kilometres 30

0 miles 20

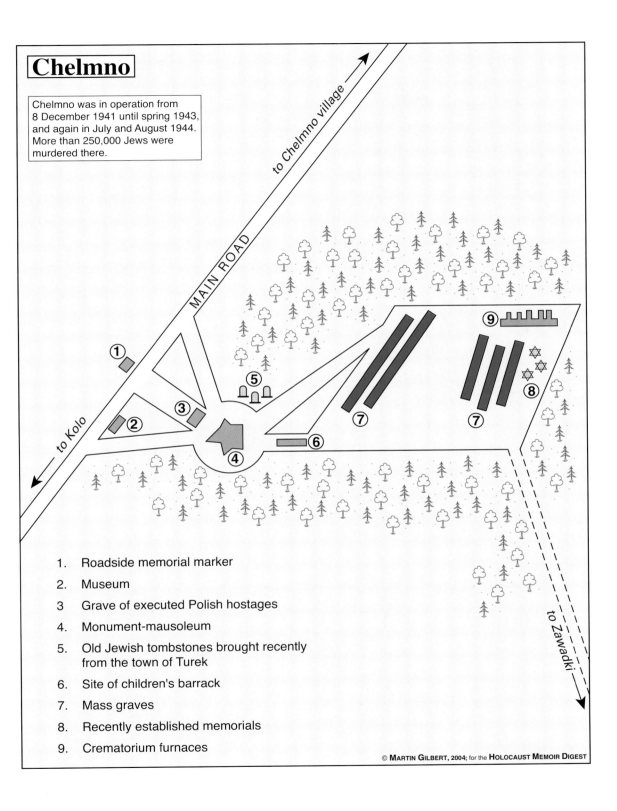

Chelmno

Chelmno was in operation from
8 December 1941 until spring 1943,
and again in July and August 1944.
More than 250,000 Jews were
murdered there.

MAIN ROAD

to Chelmno village

to Kolo

to Zawadki

1. Roadside memorial marker

2. Museum

3. Grave of executed Polish hostages

4. Monument-mausoleum

5. Old Jewish tombstones brought recently
   from the town of Turek

6. Site of children's barrack

7. Mass graves

8. Recently established memorials

9. Crematorium furnaces

© MARTIN GILBERT, 2004; for the HOLOCAUST MEMOIR DIGEST

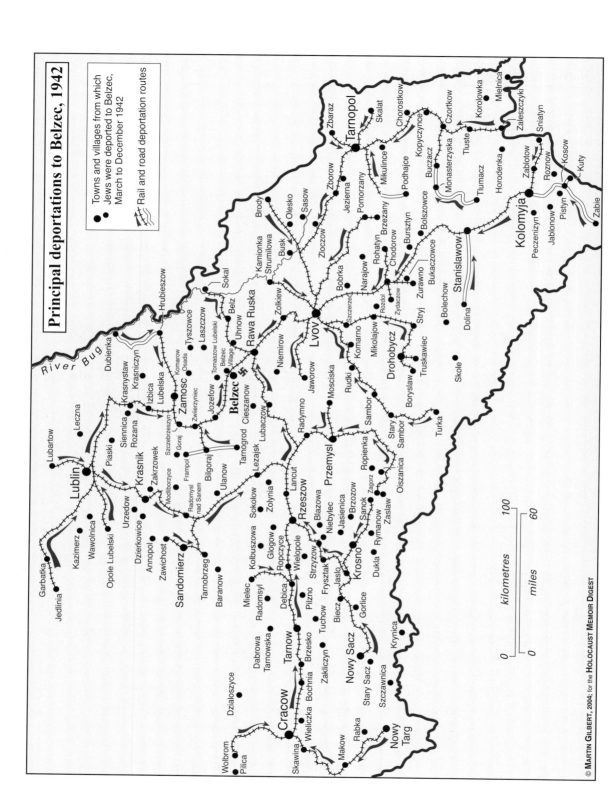

Principal deportations to Belzec, 1942

● Towns and villages from which Jews were deported to Belzec, March to December 1942

〜〜 Rail and road deportation routes

River Bug

Mielnica
Korolowka
Zaleszczyki
Sniatyn
Kosow
Kuty
Zabie
Roznow
Zablotow
Jablonow
Pistyn
Peczenizyn
KOLOMYJA
Horodenka
Tlumacz
Monasterzyska
Tluste
Czortkow
Buczacz
Chorostkow
Skalat
Kopyczynce
Podhajce
Mikulince
STANISLAWOW
Bolechow
Dolina
Skole
Bukaczowce
Bolszowce
Zurawno
Stryj
Rozdol
Zydaczow
Bolechow
Chodorow
Bursztyn
Brzezany
Narajow
Rohatyn
Pomorzany
Jezierna
Zborow
Zbaraz
TARNOPOL
Skole
Truskawiec
Boryslaw
DROHOBYCZ
Mikolajow
Komarno
Rudki
Szczerzec
Bobrka
Zloczow
Sasow
Olesko
Brody
Turka
Stary Sambor
Sambor
Mosciska
LVOV
Busk
Strumilowa
Kamionka
Zolkiew
Niemirow
Jaworow
Uhnow
Belz
Sokal
RAWA RUSKA
Cieszanow
Lubaczow
Tomaszow Lubelski
Belzec
Village
Osada
Komarow
Tyszowce
LASZCZOW
Hrubieszow
Dubienka
Krasniczyn
Krasnystaw
Izbica
Lubelska
ZAMOSC
Zwierzyniec
Jozefow
Szczebrzeszyn
Goraj
Frampol
Bilgoraj
Tarnogrod
Ulanow
Lezajsk
Lancut
Radymno
PRZEMYSL
Olszanica
Ropienka
Zagorz
Rymanow
Zaslaw
SANOK
Brzozow
Jasienica
Niebylec
Blazowa
RZESZOW
Zolynia
Sokolow
Glogow
Kolbuszowa
Ropczyce
Wielopole
Strzyzow
Frysztak
Jaslo
KROSNO
Dukla
Gorlice
Biecz
Pilzno
Debica
Tuchow
Mielec
Radomysl
Dabrowa Tarnowska
TARNOW
Brzesko
Zakliczyn
Bochnia
Wieliczka
Skawina
CRACOW
Makow
Rabka
NOWY TARG
Szczawnica
Stary Sacz
NOWY SACZ
Krynica
Baranow
Tarnobrzeg
SANDOMIERZ
Zawichost
Annopol
Dzierkowice
Opole Lubelski
Urzedow
Zakrzowek
Modliborzyce
Radomysl nad Sanem
KRASNIK
Rozana
Siennica
Piaski
LUBLIN
Leczna
Lubartow
Wawolnica
Kazimerz
Garbatka
Jedlinia
Pilica
Wolbrom
Dzialoszyce

kilometres 0 — 100
miles 0 — 60

© **MARTIN GILBERT**, 2004; for the **HOLOCAUST MEMOIR DIGEST**

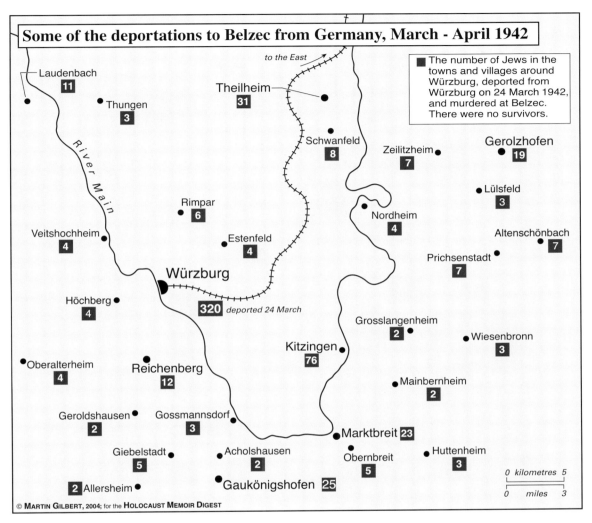

Some of the deportations to Belzec from Germany, March - April 1942

to the East

■ The number of Jews in the towns and villages around Würzburg, deported from Würzburg on 24 March 1942, and murdered at Belzec. There were no survivors.

Laudenbach **11**

Thungen **3**

Theilheim **31**

Schwanfeld **8**

Zeilitzheim **7**

Gerolzhofen **19**

Lülsfeld **3**

River Main

Rimpar **6**

Estenfeld **4**

Nordheim **4**

Altenschönbach **7**

Veitshochheim **4**

Prichsenstadt **7**

Würzburg **320** *deported 24 March*

Höchberg **4**

Grosslangenheim **2**

Wiesenbronn **3**

Kitzingen **76**

Oberalterheim **4**

Reichenberg **12**

Mainbernheim **2**

Geroldshausen **2**

Gossmannsdorf **3**

Marktbreit **23**

Huttenheim **3**

Giebelstadt **5**

Acholshausen **2**

Obernbreit **5**

2 Allersheim

Gaukönigshofen **25**

0 kilometres 5

0 miles 3

© **Martin Gilbert**, 2004; for the **Holocaust Memoir Digest**

Dortmund

Julich

G R E A T E R

Piaski

● Some of the towns in Germany
● from which Jews were deported
to Belzec in March and April 1942

Rail deportation routes from Germany
to Belzec, March and April 1942

Izbica
Lubelska

Belzec

Bad Kissingen

Bamberg

Würzburg
see map above

Nuremburg

Augsburg

G E R M A N Y

S L O V A K I A

Lindau

SWITZERLAND
neutral

0 kilometres 150

0 miles 0

© **Martin Gilbert**, 2004; for the **Holocaust Memoir Digest**

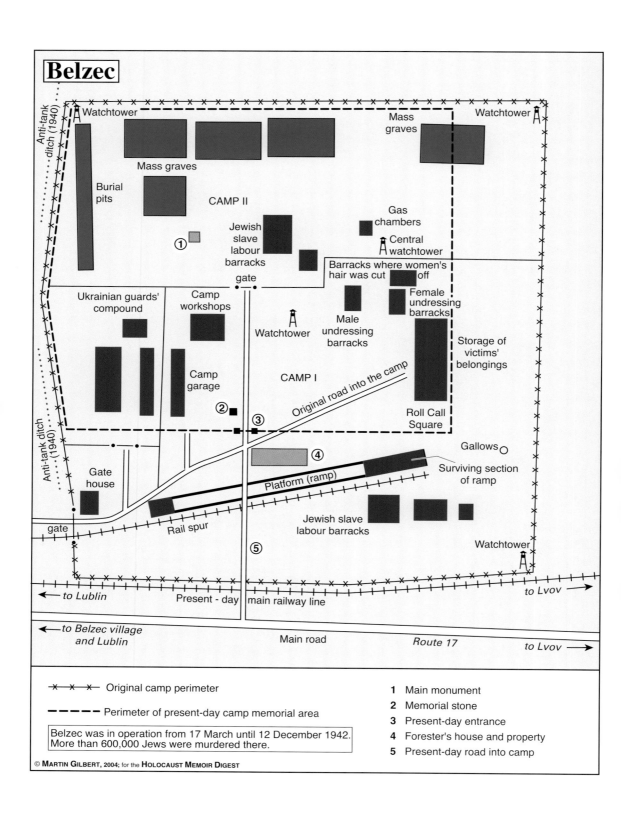

Belzec

Anti-tank ditch (1940)

Watchtower

Mass graves

Watchtower

Burial pits

Mass graves

CAMP II

①

Jewish slave labour barracks

Gas chambers

Central watchtower

gate

Barracks where women's hair was cut off

Ukrainian guards' compound

Camp workshops

Watchtower

Male undressing barracks

Female undressing barracks

Storage of victims' belongings

Anti-tank ditch (1940)

Camp garage

CAMP I

Original road into the camp

Roll Call Square

② ■

③ ■

Gallows ○

④

Surviving section of ramp

Gate house

Platform (ramp)

Rail spur

Jewish slave labour barracks

Watchtower

gate

⑤

← to Lublin

Present - day

main railway line

to Lvov →

← to Belzec village and Lublin

Main road

Route 17

to Lvov →

—✕—✕—✕— Original camp perimeter

— — — — Perimeter of present-day camp memorial area

Belzec was in operation from 17 March until 12 December 1942. More than 600,000 Jews were murdered there.

1 Main monument
2 Memorial stone
3 Present-day entrance
4 Forester's house and property
5 Present-day road into camp

© MARTIN GILBERT, 2004; for the HOLOCAUST MEMOIR DIGEST

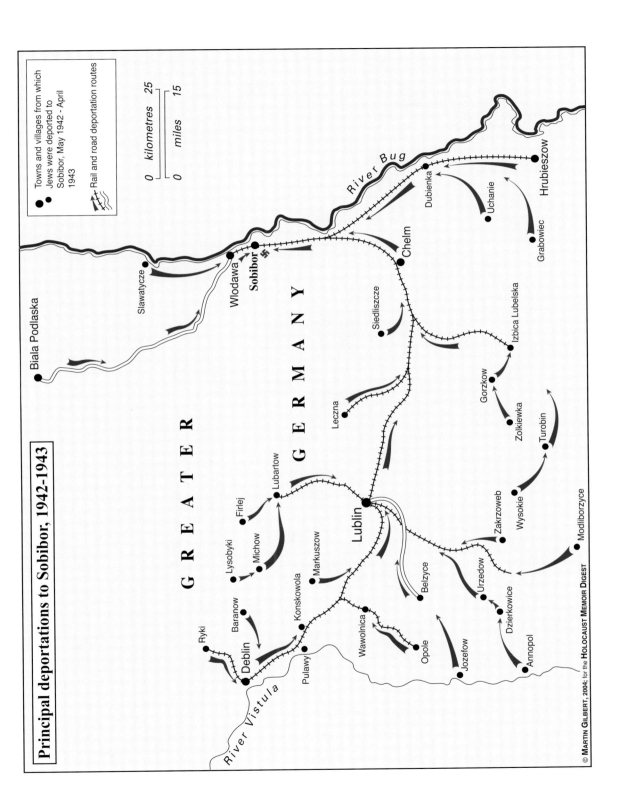

Principal deportations to Sobibor, 1942-1943

Towns and villages from which Jews were deported to Sobibor, May 1942 - April 1943

Rail and road deportation routes

0   kilometres   25

0   miles   15

Biala Podlaska

Slawatycze

Wlodawa

Sobibor

River Bug

Dubienka

Uchanie

Grabowiec

Hrubieszow

Chelm

Siedliszcze

Izbica Lubelska

Gorzkow

Zolkiewka

Turobin

Leczna

Lubartow

Firlej

Lysobyki

Michow

Ryki

Baranow

Deblin

Konskowola

Markuszow

Pulawy

River Vistula

Lublin

Belzyce

Wawolnica

Opole

Jozefow

Urzedow

Dzierkowice

Annopol

Zakrzoweb

Wysokie

Modliborzyce

G R E A T E R

G E R M A N Y

© Martin Gilbert, 2004; for the HOLOCAUST MEMOIR DIGEST

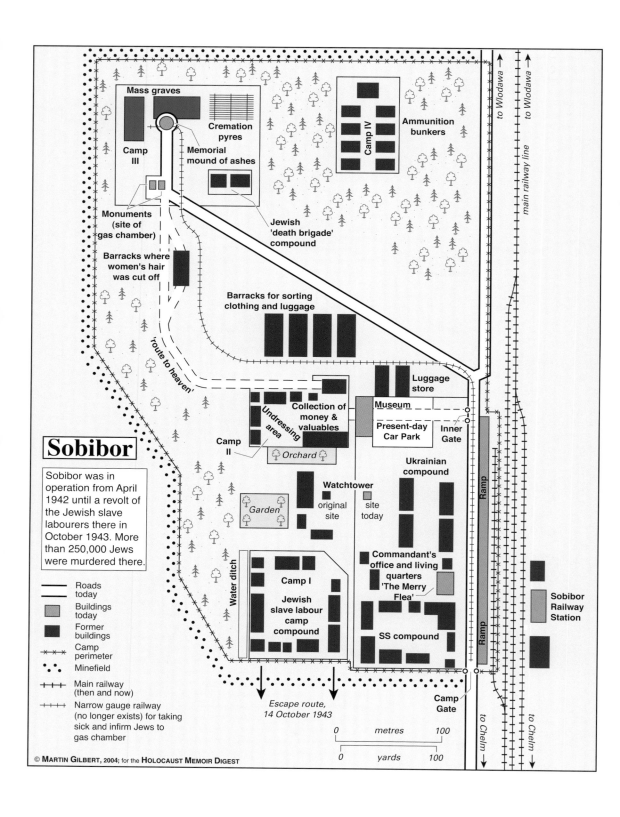

Sobibor

Sobibor was in operation from April 1942 until a revolt of the Jewish slave labourers there in October 1943. More than 250,000 Jews were murdered there.

Mass graves

Camp III

Cremation pyres

Memorial mound of ashes

Monuments (site of gas chamber)

Barracks where women's hair was cut off

'route to heaven'

Camp IV

Ammunition bunkers

Jewish 'death brigade' compound

Barracks for sorting clothing and luggage

Luggage store

Museum

Present-day Car Park

Inner Gate

Collection of money & valuables

Undressing area

Camp II

Orchard

Ukrainian compound

Watchtower

original site

site today

Garden

Commandant's office and living quarters 'The Merry Flea'

Camp I

Jewish slave labour camp compound

SS compound

Water ditch

Ramp

Ramp

Sobibor Railway Station

Camp Gate

Escape route, 14 October 1943

to Włodawa

main railway line

to Chełm

Legend

— Roads today
--- today
Buildings today
Former buildings
×-×-× Camp perimeter
•••• Minefield
+++ Main railway (then and now)
++++ Narrow gauge railway (no longer exists) for taking sick and infirm Jews to gas chamber

0   metres   100
0   yards   100

© MARTIN GILBERT, 2004; for the HOLOCAUST MEMOIR DIGEST

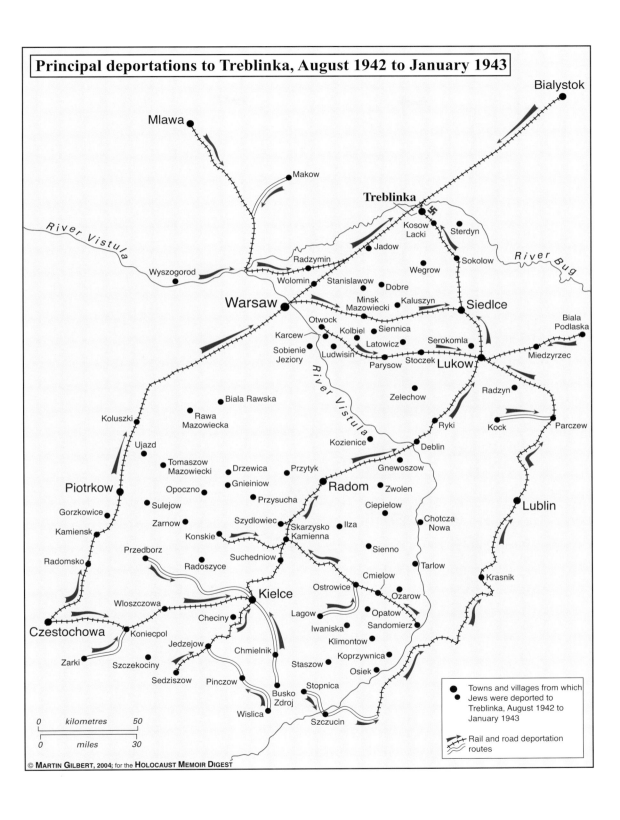

Principal deportations to Treblinka, August 1942 to January 1943

Bialystok

Mlawa

Makow

Treblinka

River Vistula

Kosow Lacki

Sterdyn

Jadow

Sokolow

Radzymin

Wegrow

River Bug

Wyszogorod

Wolomin

Stanislawow

Dobre

Warsaw

Minsk Mazowiecki

Kaluszyn

Siedlce

Otwock

Biala Podlaska

Karcew

Kolbiel

Siennica

Serokomla

Sobienie Jeziory

Latowicz

Ludwisin

Parysow

Stoczek

Lukow

Miedzyrzec

Biala Rawska

Zelechow

Radzyn

Koluszki

Rawa Mazowiecka

Ryki

Kock

Parczew

Ujazd

Kozienice

Deblin

Tomaszow Mazowiecki

Drzewica

Przytyk

Gnewoszow

Piotrkow

Opoczno

Gnieiniow

Radom

Zwolen

Gorzkowice

Przysucha

Ciepielow

Lublin

Sulejow

Kamiensk

Zarnow

Szydlowiec

Skarzysko Kamienna

Ilza

Chotcza Nowa

Konskie

Radomsko

Przedborz

Suchedniow

Sienno

Radoszyce

Cmielow

Tarlow

Krasnik

Wloszczowa

Ostrowice

Ozarow

Kielce

Checiny

Lagow

Opatow

Czestochowa

Koniecpol

Iwaniska

Sandomierz

Zarki

Jedzejow

Chmielnik

Klimontow

Szczekociny

Staszow

Koprzywnica

Sedziszow

Pinczow

Busko Zdroj

Stopnica

Osiek

Wislica

Szczucin

River Vistula

	Towns and villages from which Jews were deported to Treblinka, August 1942 to January 1943
	Rail and road deportation routes

0   kilometres   50

0   miles   30

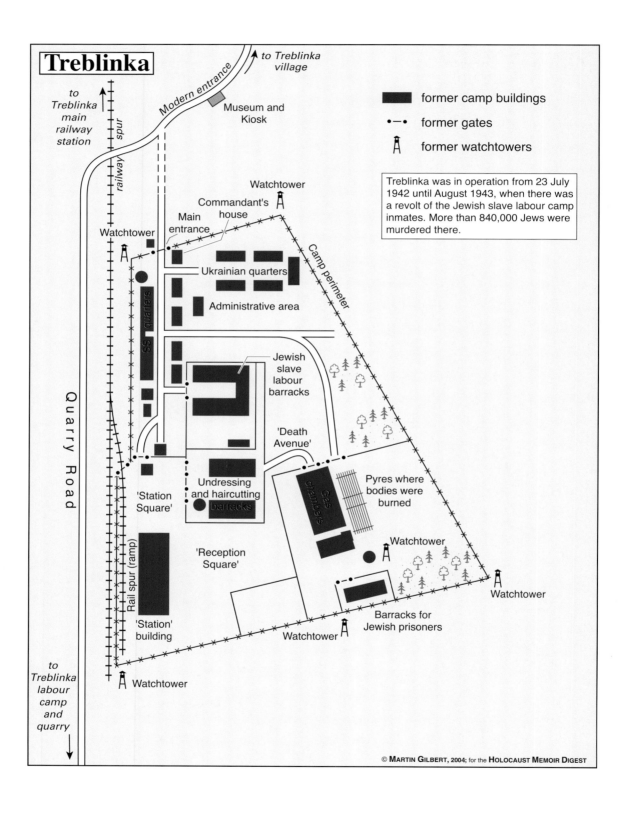

Treblinka

to Treblinka village

Modern entrance

Museum and Kiosk

to Treblinka main railway station

railway spur

■ former camp buildings
•–• former gates
♟ former watchtowers

Treblinka was in operation from 23 July 1942 until August 1943, when there was a revolt of the Jewish slave labour camp inmates. More than 840,000 Jews were murdered there.

Watchtower

Commandant's house

Main entrance

Watchtower

Camp perimeter

Ukrainian quarters

Administrative area

SS quarters

Jewish slave labour barracks

Quarry Road

'Death Avenue'

'Station Square'

Undressing and haircutting barracks

Gas chambers

Pyres where bodies were burned

Watchtower

'Reception Square'

Rail spur (ramp)

'Station' building

Barracks for Jewish prisoners

Watchtower

Watchtower

Watchtower

to Treblinka labour camp and quarry

© MARTIN GILBERT, 2004; for the HOLOCAUST MEMOIR DIGEST

Deportations across Europe to Sobibor and Treblinka, 1943

● Towns and villages from which
● Jews were deported across
Europe to Treblinka and
Sobibor, March - July 1943

Rail and river deportation routes

North Sea

Baltic Sea

Westerbork

Treblinka

HOLLAND

to Sobibor

Berlin

Siedlce

Sobibor

Vught

**GREATER
GERMANY**

Kielce   Radom

Teschen

to Treblinka

River Danube

Vienna

SWITZERLAND
neutral

Zagreb

to Treblinka

*Iron
Gates*

River Danub

Belgrade

Lom

Black Sea

Nis

Pirot

Adriatic Sea

Pristina

Kriva
Palanka

Sofia

THRACE

Kumanova

Zilianovo
Drama
Paranestion
Xanthi
Komotini

Nea Orestia
Didimoticon

Skopje

Stip

Souflion

MACE-
DONIA

Veles

Darzhsbabin

Seres   Kavalla

Bitola

Gevgelija

Thassos

Dedeagatch
Samothrace

Aegean Sea

Between 3 and 22 March 1943 more than 9,000
Jews were deported from Macedonia and Thrace
to Treblinka. Almost all were murdered within a
few hours of reaching the camp. Twenty trains
were used for these deportations. The deportations
from Thrace included a long section by barge from
the Bulgarian town of Lom to Vienna.

Most Dutch Jews were deported to Auschwitz,
but between 2 March and 20 July 1943 more than
34,000 were deported to Sobibor. All but twenty
of them were murdered there - most of them
within a few hours of reaching the camp.

| 0 | kilometres | 300 |
| 0 | miles | 200 |

© **MARTIN GILBERT, 2004**; for the **HOLOCAUST MEMOIR DIGEST**

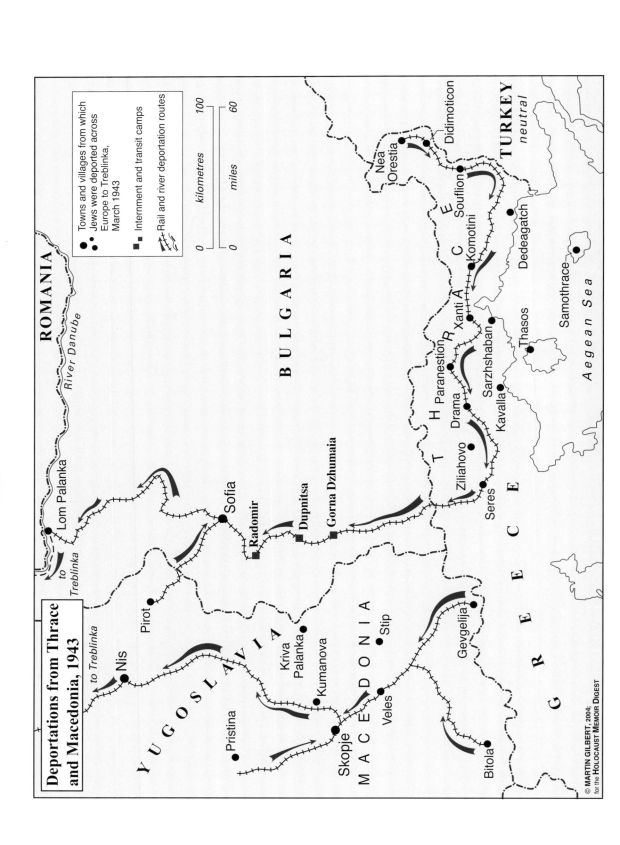

Deportations from Thrace and Macedonia, 1943

ROMANIA

River Danube

to Treblinka

Lom Palanka

to Treblinka

Nis

Pirot

YUGOSLAVIA

Pristina

Kriva Palanka

Kumanova

Skopje

MACEDONIA

Veles

Stip

Bitola

Gevgelija

Sofia

Radomir

Dupnitsa

Gorna Dzhumaia

BULGARIA

Ziliahovo

Seres

Drama

Paranestion

Xanti

Sarzhshaban

Kavalla

T H R A C E

Komotini

Souflion

Nea Orestia

Didimoticon

TURKEY
neutral

Dedeagatch

Thasos

Samothrace

Aegean Sea

G R E E C E

Towns and villages from which
Jews were deported across
Europe to Treblinka,
March 1943

■ Internment and transit camps

Rail and river deportation routes

kilometres   0   100

miles   0   60

© MARTIN GILBERT, 2004;
for the HOLOCAUST MEMOIR DIGEST

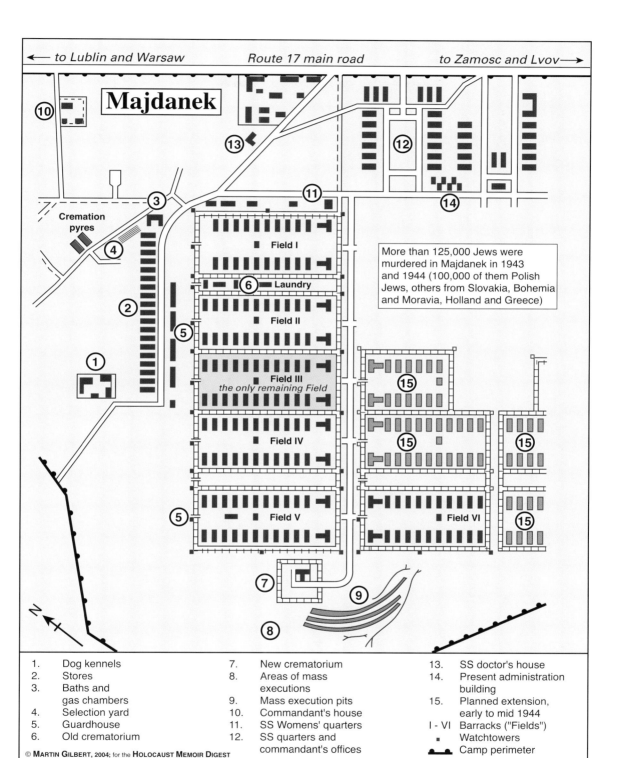

Majdanek

← to Lublin and Warsaw   Route 17 main road   to Zamosc and Lvov →

Cremation pyres

Field I

Laundry

Field II

Field III
the only remaining Field

Field IV

Field V

Field VI

More than 125,000 Jews were murdered in Majdanek in 1943 and 1944 (100,000 of them Polish Jews, others from Slovakia, Bohemia and Moravia, Holland and Greece)

N

1. Dog kennels
2. Stores
3. Baths and gas chambers
4. Selection yard
5. Guardhouse
6. Old crematorium
7. New crematorium
8. Areas of mass executions
9. Mass execution pits
10. Commandant's house
11. SS Womens' quarters
12. SS quarters and commandant's offices
13. SS doctor's house
14. Present administration building
15. Planned extension, early to mid 1944
I - VI Barracks ("Fields")
■ Watchtowers
▬▬▬ Camp perimeter

© MARTIN GILBERT, 2004; for the HOLOCAUST MEMOIR DIGEST

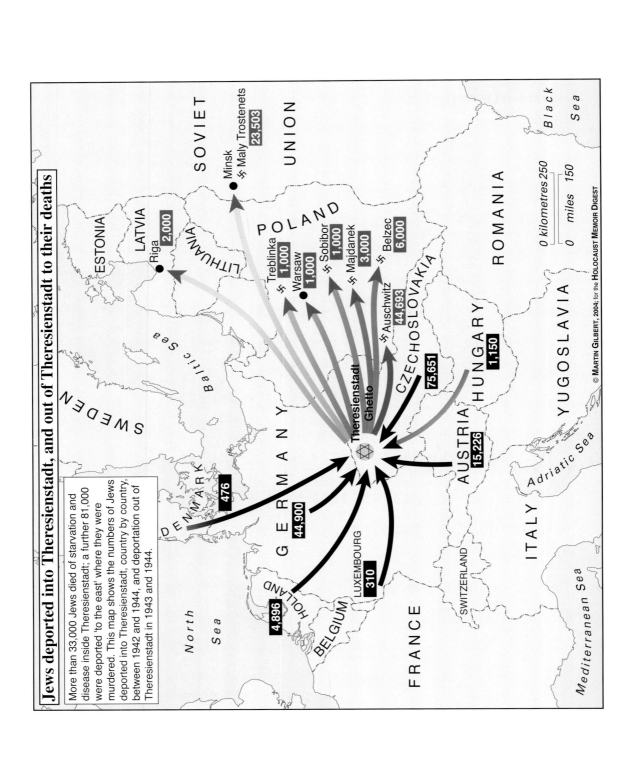

Jews deported into Theresienstadt, and out of Theresienstadt to their deaths

More than 33,000 Jews died of starvation and disease inside Theresienstadt; a further 81,000 were deported 'to the east' where they were murdered. This map shows the numbers of Jews deported into Theresienstadt, country by country, between 1942 and 1944, and deportation out of Theresienstadt in 1943 and 1944.

SWEDEN

ESTONIA

LATVIA

Riga **2,000**

LITHUANIA

SOVIET UNION

Minsk

Maly Trostenets **23,503**

POLAND

Treblinka **1,000**

Warsaw **1,000**

Sobibor **1,000**

Majdanek **3,000**

Belzec **6,000**

Auschwitz **44,693**

Baltic Sea

North Sea

DENMARK **476**

GERMANY **44,900**

HOLLAND **4,896**

BELGIUM

LUXEMBOURG **310**

FRANCE

SWITZERLAND

Theresienstadt Ghetto

CZECHOSLOVAKIA **75,651**

AUSTRIA **15,226**

HUNGARY **1,150**

ROMANIA

YUGOSLAVIA

ITALY

Adriatic Sea

Mediterranean Sea

Black Sea

0 kilometres 250

0 miles 150

© MARTIN GILBERT, 2004; for the HOLOCAUST MEMOIR DIGEST

The Theresienstadt Ghetto

More than 33,000 Jews died of starvation and disease inside Theresienstadt; a further 81,000 were deported 'to the east' where they were murdered, 44,693 of them at Auschwitz and 25,503 at Maly Trostenets, outside Minsk.

N

to Dresden

Ebergasse

PODMOKLY BARRACKS

Postgasse

DRESDEN BARRACKS

Brunnenpark

Berggasse

Stadtpark

to Prague

SUDETEN BARRACKS

CAVALRY BARRACKS

Rathausgasse

Seestrasse

Bahnhofstrasse

Langestrasse

Marktplatz

Hauptstrasse

Parkstrasse

Wallstrasse

Neue Gasse

Badhausgasse

Westgasse

HAMBURG BARRACKS

Jägergasse

HANOVER BARRACKS

MAGDEBURG BARRACKS

Südberg

Kleiner Park

Bäckergasse

to the cemetery

Südstrasse

railway to the main Dresden-Prague line

1. Children's House and School
2. Post Office, Bank, Theatre
3. Home for young people
4. Home for girls aged eight to sixteen
5. Tent for forced labour tasks (1,000 prisoners)
6. Ghetto shop used for clothing
7. Café, cabaret shows
8. SS Camp Command Headquarters
9. Housing for elderly Jews. Hospital
10. Jewish Ghetto Guard (100 men)
11. Infant school, kitchen, bakery
12. Homes for children and apprentices, and a library
13. Barracks of Czech gendarmes guarding perimeter
14. Craft workshops
15. SS dormitory and restaurant

16. SS Archives brought here from Berlin, 1943
17. Confiscated belongings sorted here
18. Women's barracks, concert performances, football in the yard
19. Housing for mothers and children under three years old
20. Playground for children; only allowed during the making of the Nazi propaganda film
21. Central hospital, public baths, showers
22. Home for old and insane deportees

23. Disinfection centre, laundry, shower room
24. Joiners workshop
25. Jewish Council of Elders office and rooms; theatrical performances
26. Men's barracks
27. Bakery and central food store
28. Railway siding
29. Main women's barracks later used for deportees to Auschwitz
30. Barracks for very old deportees
31. Sports arena
32. Earliest deportees lived here
33. Jews with encephalitis housed here. Briefly a culture hall and synagogue during the making of a Nazi propaganda film
34. Columbarium: urns with ashes placed here; the limit of mourners' journey
35. Allotments and a garden - these existed only during the making of the Nazi propaganda film

© MARTIN GILBERT, 2004; for the HOLOCAUST MEMOIR DIGEST

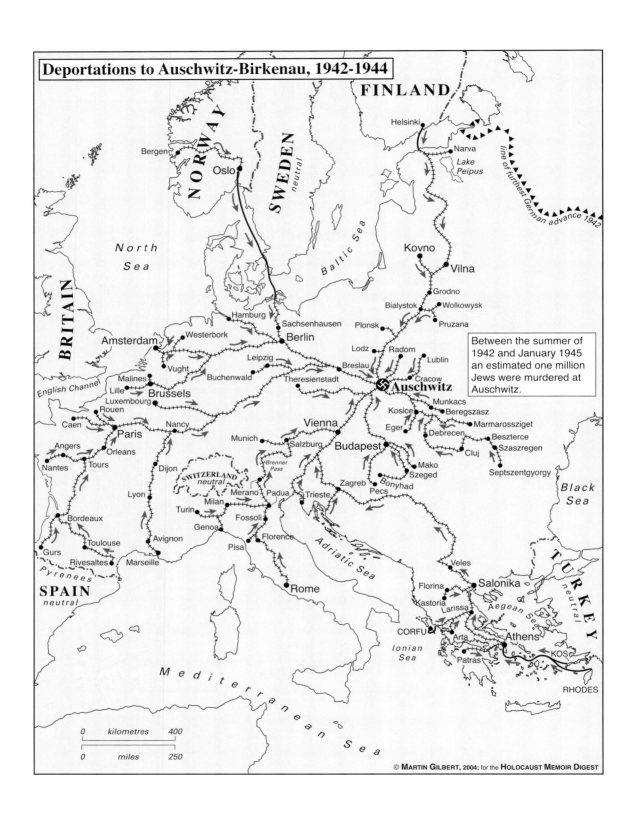

Deportations to Auschwitz-Birkenau, 1942-1944

Between the summer of 1942 and January 1945 an estimated one million Jews were murdered at Auschwitz.

FINLAND

NORWAY

SWEDEN neutral

BRITAIN

SPAIN neutral

SWITZERLAND neutral

TURKEY neutral

North Sea

Baltic Sea

English Channel

Adriatic Sea

Black Sea

Aegean Sea

Ionian Sea

Mediterranean Sea

Pyrenees

line of furthest German advance 1942

Helsinki
Narva
Lake Peipus
Bergen
Oslo
Kovno
Vilna
Grodno
Bialystok
Wolkowysk
Pruzana
Hamburg
Plonsk
Westerbork
Berlin
Sachsenhausen
Amsterdam
Leipzig
Lodz
Radom
Lublin
Vught
Buchenwald
Breslau
Malines
Theresienstadt
Cracow
Lille
Auschwitz
Brussels
Munkacs
Luxembourg
Kosice
Beregszasz
Rouen
Eger
Marmarossziget
Caen
Nancy
Vienna
Debrecen
Beszterce
Angers
Munich
Salzburg
Budapest
Cluj
Szaszregen
Orleans
Paris
Mako
Nantes
Tours
Szeged
Septszentgyorgy
Dijon
Bonyhad
Lyon
Merano
Padua
Zagreb
Pecs
Trieste
Turin
Milan
Fossoli
Bordeaux
Genoa
Florence
Avignon
Toulouse
Pisa
Gurs
Rome
Veles
Rivesaltes
Marseille
Florina
Salonika
Kastoria
Larissa
CORFU
Arta
Athens
Patras
KOS
RHODES

Brenner Pass

0   kilometres   400

0   miles   250

© MARTIN GILBERT, 2004; for the HOLOCAUST MEMOIR DIGEST

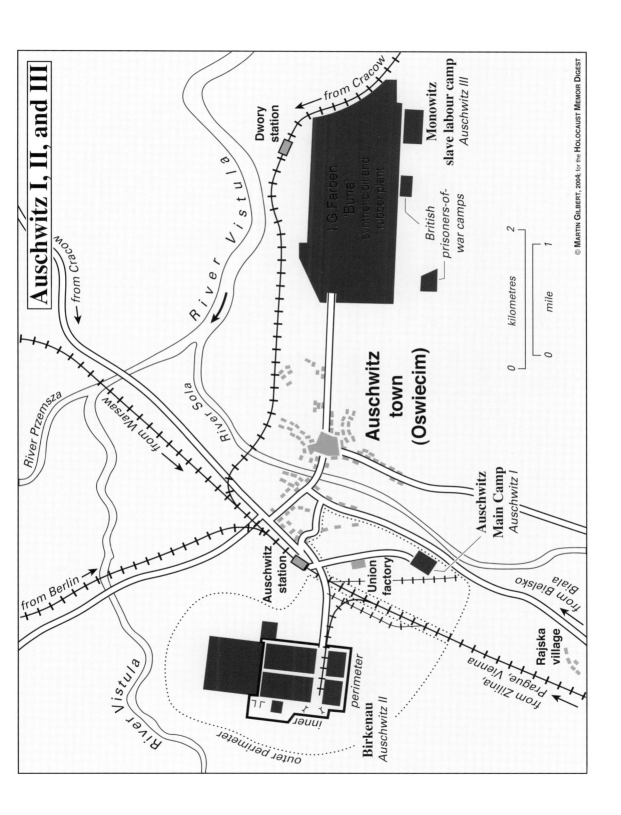

Auschwitz I, II, and III

from Cracow

River Vistula

Dwory station

from Cracow

I.G.Farben 'Buna' synthetic oil and rubber plant

British prisoners-of-war camps

Monowitz slave labour camp
Auschwitz III

River Przemsza

from Warsaw

River Sola

from Berlin

River Vistula

Auschwitz town (Oswiecim)

Auschwitz station

Union factory

Auschwitz Main Camp
Auschwitz I

inner perimeter

outer perimeter

Birkenau
Auschwitz II

from Bielsko Biala

from Zilina, Prague, Vienna

Rajska village

| 0 | 1 | 2 kilometres |
| 0 | 1 mile | |

© MARTIN GILBERT, 2004; for the HOLOCAUST MEMOIR DIGEST

Auschwitz Main Camp (Auschwitz I)

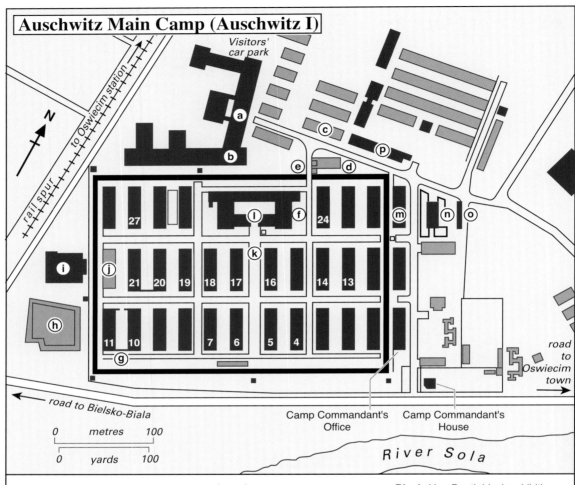

a. Entrance
b. Reception building for new prisoners
c. Stores, warehouse, workshops
d. SS Guardroom
e. Entrance gate inscribed 'Arbeit macht frei' (work makes you free)
f. Place where camp orchestra played
g. Wall of Death, where prisoners were executed by shooting
h. Gravel pit, site of executions
i. Warehouse for belongings taken from deportees. The poison gas canisters were also stored here

j. Laundry
k. Assembly Square (Appelplatz)
l. Camp kitchen
m. SS hospital
n. Gas chamber and Crematorium (Crematorium I)
o. Political section (Camp Gestapo)
p. SS garages, stables and stores

Block 4: Extermination exhibition
Block 5: Exhibition of material evidence of crimes
Block 6: Exhibition of everday life of prisoners
Block 7: Exhibition of living and sanitary conditions
Block 10: Exhibition of sterilization experiments

Block 11: Death block exhibition
Block 13: Denmark and Germany exhibitions
Block 14: National exhibition, formerly Soviet exhibition
Block 16: Czechoslovak exhibition
Block 17: Yugoslavia and Austria exhibition
Block 18: Hungarian and Bulgarian exhibitions
Block 19: Prisoners' hospital
Block 20: Prisoners' hospital
Block 21: Prisoners' hospital
Block 24: Museum archive
Block 27: Exhibition, 'Suffering and struggle of Jews'

▬▬ Brick perimeter wall   ■ Watchtowers

Birkenau (Auschwitz II)

Between the summer of 1942 and November 1944 an estimated one million Jews were murdered at Birkenau.

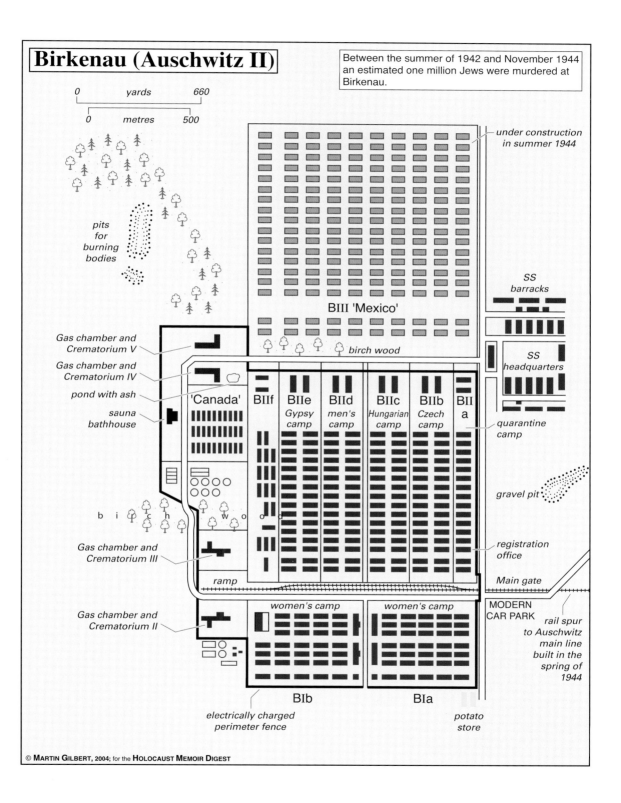

0 — yards — 660

0 — metres — 500

pits for burning bodies

birch wood

BIII 'Mexico'

under construction in summer 1944

SS barracks

SS headquarters

Gas chamber and Crematorium V

Gas chamber and Crematorium IV

pond with ash

sauna bathhouse

'Canada'

BIIf

BIIe
Gypsy camp

BIId
men's camp

BIIc
Hungarian camp

BIIb
Czech camp

BIIa

quarantine camp

b   i   r   c   h   w   o   o   d

gravel pit

Gas chamber and Crematorium III

ramp

registration office

Main gate

Gas chamber and Crematorium II

women's camp

women's camp

MODERN CAR PARK

rail spur to Auschwitz main line built in the spring of 1944

BIb

BIa

electrically charged perimeter fence

potato store

© **MARTIN GILBERT**, 2004; for the **HOLOCAUST MEMOIR DIGEST**

Escape route of Rudolf Vrba and Alfred Wetzler, 7-25 April 1944

Oswiecim

River Vistula

Birkenau

Buna-
Monowitz

Auschwitz

E A S T
U P P E R
S I L E S I A

River Sola

P O L A N D

Pisarowice

Porabka

River Vistula

Bielsko-
Biala

fired on by a
German patrol

F o r e s t

Zywiec

Milowka

Zwardon

Skalite

Sol

Rajcza

B e s k i d   M o u n t a i n s

Cadca

Southward route of the two escapees
Railway from Poland to Slovakia
International borders, 1937
SS-run camps

S L O V A K I A

| 0 | kilometres | 15 |
| 0 | miles | 10 |

Zilina

© MARTIN GILBERT, 2004; for the HOLOCAUST MEMOIR DIGEST

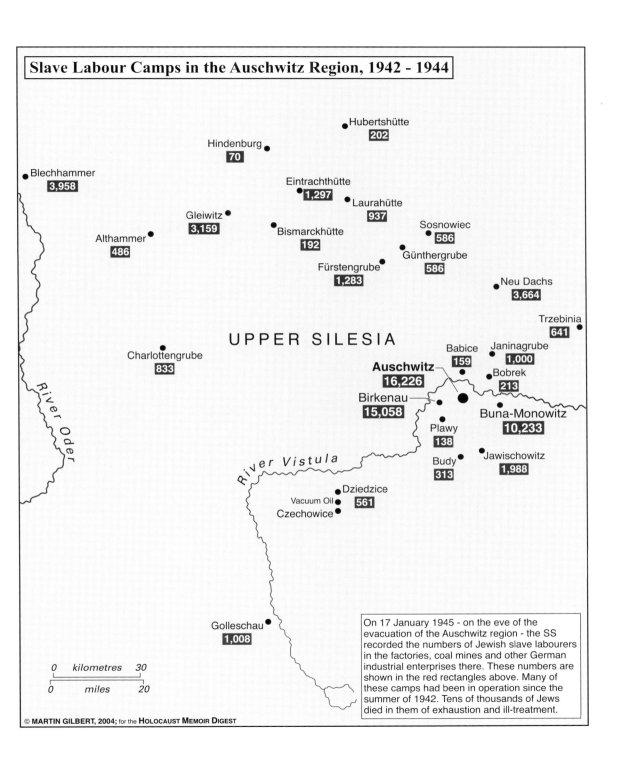

Slave Labour Camps in the Auschwitz Region, 1942 - 1944

Hubertshütte
202

Hindenburg
70

Blechhammer
3,958

Eintrachthütte
1,297

Laurahütte
937

Gleiwitz
3,159

Bismarckhütte
192

Sosnowiec
586

Althammer
486

Günthergrube
586

Fürstengrube
1,283

Neu Dachs
3,664

Trzebinia
641

UPPER SILESIA

Charlottengrube
833

Babice
159

Janinagrube
1,000

Auschwitz
16,226

Bobrek
213

Birkenau
15,058

Buna-Monowitz
10,233

Plawy
138

Jawischowitz
1,988

Budy
313

River Oder

River Vistula

Dziedzice
Vacuum Oil   561
Czechowice

Golleschau
1,008

0   kilometres   30

0   miles   20

On 17 January 1945 - on the eve of the
evacuation of the Auschwitz region - the SS
recorded the numbers of Jewish slave labourers
in the factories, coal mines and other German
industrial enterprises there. These numbers are
shown in the red rectangles above. Many of
these camps had been in operation since the
summer of 1942. Tens of thousands of Jews
died in them of exhaustion and ill-treatment.

© MARTIN GILBERT, 2004; for the HOLOCAUST MEMOIR DIGEST

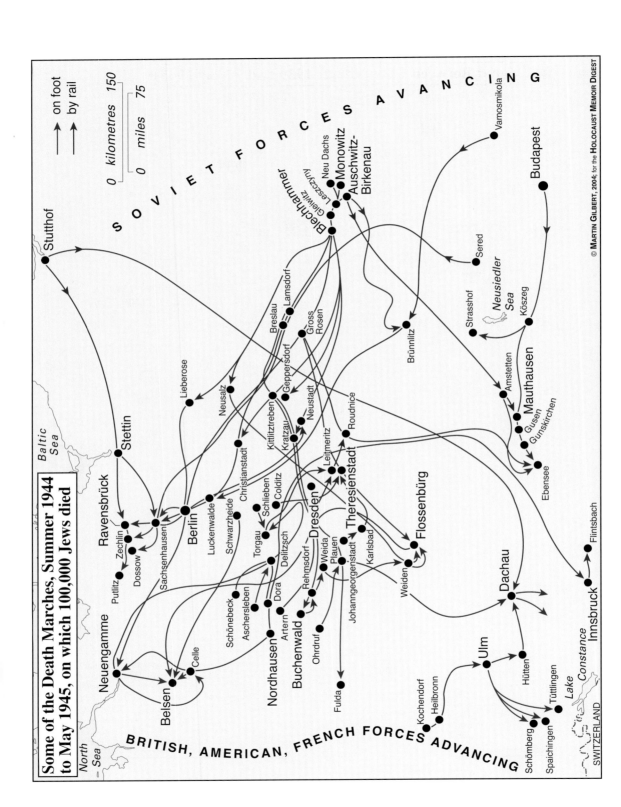

Some of the Death Marches, Summer 1944 to May 1945, on which 100,000 Jews died

on foot
by rail

0 kilometres 150
0 miles 75

North
— Sea

Baltic Sea

SOVIET FORCES AVANCING

BRITISH, AMERICAN, FRENCH FORCES ADVANCING

SWITZERLAND

Lake Constance

Neusiedler Sea

Stutthof
Stettin
Ravensbrück
Zechlin
Dossow
Putlitz
Neuengamme
Belsen
Celle
Sachsenhausen
Berlin
Luckenwalde
Schwarzheide
Lieberose
Neusalz
Christianstadt
Schlieben
Colditz
Torgau
Delitzsch
Schönebeck
Aschersleben
Dora
Artern
Nordhausen
Buchenwald
Ohrdruf
Rehmsdorf
Weida
Plauen
Johanngeorgenstadt
Fulda
Karlsbad
Dresden
Theresienstadt
Leitmeritz
Roudnice
Flossenbürg
Weiden
Kittlilztreben
Kratzau
Neustadt
Geppersdorf
Gross Rosen
Breslau
Lamsdorf
Blechhammer
Gleiwitz
Leszczyny
Neu Dachs
Monowitz
Auschwitz-Birkenau
Brünnlitz
Sered
Strasshof
Koszeg
Amstetten
Mauthausen
Gusen
Gunskirchen
Ebensee
Vamosmikola
Budapest
Dachau
Flintsbach
Innsbruck
Ulm
Hütten
Tüttlingen
Schömberg
Spaichingen
Heilbronn
Kochendorf

© MARTIN GILBERT, 2004; for the HOLOCAUST MEMOIR DIGEST

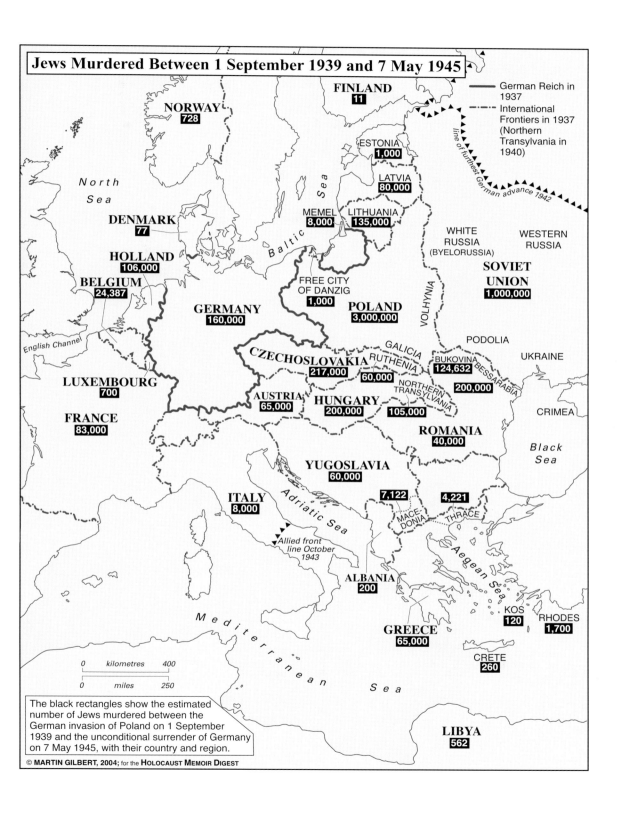

Jews Murdered Between 1 September 1939 and 7 May 1945

— German Reich in 1937

—·—·— International Frontiers in 1937 (Northern Transylvania in 1940)

line of furthest German advance 1942

FINLAND 11

NORWAY 728

ESTONIA 1,000

LATVIA 80,000

DENMARK 77

MEMEL 8,000   LITHUANIA 135,000

WHITE RUSSIA (BYELORUSSIA)

WESTERN RUSSIA

HOLLAND 106,000

BELGIUM 24,387

FREE CITY OF DANZIG 1,000

SOVIET UNION 1,000,000

GERMANY 160,000

VOLHYNIA

North Sea

Baltic Sea

English Channel

POLAND 3,000,000

PODOLIA

GALICIA

RUTHENIA

CZECHOSLOVAKIA 217,000   60,000

BUKOVINA 124,632

BESSARABIA 200,000

UKRAINE

LUXEMBOURG 700

AUSTRIA 65,000

HUNGARY 200,000

NORTHERN TRANSYLVANIA 105,000

CRIMEA

FRANCE 83,000

ROMANIA 40,000

Black Sea

YUGOSLAVIA 60,000

ITALY 8,000

Adriatic Sea

7,122

MACEDONIA

4,221

THRACE

Allied front line October 1943

Aegean Sea

ALBANIA 200

KOS 120

RHODES 1,700

GREECE 65,000

CRETE 260

Mediterranean Sea

0   kilometres   400

0   miles   250

LIBYA 562

The black rectangles show the estimated number of Jews murdered between the German invasion of Poland on 1 September 1939 and the unconditional surrender of Germany on 7 May 1945, with their country and region.

© **MARTIN GILBERT, 2004;** for the **HOLOCAUST MEMOIR DIGEST**

Non-Jews Recognised For Having Saved Jews From Death, 1939 - 1945

North Sea

Baltic Sea

NORWAY 24

SWEDEN 10

ESTONIA 2

RUSSIA 93

DENMARK 17

LATVIA 93

LITHUANIA 513
• Kaunas

GREAT BRITAIN 13

HOLLAND 4,513

BELARUS 512

Berlin •

GERMANY 376

POLAND 5,733

Kharkov →

1,357

CZECH REPUBLIC 104

UKRAINE 1,881

BELGIUM 1

LUXEMBOURG

Vienna •

SLOVAKIA 428

AUSTRIA 84

Budapest •

MOLDOVA 53

SWITZ. 38

HUNGARY 617

FRANCE 2,262

SLOVENIA 6

ROMANIA 48

Bordeaux •

CROATIA 93

SERBIA 116

BOSNIA 34

Marseille •

ITALY 325

Adriatic Sea

YUGOSLAVIA

BULGARIA 16

SPAIN 3

MACEDONIA 10

Black Sea

61

GREECE 253

TURKEY 1

ALBANIA

Mediterranean Sea

Aegean Sea

| 0 | kilometres | 300 |
| 0 | miles | 200 |

Rhodes •

— · — · International borders, 1937
·········· Post-1991 divisions of the Soviet Union

© MARTIN GILBERT, 2004; for the HOLOCAUST MEMOIR DIGEST

The total number of non-Jews who saved Jewish lives during the Holocaust, and have been honoured by the State of Israel and the Yad Vashem Holocaust memorial in Jerusalem since 1953 reached 19,706 on 1 January 2003 (as shown on this map). They are given the title 'Righteous Among the Nations'. They are also known as 'Righteous Gentiles'. This map shows the awards given country by country, during that fifty-year period.

Also shown on the map are the cities where Jewish lives were saved by individuals who have been recognized by Yad

Vashem as Righteous: ten Armenians (including one in Budapest and one in Vienna), two Chinese (one in Kharkov, the other in Vienna), a Brazilian diplomat (in Berlin), a Portuguese diplomat (in Bordeaux), a Japanese diplomat (in Kaunas), and a United States citizen, Varian Fry, who, from Marseille, enabled many hundreds of Jews to leave Europe. The one Turkish citizen indicated on the map was also a diplomat, the Turkish Consul on the island of Rhodes.

At their own request, the Norwegian and Danish resistance movements received their honours collectively.

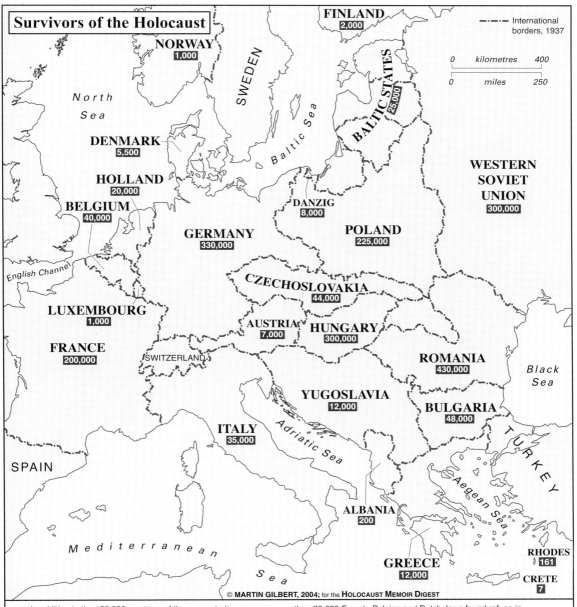

Survivors of the Holocaust

FINLAND
2,000

NORWAY
1,000

SWEDEN

North
Sea

Baltic Sea

BALTIC STATES
25,000

International
borders, 1937

0   kilometres   400
0   miles   250

DENMARK
5,500

HOLLAND
20,000

BELGIUM
40,000

DANZIG
8,000

GERMANY
330,000

POLAND
225,000

WESTERN
SOVIET
UNION
300,000

English Channel

CZECHOSLOVAKIA
44,000

LUXEMBOURG
1,000

AUSTRIA
7,000

HUNGARY
300,000

FRANCE
200,000

SWITZERLAND

ROMANIA
430,000

Black
Sea

YUGOSLAVIA
12,000

BULGARIA
48,000

TURKEY

ITALY
35,000

Adriatic Sea

SPAIN

Aegean Sea

ALBANIA
200

Mediterranean

RHODES
161

GREECE
12,000

CRETE
7

Sea

© **MARTIN GILBERT**, 2004; for the HOLOCAUST MEMOIR DIGEST

In addition to the 100,000 survivors of the concentration camps, more than a million and a half European Jews survived Hitler's efforts to destroy them. The numbers are shown on this map, country by country.

Some Jews were fortunate, as in Germany, to escape from Europe before the outbreak of war, or, as in Italy, to be liberated by the Allies before the plans for their destruction could be completed. Others, as in Romania, were saved when their Government, previously anti-Jewish, changed its policy in anticipation of an Allied victory. All 48,000 Jews of Bulgaria were saved by the collective protest of the Bulgarian church, parliament and people.

The majority of the Polish Jews shown here survived because they found refuge at the beginning of the war in Soviet Central Asia. More than 20,000 French, Belgian and Dutch Jews found refuge in Switzerland, Spain and Portugal. Almost all Denmark's 7,000 Jews were smuggled to safety in Sweden. Many Greek Jews found refuge in Turkey.

Some Jews everywhere, particularly in France, Belgium, Holland and Italy, survived because the Germans took longer to deport them than the course of the war allowed: the Allied landings on continental Europe in June 1944 coming while the deportations were still in progress.

As many as 100,000 Jews escaped death because they were hidden by non-Jews who risked their own lives to save Jews.

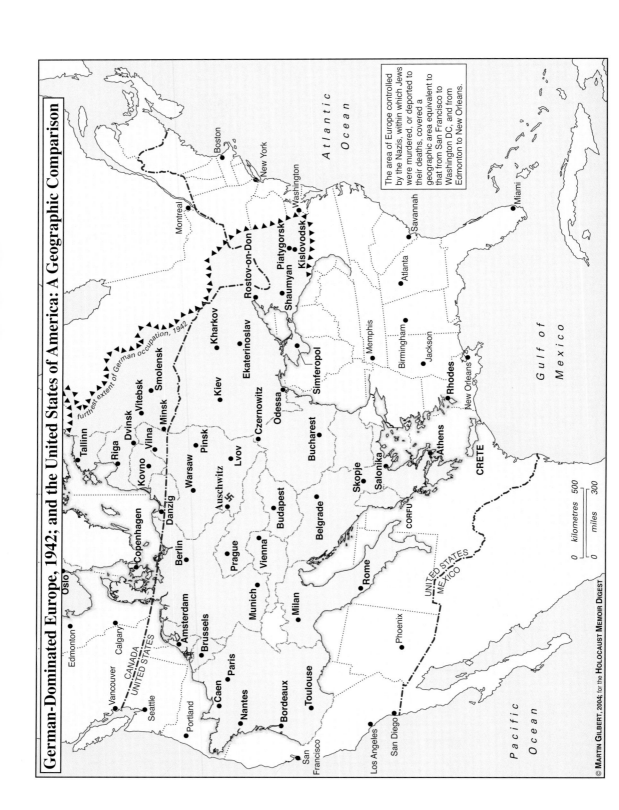

German-Dominated Europe, 1942; and the United States of America: A Geographic Comparison

The area of Europe controlled by the Nazis, within which Jews were murdered, or deported to their deaths, covered a geographic area equivalent to that from San Francisco to Washington DC, and from Edmonton to New Orleans.

furthest extent of German occupation, 1942

Atlantic Ocean

Pacific Ocean

Gulf of Mexico

UNITED STATES
MEXICO

CANADA
UNITED STATES

0   kilometres   500
0   miles   300

© MARTIN GILBERT, 2004; for the HOLOCAUST MEMOIR DIGEST

Edmonton • Calgary • Vancouver • Seattle • Portland • San Francisco • Los Angeles • San Diego • Phoenix

Boston • New York • Washington • Montreal • Atlanta • Savannah • Birmingham • Jackson • Memphis • New Orleans • Miami

Oslo • Copenhagen • Berlin • Tallinn • Riga • Dvinsk • Vilna • Kovno • Minsk • Vitebsk • Smolensk • Kharkov • Rostov-on-Don • Platygorsk • Shaumyan • Kislovodsk • Simferopol

Amsterdam • Brussels • Paris • Caen • Nantes • Bordeaux • Toulouse • Munich • Prague • Vienna • Milan • Rome

Danzig • Warsaw • Auschwitz • Pinsk • Lvov • Kiev • Czernowitz • Ekaterinoslav • Odessa • Bucharest • Budapest • Belgrade • Skople • Salonika • Athens • Rhodes

CRETE • CORFU